To Clark Nixon,
Some good memories
Gail K. Cleary

Brewed with Style

The Story of the House of Heileman

Paul D. Koeller • David H. DeLano

Published by

University of Wisconsin-La Crosse Foundation, Incorporated
Cleary Alumni & Friends Center
615 East Avenue North
La Crosse, Wisconsin, 54601

Cover design: Kurt Friederichs

Main editors: Frances and John Edstrom

Book design and editing: Ken Brekke and Sue Knopf

RC Printing
127 South Sixth Street
La Crosse, Wisconsin 54601

ISBN 0-9605832-2-X

2004

Contents

Part III—People

Heileman brewery, postcard view, pre-Prohibition. PHOTO COURTESY OF MURPHY LIBRARY, UNIVERSITY OF WISCONSIN-LA CROSSE

Introduction

In the fall of 2000, my wife, Karen, and I sent our daughter, Mara, off to school at the University of Wisconsin in Madison. Afterwards, we talked about our plans as we faced an "empty nest." We decided that we needed some ways to fill the extra hours that previously we'd spent with Mara and her school activities. In addition to our existing hobbies, we wanted to travel and look for some volunteer activities. One of the things we talked about was some kind of volunteer activity related to my interest in history.

In October 2000, we made good on our plans to travel by taking a five-day trip to New England to see the fall foliage. As part of that trip we visited Lowell, Massachusetts, to see the New England Quilt Museum. During our visit, we learned that Lowell had been the birthplace of the Industrial Revolution in the United States. Sadly, most of the textile mills had closed and many of them stand empty today with the windows broken out. However, several of the mills were converted into museums dedicated to preserving the history of the mills and their importance to the city of Lowell.

Our visit to Lowell made me think about the similarity of the mills to the G. Heileman Brewing Company in La Crosse, Wisconsin. The brewery played a big role in my life. My father worked in the bottle house at Heileman for more than 40 years. As a child, my father used to take me down to Heileman to pick up his pay check when he was on vacation. I used to collect bottle caps from the brewery. Unfortunately, somewhere along the way all those bottle caps were lost or thrown away. However, I still remember many of the brands from the bottle caps: Old Style, Special Export, Fox Head, Kingsbury, Wisconsin Premium, and more. In the early 1980s, Heileman started issuing beer steins, and I began collecting them. Today, I own the entire collection of Heileman steins.

Like the textile mills in Lowell, Heileman played an important role for the city of La Crosse. Also, like the Lowell mills, Heileman closed down and the workers lost their jobs. Since that time, the brewery has been reopened as The City Brewery. This reverts to the original name of the Heileman Brewery before Gottlieb Heileman took over as sole owner.

With that as motivation, I returned home knowing I had found another way to fill those extra hours. I decided to research and document the history of G. Heileman Brewing Company. I started my research on October 22, 2000. Thanks to the Internet, I was quickly able to make some initial progress. After several days of researching, I remembered that my collection of Heileman beer steins might also be a good source of information. The steins provided me with plenty of new leads to follow. After a few trips to the public library, I discovered I had found a wealth of information.

In the spring of 2002, I connected with David DeLano. David had worked at Heileman and one of his roles was as company historian. David also had plans to write a book on Heileman. We decided to collaborate and spent the next two years conducting interviews and finalizing the book.

My goal was to leave behind a history of the company that meant so much to La Crosse, my family, and to me. I've enjoyed many hours compiling the information and learning the history of the brands that appeared on those bottle caps and the breweries that appear on the Heileman steins. I hope you enjoy reading about it.

—Paul D. Koeller

This book is dedicated to the memory of my father,
Paul Edward Koeller.
He was a life-long resident of La Crosse,
and a loyal employee of G. Heileman Brewing Company
for more than 40 years.
He passed away in 1994, but would have loved this book.

PAUL D. KOELLER

This book is dedicated to
all of my fellow Heileman employees
who diligently worked for the company
over a span of almost 138 years.
What a great run it was.

DAVID H. DELANO

PART I

History

Roy Kumm, Heileman president from 1957 to 1971, opened the door to growth within the brewing industry by instituting a strategy of acquiring troubled breweries, adding brands and wholesalers, and diversifying into other businesses. With Kumm at the helm, Heileman grew from the 39th largest brewery in the country to the nation's 15th largest.

PHOTO COURTESY CLEARY-KUMM FOUNDATION

This is the story of a few visionary leaders,
a supportive community in La Crosse,
thousands of dedicated Heileman employees,
and millions of satisfied customers around the world.

Chapter 1

Germany Comes to America

EARLY HISTORY 1858–1919

Gottlieb Heileman "built a business which extended over a vast territory."

—FROM THE BREWERY FOUNDER'S 1878 OBITUARY

Legend says Gottlieb Heileman searched for two years in the 1850s and tested hundreds of sites on his quest for a place to brew the perfect beer.

Gottlieb Heileman
PHOTO COURTESY OF MURPHY LIBRARY, UNIVERSITY OF WISCONSIN-LA CROSSE

While we'll never know if that is true, we do know that he eventually settled on La Crosse, Wisconsin, as the place to demonstrate his old-country brewing skills. Here the pure ice age water was 7,500 years old and crystal clear, having traveled hundreds of miles from the north through unending strata of limestone and gravel formations.

Little did he know of the profound impact that his dream would have on his new home over the next 140 years. By 1983, G. Heileman Brewing Company was the fourth-largest brewery in the United States with annual sales exceeding $1.3 billion. It had become one of the largest companies in La Crosse and employed more than 1,700 people there and thousands more around the country. Tens of thousands of tourists flocked to La Crosse to tour the brewery and millions worldwide became loyal drinkers of Heileman's beer.

But, less than 15 years after reaching the pinnacle of its success, the company would become the victim of the same thing that made it successful. Through a series of buyouts and failed business ventures, the brewery in La Crosse was closed and G. Heileman Brewing Company ceased to exist.

This is the story of a few visionary leaders, a supportive community in La Crosse, thousands of dedicated Heileman employees, and millions of satisfied customers around the world.

This is the story of the G. Heileman Brewing Company.

Wisconsin had one of the largest German settlements in America, and Germans made up the largest ethnic group in Wisconsin. Here they found a climate and topography similar to their homeland, perfectly suited for growing grains, with an abundant supply of crystal pure spring water for brewing the beer they loved so much.

There were already 22 breweries in Wisconsin by 1849, and within the next decade the number would grow to 166. In Milwaukee, Jacob Best, Joseph Schlitz, Val Blatz and others established successful breweries.

La Crosse sits on the shores of the Mississippi River in Western Wisconsin, the limestone bluffs towering above it. The Mount Simon aquifer lies beneath the river. While most of Wisconsin was scoured by glaciers during the Ice Age, the area surrounding La Crosse is in what geologists call the Driftless Area.

Dating back several centuries, the prairie around La Crosse was a camp and village site for Native Americans. The first European immigrants in the area were French Catholic missionaries, who named the area Prairie la Crossette after seeing the Native Americans playing a game that resembled lacrosse. In 1805, Major Zebulon Pike arrived in the area, climbed a bluff, and wrote the following description in his journal on September 5: "It is altogether a prospect so varied and romantic that a man may scarcely expect to enjoy such a one but twice or thrice in the course of his life."

Nathan Myrick was the first white settler and postmaster who took up residence there in November 1841. He opened a trading post near the Mississippi River in an area now known as Riverside Park, serving only a handful of structures and a few residents. However, as navigation on the Mississippi River expanded, La Crosse grew rapidly and soon became an important trading center along with other bustling river towns such as Prairie du Chien, Wisconsin, Galena, Illinois, Dubuque, Iowa, and Winona, Minnesota.

As migration continued westward, La Crosse grew into a beautiful city of about 4,000 people.

The first Germans began arriving in 1850, and these beer-loving German immigrants soon became the largest ethnic group, with their own German newspapers, churches, and social groups.

In October 1858 the railway spur between Milwaukee and La Crosse was connected, and the first train arrived from Milwaukee with 14 passenger cars. The trains provided a steadily growing westward population expansion, and a great opportunity for a brewer to ply his trade for the new arrivals.

John Gund and Gottlieb Heileman recognized the opportunity in La Crosse, and in 1858 they formed a historic partnership to build the City Brewery at 1018 South Third Street, near the banks of the Mississippi River. A newspaper article in the September 14, 1858, *National Democrat* stated: "The cellar of John Gund and Co.'s new brewery is now nearing completion. (It) will be the same size as Michel's and the beer to be manufactured will be equal to that of any one in the City."

City Brewery opened for business on November 13, 1858, with a modest initial production of less than five hundred 31-gallon barrels per year. Nonetheless, the product was well received by the citizens of La Crosse, and an advertisement placed in the

June 7, 1859, *La Crosse National Democrat* read as follows: "City Brewry (sic) John Gund & Co. at his Brewry (sic) in La Crosse is prepared to furnish Lager Beer in any quantity to Hotel or Saloon Keepers, or to families. Orders from any other town will be promptly attended to."

From the beginning, the market in La Crosse demanded a light-bodied beer known as lager beer that requires fermentation at a lower temperature than ale, with a yeast that drops to the bottom of the fermenting vessels. In the early years City Brewery brewed beer only during the winter, kegged and transported in large sleighs to the bluff caves in Mormon Coulee. There the beer was pumped into large wooden vats for aging in the cool confines of caves. By the 1860s, brewery workers began to cut ice from the Mississippi River and pack it away in stone buildings, thus providing a primitive refrigeration system that eliminated the arduous project of hauling the fresh beer to the caves. Electrical refrigeration would not be available until the 1890s.

By 1870, the city of La Crosse had grown to 7,785 inhabitants and City Brewery's production had increased to 3,000 barrels a year. During this time most breweries provided boardinghouses for their employees, and the average working day was 12 to 18 hours. Heileman's wife, Johanna, was known to provide lunches for the brewery's single workers, but felt that

The Heileman home at 925 South Third Street, in the 1890s.

PHOTO COURTESY OF MURPHY LIBRARY, UNIVERSITY OF WISCONSIN-LA CROSSE

the wives of the married workers should take care of their husbands' lunches.

Originally the Heilemans lived at 126 South Third Street, but tradition in those days was for the brewery owner to build his home adjacent to the brewery. Profits from City Brewery allowed Heileman to build a grand new home in 1870 for his family at 925 South Third Street. The same German craftsmen who in 1869 built La Crosse's largest Catholic church, Saint Joseph the Workman Cathedral at Sixth and Main streets, probably built the large brick Heileman house.

Heileman and Gund apparently had had a falling out by 1872, and they decided to part ways. In addition to the brewery, they also owned the International Hotel and Saloon in La Crosse, and legend says the two men flipped a coin to determine who would get the brewery and who would get the hotel and some other jointly owned properties. Heileman won the toss, took sole ownership of the brewery, and changed the name to G. Heileman's City Brewery.

Johanna Heileman

PHOTO COURTESY OF LA CROSSE COUNTY HISTORICAL SOCIETY

Gottlieb Heileman died on February 19, 1878, at the age of 54, following an illness of several weeks.

Johanna Heileman takes over

Heileman's widow, Johanna, was heiress to the estate and became president of the brewery. With the assistance of her sister Caroline's husband, Reinhard Wacker, she carried on the management of the brewery. Wacker was said to possess technical expertise in management and held the title of foreman. In 1879, the number of breweries in the United States peaked at 2,520, most of them opened by German immigrants. Heileman's was the third-largest brewery in La Crosse by 1880, using 17,295 bushels of malt and 9,560 pounds of hops to produce 7,170 barrels of beer. It employed 12 men and three boys at a total annual compensation of $7,200.

In the 1880s and 1890s, the Heileman brewery consisted of the brewery proper, the malt house, ice house, and bottling department. All of the buildings were made of stone to reduce the risk of fire. The malt house was designed and built by a German contractor and mason named John Fox. C.F. Struck, a Norwegian architect who arrived in La Crosse in 1877, designed the ice house for Heileman and several other breweries, and also was the architect for Germania Hall and numerous other buildings in La Crosse.

Fire was one of the major risks to a brewing operation in the late 1800s, because open fires were used in the brewing process and so many breweries were built of wood. Nearly every brewery in La Crosse experi-

Sketch of City Brewery in the 1890s. PHOTO COURTESY OF MURPHY LIBRARY, UNIVERSITY OF WISCONSIN-LA CROSSE

enced at least one serious fire in its history. In 1879, a fire at the Heileman household was extinguished by volunteer firefighters, who afterwards were served a cold luncheon, and beer, of course. One of the firefighters, Emil Traugott (E.T.) Mueller, was introduced to the Heilemans' daughter, Louisa. Romance blossomed, and they were married on May 17, 1881. Mueller, trained as an accountant, accepted a position as assistant manager and bookkeeper at Heileman, and in 1884 he was promoted to general manager. In this position he would preside over the management and growth of the brewery for the next several decades.

On May 1, 1890, the business was incorporated as The G. Heileman Brewing Company. Johanna carefully controlled the stock of the company, and chose to keep her daughters mostly in the background of the business. Instead, she relied on her sons-in-law (particularly Mueller) to manage the business following the incorporation. The Heilemans' only son, Henry, was a vice president and the assistant manager.

Heileman office, with a goat, company mascot, looking north on Third Street about 1910. The brewery's offices are on the right and the Heileman house is in the background. PHOTO COURTESY OF MURPHY LIBRARY, UNIVERSITY OF WISCONSIN-LA CROSSE

Early on the morning of August 15, 1895, Henry G. Heileman climbed into the hayloft of the barn behind the Heileman family residence, put a revolver to his head and took his own life. A La Crosse newspaper article claimed his suicide was "attributed to melancholia brought on by continued ill health. He had been complaining of not feeling well for several months and had given up his duties at the brewery. He had been subject to fits of despondency."

Suicide is a difficult subject to comprehend even with our enlightened understanding in the 21st century. At the time of his death, 26-year-old Henry Heileman was a bachelor who had lived with his mother and sisters his entire life. It was said the well-educated Henry rarely engaged in society and that he had but a few intimate friends. The precise reasons for Henry Heileman's action will never be known. His father, Gottlieb, died when Henry was 10 years old. Following the death of his father, the only male Heileman heir grew up and lived with a matriarchal mother and seven sisters as the brewery thrived and grew.

Henry became an adult and began work at the brewery at a time when his very capable older brother-in-law, E.T. Mueller, already had begun to assert himself in the management of the business. One could reasonably presume this environment created pressure on Henry to carry on with the family brewery business. Perhaps Henry may have been incapable of fulfilling that role, perhaps he simply chose not to, or perhaps there were other reasons. Nonetheless, Henry chose suicide.

When interviewing elderly Heileman descendants almost 100 years after Henry's death, the circumstances were still considered a dark and mysterious twist of fate. One elderly woman recalled that Johanna Heileman chose not to speak of the event at all in her later years due to the painful memories. Johanna chose to make Henry's suicide a family secret.

The product—Old Style is born

Around the turn of the 20th century, beer brand marketing in the United States came of age. Whereas breweries until then generally sold their product as Pilsner, Bohemian, Wiener or perhaps an Export-type beer, competition now dictated that distinct beer brands be developed and aggressively marketed. This was partially due to the increasing popularity of bottled beer, which encouraged early beer marketers to develop brand names and logos for the bottle labels.

Heileman's Wiener beer was advertised in a November 17, 1884, edition of *Nord Stern* (North Star), a German language magazine published in La Crosse. This is the first known reference to bottled beer produced at Heileman brewery, described as a light lager beer. In 1885, the label verbiage was all in German and the company was referred to as "Heilemann City

Heileman employees about 1900.
PHOTO COURTESY OF MURPHY LIBRARY, UNIVERSITY OF WISCONSIN-LA CROSSE

This 1899 photo shows the bottling department crew at G. Heileman Brewing Company in La Crosse. The picture was taken on the west side of Third Street, on a site now occupied by a statue of King Gambrinus. The brewery's main label at that time was Golden Leaf, although that brand was replaced within about two years by the introduction of Old Style Lager. In the picture, from left, are: front row – Peter Osweiler, Oscar Schoenfeld, Louis Gerke, Joseph Bogner, John Gessler (the brewmaster), Franz Mueller (bottle house foreman), Otto Kanard, Henry Platz, Otto Huebner and Herman Werth; second row – Martin Walchak, Anton Walchak, William Ryan, Emil Kapanke, George Bell (chief engineer), Sylvia Lauer, Agnes Beranek, Lena Putsch, Mary Kreitz and Joe Kaiser; third row – Fred Schultz, Adolph Luedke, Christ Duerrwaechter, Frank Lapitz, Hans Goetzke, William Hauswirth, Benny Schoenfeld and Joe Ziegler; top row – August Helke, Gust Schultz, John Fiedler, unidentified, Louis Schoen, Martin Alberts and Andrew Wangen. The girl on Gessler's lap in the front row is unidentified. The two dogs are Otis, the rat terrier being held by Platz, and Prince, who belonged to Gust Kanard, who operated a grocery store and tavern at Third and Mississippi streets for many years.

PHOTO COURTESY OF MURPHY LIBRARY, UNIVERSITY OF WISCONSIN-LA CROSSE

Brauerei." In 1890, Heileman introduced Picnic Beer, sold in 64-ounce bottles, a package known generically as "Picnics," which were intended to enhance the growing carry-home business. By 1892, Hofbrau, a dark brew, was also offered in bottles.

In 1885, Heileman's City Brewery opened its first agency in Glencoe, Minnesota. Agencies were brewery-owned distributorships that quickly proved to be an excellent way to expand sales beyond the limited delivery radius of the brewery. They were forebears of the modern beer distributors. Other agencies were opened over the next few years: Aberdeen, Milbank, Mobridge, Bowdle, and Sioux Falls in South Dakota; Wahpeton in North Dakota; and Albert Lea, Moorhead, East Grand Forks, Glenwood, Belgrade, Breckenridge, Duluth, Thief River Falls, and Waterville, all in Minnesota. Wisconsin agencies were established in Prairie du Chien and Independence, and Illinois agencies were established in Chicago and Rock Island. Sales in 1885 were 12,000 barrels. A year later, sales had increased to 16,000 barrels. Employment at the brewery in 1887 was 35 men.

William Hauswith was born October 20, 1858, in Milwaukee, and in 1879 moved to La Crosse and became a cooper (barrel maker). In 1886, he went to work in the Heileman cooperage department and worked there for 32 years, until Prohibition. Barrel making and maintenance were enormously important for brewers prior to the bottling of beer, which continues to be sold in barrels. Technology has greatly changed the painstaking effort necessary to produce pitch-lined kegs, made of oak and iron staves in leak-proof form in the old days.

During most of the 19th century, a large majority of American brewers, including Heileman, shied away from bottling beer. Spoilage was a problem, as was finding a stopper that worked, and federal regulations regarding the taxing of bottled beer were difficult and outdated. Beer had to be put in kegs first, taxed via tax stamps affixed to each barrel, and then removed from the kegs and bottled. Most brewers chose not to bottle. However, in 1887, Heileman introduced a patented white flint porcelain bottle stopper with a rubber grommet that replaced the customary cork stopper.

Heileman's Wiener beer was then offered in wooden cases packaged in the following configurations: twenty-four 32-ounce bottles, twelve 32-ounce bottles, thirty-six 12-ounce bottles, and twenty-four 12-ounce bottles.

In 1892, a Baltimore machinist named William Painter patented a crowned cork bottle cap. Previously, 1,500 other bottle-stopping devices had already been patented, but the crown top was the first one that really worked. It kept carbonation in and dirt out, and was to prove a boon to the sale of bottled beer. By the late 1890s, the discovery of pasteurization, along with the invention of the crowned cork cap and more sensible government regulations, had combined to create an environment much more hospitable for the widespread sale of bottled beer.

On December 20, 1899, the Golden Leaf trademark was purchased from Wilmann's Brothers Lithography of Milwaukee, and the Golden Leaf brand was introduced shortly thereafter, marketed as "a light body beer." The Old Times Lager brand was introduced in 1900, marketed as "a heavy body beer" and as "a Strong Old Beer of Golden Color." It was offered in dark green 16-ounce bottles only and was advertised in the La Crosse City Directory of 1900 by a jolly fat man saying, "Ha! Ha! That's the stuff."

Another brewery, however, claimed brand infringement and, to settle the issue, the word "Style" was substituted for "Times" in 1902, when plans were made to increase capacity to 175,000 barrels. Heileman's main brand was still "Golden Leaf Beer," but it was soon to be replaced with "Old Style Lager."

Early Brewery Success

The brewery's success in the first decade of the 20th century was quite remarkable, as indicated by records of the production barrelage on which Heileman paid federal excise tax from 1900 to 1913. Note the especially dramatic rise in bottled beer sales.

YEAR	BARRELS SOLD IN BOTTLES	BARRELS SOLD IN KEGS	TOTAL BARRELS SOLD
1900	5,117	25,484	30,601
1901	6,634	28,230	34,864
1902	9,200	28,262	37,462
1903	10,276	27,781	38,057
1904	14,082	29,851	43,933
1905	17,588	35,245	52,833
1906	22,357	41,632	63,989
1907	24,684	44,806	69,490
1908	30,366	46,370	76,736
1909	45,046	47,795	92,841
1910	44,256	53,909	98,165
1911	43,049	59,152	102,201
1912	N/A	N/A	114,441
1913	N/A	N/A	131,966

Old Style Lager was an immediate success. While Mueller got credit for the label creativity and the marketing savvy that would follow, Heileman brewmaster John Gessler was responsible for the recipe and the quality of the product. In 1898, Gessler had taken over as brewmaster from Wacker and served in this role from 1898 to 1912, assisted by Louis Schoen during later years. Their achievements were apparently well appreciated—at the annual Heileman stockholder's meeting, held on February 4, 1905, the board authorized that Gessler's salary be increased $300 and Mueller's increased by $600 a year. Gessler died in 1913 and was replaced by Otto E. Mueller, son of E.T., as brewmaster. He served in that role until 1930.

In March 1902, Old Style Lager was introduced to the public, and in 1905 Heileman got the rights to the "Old Style" label with a grenadier holding a bottle and stein. Demand was increasing for the new Old Style Lager and the company was taxed to supply it. Promoted heavily in La Crosse newspapers throughout its launching year of 1902, Old Style Lager sold 537,000 bottles from May 4 to December 4, 1902.

Old Style's unique bottle label was created through the marketing genius of Mueller, who said that the predominately green label, with its many interesting caricatures, illustrated the history of brewing, from ancient Teutonic times through the medieval monasteries of Europe to the modern day. The words Old Style Lager were quite small on the body label, but prominently displayed on the neck label. The 1902 body label also contained the lyrics to an old German drinking song (see box below).

Old Style Lager was originally marketed only in clear glass bottles that had raised *Old Style Lager* letters scripted in the glass above the body label. On the opposite side raised lettering specified "G. HEILEMAN BRG. CO. LA CROSSE, WIS.," and the bottle was capped with the cork-lined steel crown that had been patented 10 years earlier.

So successful was the brand in the pre-Prohibition years that many other breweries came out with similar sounding brand names, and by 1913 Old Style Lager had lots of competition. Other brewers were offering brands such as Old German Lager, Old Tavern Beer, Old Lager, Old Style Brew, Old Style Beer, Old German Beer, Old German Style Beer, Old Fashioned Beer, Old Settlers Beer, Old Style Select Beer, Ye Old Lager, and An Old Style Lager. It got to the point where Heileman launched an advertising campaign thanking "brother brewers for trying to imitate the snappy flavor and zest of Heileman's Old Style Lager, the bottle with the green label."

Heileman pursued litigation for brand infringement in at least one instance, but Mueller generally thought it best to use the imitators as a source of flattery in various advertising themes. The addition of a red triangle to the Old Style Lager label in 1914, which stated, "*none genuine without this signature— G. Heileman Brewing Company,*" was clearly intended to distinguish Heileman's Old Style Lager from the impostors. Old Style was soon being distributed nationwide and even internationally in Canada and the Caribbean.

The business continues to grow

During the last two decades of the 19th century, and continuing into the 20th century, brewers discovered another way to enhance beer sales through the control or ownership of "selling properties," such as beer gardens, restaurants, taverns, and hotels. This system was referred to as the "tied house," as breweries would have exclusive selling privileges there once ownership was established.

The Heileman Saloon, located in downtown La Crosse on the north side of Main Street between Second and Third streets, was one such property. Another was the "Corner Saloon," which Heileman purchased in downtown Cashton, Wisconsin. That building, still standing today, has "G. Heileman Brewing" inscribed in the corner turret. A 1912 picture

German verbiage on the label:	*English translation:*
Es lagen die alten Germanen	In olden days along the Rhein
An beiden Ufern des Rheins	The Germans could be found
Sie lagen auf Lowen Hauten	Lying around on lion skins,
Und tranken immer noch eins.	Drinking another round.

Brewery workers
PHOTO COURTESY OF MURPHY LIBRARY, UNIVERSITY OF WISCONSIN-LA CROSSE

of it shows a sign on the outside wall that states, "DRINK THAT GOOD OLD STYLE LAGER. MADE IN LACROSSE." The awning above the windows states the name of the saloon, "THE PALM GARDEN." "Tied house" systems were made illegal by federal law following Prohibition.

La Crosse brewers in the 19th century did not have antitrust laws to be concerned about, which enabled breweries to fix uniform prices. On May 1, 1898, the La Crosse brewers boldly posted prices as a unified group, announcing a price increase due to a hike in the federal excise tax. The notice read, "We the undersigned Brewers . . . hereby give notice that, owing to the increased Government Tax on Beer . . . the following uniform prices will be in force: KEG BEER per barrel . . . $8; BOTTLE BEER, 2 doz. quarts, $2.20; 1 doz. quarts, $1.20; 2 doz. quarts (export), $1.90: 2 doz. pints, $1.35; 2 doz. half pints, $.80; Pic-Nics, $1.10. Very respectfully, John Gund Brewing Co., C&J Michel Brewing Co., G. Heileman Brewing Co., Geo. Zeisler & Sons, Franz Bartl Hussa Brewing Co."

Major expansion took place in December 1902 to increase brewing capacity from 30,000 barrels to 160,000 barrels. The brewhouse, mill house, and beer storage cellars were constructed entirely of stone,

The brewery's working women
PHOTO COURTESY OF MURPHY LIBRARY, UNIVERSITY OF WISCONSIN-LA CROSSE

iron, asphalt, and concrete. All of the woodwork was removed to reduce the risk of fire, and new updated machinery was installed. The beer cellars now contained monster oak casks that held 500 barrels each.

Earlier in the year, Heileman was the largest nonunion brewery in La Crosse, but on August 23 a union was voted in. Total company payroll reached $200,000. By 1910, Heileman employed 285 people, including salesmen and agents.

Mueller wrote the following in 1911:

> *The Chicago market was modestly entered in 1908, with an equipment of two rigs, three horses, a manager and two helpers. The success of Old Style Lager in Chicago was instantaneous and created a widespread demand, from which much new and valuable business resulted. Our Chicago business is now well developed, and a regular sale is insured by the sale of our keg beer at $8 per barrel to 55 saloons, most of which we control. New saloon propositions are offered to us daily, three of which are now under consideration and these three will sell in the aggregate 400 barrels per month the year round. The control of a few more such stands will guarantee a good, steady profit from this regular*

business, while new trade will yield profits at an even greater ratio. The advantage gained by the great popularity of Old Style Lager in Chicago is priceless, as new business from all parts of the country comes to us daily as a direct result of it.

In 1914, as the original bottle house became inadequate to handle the increasing business, a new 90,000-square-foot, three-story bottle house, equipped with the most modern bottling machinery and with full basement, was built on the west side of Third Street. Even with this facility addition, business was brisk enough to require day and night shifts during the peak summer months. The old bottle house, on the east side of Third Street, was used as an office building until 1959 when it was destroyed by fire.

Old Style Lager beer was being shipped to 34 states by 1915. The total railroad carload shipments in 1916 (incoming and outgoing) totaled 3,998. Two years later Heileman shipped 140,000 barrels and purchased $141,036.37 worth of empty bottles.

Old Style Lager was now a popular brand throughout the South. Heileman also had distributors in all the major cities of Texas. For example, the distributor in Fort Worth, Texas, received 28 carloads a year. In Florida the distributor in Jacksonville received 30 carloads. The beer was then distributed across Florida to places such as Pensacola and Key West. In Chicago, Heileman employed 50 people to handle distribution. Heileman's beer was also purveyed in Canada, Puerto Rico, and the West Indies.

Johanna Heileman remained president of the company until her death on January 5, 1917, at the age of 85. At the time of her death she was still living in the family home at 925 South Third Street, and was survived by six daughters. Her funeral was held in the German Lutheran Church, and she was buried in Oak Grove Cemetery next to Gottlieb. Her death preceded the near-death experience of the United States brewing industry with the passage of the Volstead Act in 1919 and the start of Prohibition.

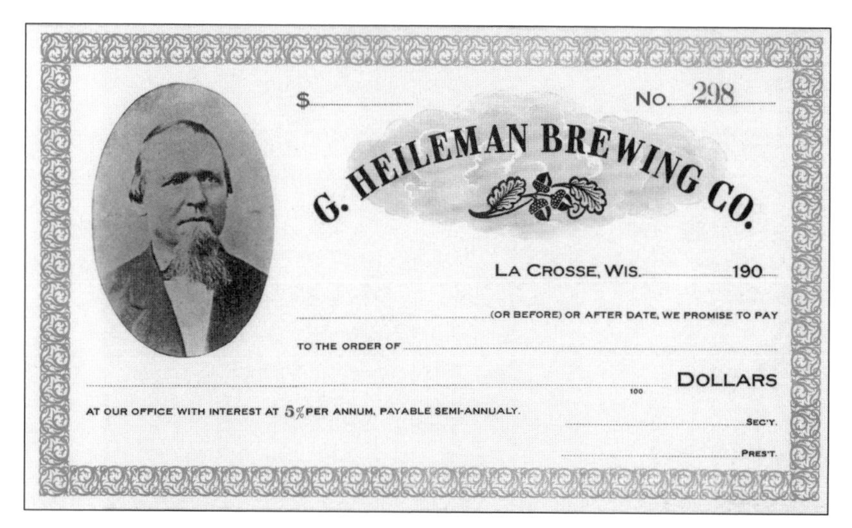
$ .... No. 298

G. HEILEMAN BREWING CO.

LA CROSSE, WIS. .... 190...

.... (OR BEFORE) OR AFTER DATE, WE PROMISE TO PAY

TO THE ORDER OF ....

.... 100 DOLLARS

AT OUR OFFICE WITH INTEREST AT 5% PER ANNUM, PAYABLE SEMI-ANNUALY.

.... SEC'Y.

.... PRES'T.

Corporate bonds like this one were issued to investors in G. Heileman Brewing Company in the early 1900s. Coupons attached to the bond could be detached and redeemed for quarterly payments.

FROM THE CLEARY-KUMM FOUNDATION

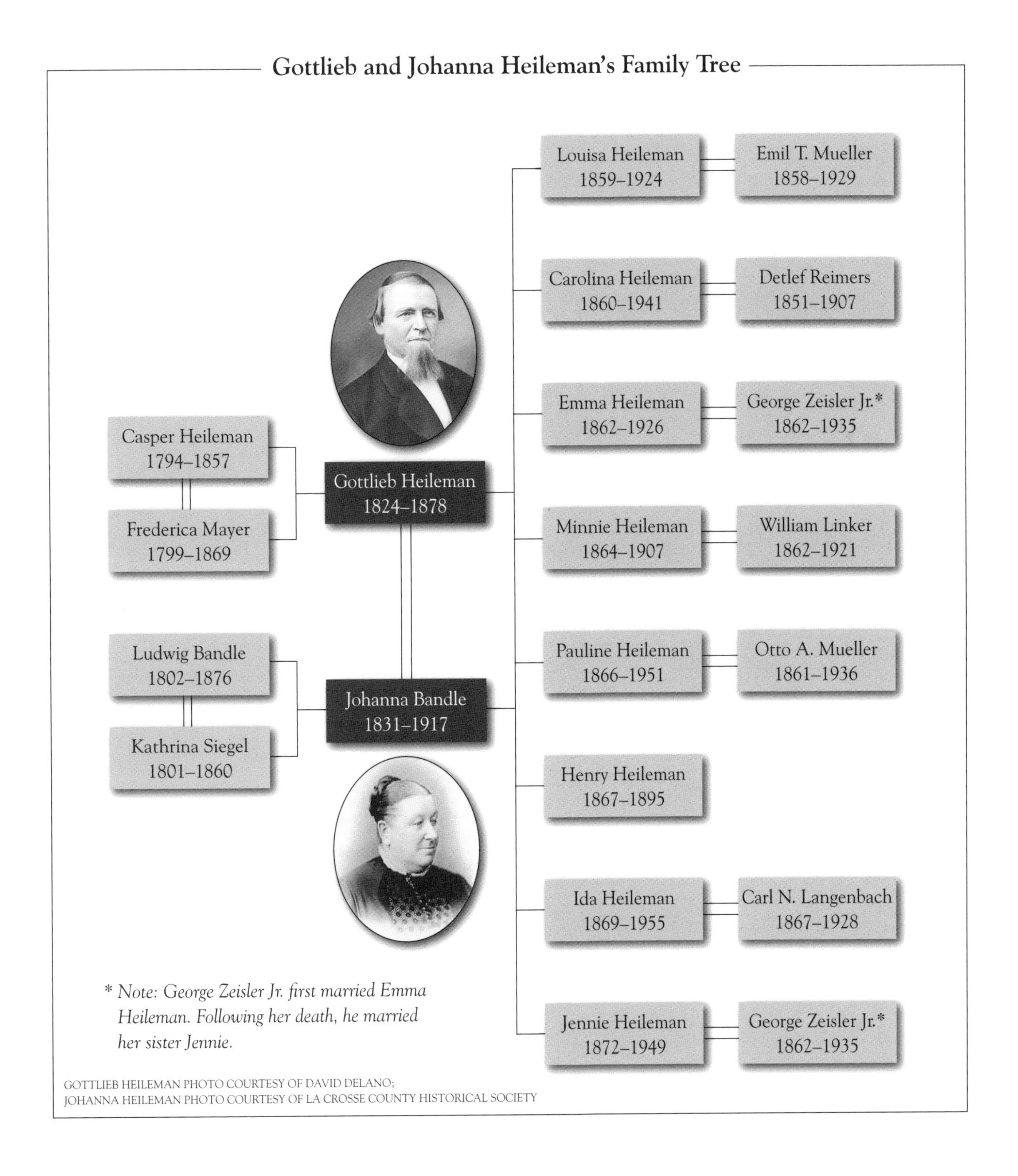

GOTTLIEB HEILEMAN PHOTO COURTESY OF DAVID DELANO;
JOHANNA HEILEMAN PHOTO COURTESY OF LA CROSSE COUNTY HISTORICAL SOCIETY

This is the way Rusty's Bar in Dresbach, Minnesota, looked in the 1940s. The bar was owned by Arthur Dickson until his death in 1938. He had a long red beard, which triggered the bar's name. The tavern was operated after his death by his wife, Ruby, and their son, Philip, who are in the picture. Note the Old Style Lager clock at upper left and the statue of a Heileman grenadier in the top center of the photo.

PHOTO COURTESY OF JON DICKSON

Chapter 2

Near Beer and Near Bankruptcy

THE BREWERY STAGGERS THROUGH PROHIBITION AND WORLD WAR II 1919–1956

You guys are nuts!

—BREWMASTER JAKE GEHRING'S RESPONSE TO EMPLOYEES SEEKING A SPECIAL BREW FOR A COMPANY PICNIC. BUT GEHRING PRODUCES A NEW BEER ANYWAY, AND SPECIAL EXPORT IS BORN.

The American Society for the Promotion of Temperance was formed in Boston in 1826. As early as 1836 the group proposed total abstinence, and in 1846 Maine was the first to pass a prohibition law. At the national level, a prohibition amendment to the U.S. Constitution was introduced in 1887.

E.T. Mueller

SKETCH COURTESY OF DAVID DELANO

The Twilight Lodge branch of the Good Templars was organized in La Crosse in October 1858, and the group later built a hall on the corner of Second and State streets. On April 12, 1873, the Sparkling Water Division No. 23, Sons of Temperance, was initiated. By 1880 it had more than 600 members. Other organizations sprang up in the 1870s. Mendotas organized on March 27, 1876, and the Temple of Honor, No. 51, was formed on April 8, 1876. The latter held meetings every Monday in the Temperance Hall for its 105 members. In 1880, a local chapter of the Women's Christian Temperance Union was founded.

Heileman jumped into the political fray in 1886 by joining the U.S. Brewers Association, and E.T. Mueller was elected secretary of the La Crosse chapter of the Personal Liberty League, founded that year as a political organization supportive of "wet" political policies and positions. At one time it had 114 members, mostly saloon owners. Their lawyer was J.W. Losey (for whom Losey Boulevard in La Crosse is named) and the president was John Pamperin, a maker of tobacco products and merchant in La Crosse. The Personal Liberty League existed until 1896.

In 1893, the Anti-Saloon League was organized in Oberlin, Ohio. In Wisconsin, more than 100 communities abolished liquor licenses in 1907 alone. In 1913 the Anti-Saloon League shifted strategies from its long-standing attempts to pass local saloon bans to an all-out effort to enact a federal constitutional amendment prohibiting all alcoholic beverage sales. The U.S. Brewers Association responded by emphasizing the difference between brewers, whose product was a beverage of moderation, and whiskey producers, who promoted drunkenness. This effort was generally unsuccessful.

The sinking of the *Lusitania* by a German submarine on May 17, 1915, and consequent loss of 125 American lives, stirred a strong anti-German sentiment throughout the United States, and brewers of mostly German descent felt the tide of public opinion turning against them. U.S. Attorney General A. Mitchell Palmer brought a variety of charges against German brewers in 1918. He suggested the brewers were supporting causes that were sympathetic to Germany, attempting to influence political candidates, and boycotting manufacturers who supported prohibition. Some of these investigations were specifically aimed at Milwaukee breweries, which, it was claimed, were owned by German aliens.

America declared war on Germany on April 6, 1917. Those of German descent in the United States, including many of the country's brewers, suddenly were on the receiving end of insults and insinuations questioning their patriotism. Much of the political success in promoting the prohibition movement was achieved by the "drys" over the next couple of years in a climate in which German-American brewers were broadly painted as pro-German.

By 1917, the District of Columbia and 21 states were dry. In May of that year, Congress banned the sale of alcoholic beverages to men in uniform as sentiment edged the country closer to national Prohibition. Then, in August, President Woodrow Wilson signed into law the Food Control Bill, which banned liquor distilling and reduced the grain supply allowed for brewers by 30 percent. Prohibition of beer and wine was temporarily delayed, but as the federal government put the squeeze on the brewing industry, the federal excise tax on beer climbed from $1.50 a barrel to $3 a barrel and finally to $6 a barrel on February 25, 1919. Effective May 1, 1919, brewing beer was prohibited, and effective July 1, 1919, its sale was prohibited.

The 18th Amendment to the Constitution, prohibiting the manufacture, sale and possession of alcoholic beverages, was passed by Congress on December18, 1917. Twenty-seven of the 48 states were already "dry," and little more than a year later, on January 16, 1919, Nebraska became the necessary 36th state to ratify the 18th Amendment. Only Connecticut and Rhode Island declined to ratify the amendment.

In May 1919, the U.S. House of Representatives initiated Bill 6810, which outlined the apparatus for enforcing prohibition. This bill was introduced by U.S. Rep. Andrew Volstead of Minnesota and thus became known as the Volstead Act. The bill was passed on October 10, 1919, but President Wilson vetoed it. Congress overrode the veto, the bill became law, and the lights totally went out on January 17, 1920, when it became illegal to manufacture, sell, transport or consume any beverage exceeding ½ of 1 percent alcohol.

Prior to Prohibition there were more than 1,700 breweries in the United States. When Prohibition ended, in 1933, fewer than 750 breweries reopened their doors.

On May 19, 1919, Heileman management revealed a new business strategy with an advertisement that appeared in the *La Crosse Tribune and Leader-Press* introducing the company's latest product—Heileman New Style Lager, a near beer that contained less than ½ of 1 percent alcohol. The advertisement described the new brew as "The Snappy Cereal Beverage" and noted the product "conforms to every government regulation."

Brewery exterior, 1920s or 1930s. PHOTO COURTESY OF MURPHY LIBRARY, UNIVERSITY OF WISCONSIN-LA CROSSE

Mueller resigned as Heileman general manager in 1919 because of failing health and was replaced by his undersecretary, R.A. Albrecht. Other officers of the company during this period included: Carl N. Langenbach, vice president; L.W. Schroeder, treasurer; Herman Jahn, accountant; Louis Schoen, brewmaster; and Theodore Solie, credit manager.

Heileman managed to survive the 13 years of Prohibition through a combination of careful management and creative products. The company produced near beer and other soft drinks, as well as malt syrup. The near beer was sold under "Delight," "New Style Lager," "Coney Island," and "King of Clubs" labels. Heileman also introduced several soda pop brands, including Old Style Grape, Old Style Ginger Ale and Old Style Root Beer, playing off the brand name without much success. Also sold was a "Malt Tonic" promoted as "a healthful and invigorating malt and hop tonic that aids both young and old in the restoration and preservation of good health."

The near beer brewing process began by brewing beer in the normal way. But after the proper aging most of the alcohol was removed, with the resulting product then again aged in large white oak storage vats, each holding 600 barrels. It was filtered four times to remove all yeast cells, then pasteurized to be free of bacteria and other dangerous elements. Heileman continued to keep its equipment in top-notch shape.

Near beer sales, never very much to start with, continued to decline in the early 1920s. Heileman nevertheless continued to ship its nonalcoholic products throughout the Midwest, with distributors located in Minnesota, North Dakota, South Dakota, Wisconsin, Illinois, Nebraska, Kansas, Iowa, Oklahoma, Wyoming, Montana, Michigan, and Indiana. By 1926, however, shipments had dropped to 20,000 barrels, down from 140,000 in the pre-Prohibition year of 1917.

It was just too easy for people to make "heimgemacht," German for home-brew. Scores of brewers, Heileman included, consequently decided they might be able to eke out a livelihood by manufacturing home-brew products. It produced malt syrups and extracts specifically for this market and introduced a near beer called "Spike" in 1922.

"Old Style Malt Syrup" was manufactured and canned under the Heileman label by the Blatz Brewery of Milwaukee. The net profit from selling the malt syrup in the first year was $10,000. In the second year, the profit was up to $25,000. The malt syrup was sold primarily in La Crosse in grocery stores, confectionery stores, butcher shops, and even barbershops. Beer-making kits were available and stills were commonly found on Mississippi River islands or in the basements of homes.

In 1927, Heileman executives publicly expressed their hope that the government would soon favor a modification of the Volstead Act. The company wanted the government to permit the manufacture and sale of pure, healthful, invigorating, and nourishing beverages, such as real beer. A product produced by a scientific process, void of all bacteria and other dangerous elements, surely was a better option than the crude stuff now made by millions throughout the land, executives suggested. It also was pointed out that bootlegging was an industry

Bob and Gerry Brenner wanted George Pierce at their wedding on August 30, 1940, but Pierce couldn't leave his job at Heileman. So the wedding came to him in the form of visits from two bridesmaids, Ilene Brenner (left) and Dorothy Kessel.

PHOTO COURTESY OF MURPHY LIBRARY, UNIVERSITY OF WISCONSIN-LA CROSSE

that paid no taxes, and police records showed that corruption, bribery, and crime prevailed throughout America from increased drunkenness. Heileman called beer "an innocent harmless beverage, a true temperance beverage," and "not liquor that creates intoxication."

Heileman operated strictly within the law during Prohibition, despite being offered $40 to $50 a barrel for real beer by those who didn't mind breaking the law to make high profits. Gangsters Al Capone, Bugs Moran and Dion O'Banion were quick to seize these opportunities with Chicago breweries, while mobsters Dutch Schultz and Waxey Gordon did the same in New York City. In La Crosse, meanwhile, Heileman was under constant scrutiny by federal agents checking to see that products did not exceed ½ percent alcohol by volume.

Ten years after the advent of Prohibition, and caught between the Depression and bootleg beer, the Heileman brewery was in a severe financial crisis and barely able to remain in business. The number of legally operating breweries in the United States had dropped from 303 in 1929 to 231 by the end of 1930.

On September 12, 1931, a massive fire at the Heileman brewery destroyed three warehouses and the roof of a fourth. The loss was estimated at $50,000. The fire consumed warehouse buildings on the east side of Third Street between Win-

Decorated truck, Prohibition era, advertising New Style Lager.
PHOTO COURTESY OF MURPHY LIBRARY, UNIVERSITY OF WISCONSIN-LA CROSSE

nebago and Mississippi streets that contained kegs and equipment unused since Prohibition. A crowd of nearly 10,000 people gathered to watch as clouds of dense black smoke, visible for miles and caused mainly by the burning of the pitch-lined kegs, made fighting the fire difficult. There was no fire insurance, and the company hit rock bottom. Albrecht stated bravely that the loss would not interfere with the plant's operations, but only a total change in the business climate could save Heileman from bankruptcy.

Fortunately for the brewery fate intervened, and the nation's 13-year social experiment was coming to an end. In 1932 Franklin Delano Roosevelt successfully campaigned on a New Deal platform that included the repeal of Prohibition. Nine days after taking office, on March 13, 1933, FDR sent a message to Congress strongly urging the "immediate modification of the Volstead Act in order to legalize the manufacture and sale of beer." Congress agreed and within 10 days a bill was passed that legalized the manufacture and sale of 3.2 percent (alcohol by volume) beer. At midnight on April 7, 1933, the sale of 3.2 percent beer would become legal again in Wisconsin, 20 other states, and the District of Columbia.

By the end of the year all but a handful of states were "wet" again. At the G. Heileman Brewing Company loading dock, late on the night of April 6, 1933, trucks waiting to pick up 3.2 percent beer were lined up for blocks. For 30 days prior to that, Heileman had been allowed by federal agents to bottle and keg beer so a supply would be available.

According to an eyewitness, a steam engine, preloaded on brewery premises, pulled out at precisely midnight. "Two or three trucks [also] left at that time. The other truck drivers got into a loud argument as to who should be loaded next. I saw trucks there from North Dakota, South Dakota, Minnesota, Iowa and Wisconsin. There were several spectators and everyone enjoyed the affair," wrote Harry C. Welch many years later. The last truck, belonging to a distributor from Viroqua, Wisconsin, was loaded long after midnight.

Now the Heileman brewery was swamped with demands for beer, and the staff worked 18 hours a day to fill orders taken by telephone, wire, and in person. Those orders came from all over the Midwest, as well as Boston, Los Angeles, Winnipeg, and even the West Indies. The plant released 2,500 barrels of beer in the next two days, but part of the staff was kept busy turning down new orders and returning checks for thousands of dollars that accompanied orders that could not be filled.

Heileman resumed full-scale brewing activities in 1933, and during the following two years an aggressive facilities upgrade was undertaken. A new brewhouse was built with a 400-barrel kettle, additional cellars, new bottling equipment, and a modernized power plant and storage vats.

It had been realized that a significant influx of capital would be needed to bring the brewery back up to speed, and the second generation of the Heileman

Heileman beer distribution warehouse, about 1940. PHOTO COURTESY OF MURPHY LIBRARY, UNIVERSITY OF WISCONSIN-LA CROSSE

family was getting on in years and had endured significant economic hardship for the previous 13 years. The time had come for a change of ownership and the Paul Davis Company of Chicago was engaged to arrange for the sale of the business from primarily Heileman family members to a public corporation. On July 19, 1933, the company incorporated as a Delaware corporation called G. Heileman Brewing Company Incorporated.

Albert C. Smith became the first president of the new corporation and his first duty was to sign stock certificates. As Smith did so, on a hot Chicago afternoon, he became sick and died of a heart attack. An emergency meeting of the board of directors took place at 10 P.M. to select a successor. Harry Dahl was chosen for the job and continued in that capacity until 1936. Directors of the new corporation were Harry Dahl, John J. Desmond, Quincy H. Hale, Nordahl Nustad, and Robert D. Gordon, all from the La Crosse area, and Fred H. Hankerson and F. B. Evans, both of Chicago.

The post-Prohibition years

The brewing industry was undergoing massive change, from a costly and labor-intensive process to a more automated one, driven by the need to produce large volumes in order to survive. Over the next two decades large breweries were able to successfully use automation to increase their production to three barrels of beer per man-hour, compared with half a barrel per man-hour for the small regional brewers. This allowed the large brewers to pass these cost savings on to the consumer, making it more difficult for the small breweries to compete.

In an attempt to regain market share in Chicago, an advertisement appeared in the *Chicago Daily Tribune* on September 27, 1933, stressing the "genuineness" of Old Style Lager (verified by the "G. Heileman Brewing Company" signature in the red triangle on the label). It also assured customers that Heileman had the same brewmaster as prior to Prohibition.

On December 5, 1933, the 21st Amendment was ratified, making "strong" beer legal once again. Except where forbidden by state or local law, hard liquor, wine, and beer of any strength could be legally manufactured and sold once again. Beginning at 12:01 A.M., Heileman shipped 11,000 cases of "strong" beer. After 2 A.M. trucks were turned away empty, as the brewery had no more beer to sell.

Louis Schoen, Heileman's brewmaster, was fired in the spring of 1934 after a disagreement with management's decision to purchase glass-lined aging tanks. He preferred the traditional pitch-lined wooden tanks. His successor was Jake Gehring, a large, burly man given to bellowing out orders to employees. He was reputed to have been involved with bootlegging operations and gangsters in Chicago during Prohibition. Gehring began his employment with Heileman in 1933 and was fired in 1937, allegedly for allowing bad product to get into the marketplace.

Gehring's claim to Heileman fame came in the summer of 1934 when, as a gag, he concocted a "special" brew for employees at the company picnic. Actually, certain members of Brewery Workers Local 81 had requested a high-alcohol "special" brew for this event. "You guys are nuts," was Gehring's response, but he went ahead and brewed it anyway.

Beer delivery truck from early 1940s. PHOTO COURTESY OF MURPHY LIBRARY, UNIVERSITY OF WISCONSIN-LA CROSSE

As it turned out, the picnickers loved this "special" brew. Some of the employees were said to have literally gone "crazy" over the product, and Special Export was born.

At that time Heileman was producing only one beer brand, Old Style Lager. Given the employees' reaction to Gehring's new recipe, and with business booming shortly after the repeal of Prohibition, a decision was made to offer this other brand to the public. Special Export's unique characteristics convinced management that it could sell itself without advertising. Thus, in the fall of 1934, Heileman Special Export was introduced to the public. The first packaging was in a 12-ounce brown bottle, and the label and crown declared, "Heileman's Old Style Lager Special Export." The neck label was yellow, which led to the brand's first nickname—"yellow necks."

The original Special Export was very strong, about 6 percent alcohol by volume. Gehring's formula included a liberal dose of corn syrup to fortify the alcohol content, and rice adjuncts were substituted for traditional corn. Brewed using the traditional kraeusening process, Special Export had a distinctive taste and soon established a place for itself in the market. Although it attracted a niche of loyal consumers, sales were but a small fraction of Old Style Lager's during the 1930s and 1940s.

In 1936 the aging tanks in the cellars of the brewery were wooden upright structures containing 350 barrels each. Gehring would occasionally draw from these tanks into a copper cup to test the beer. The aging tank that contained Special Export was next to an entryway, a location well known to the brewery workers. The workers were allowed to drink a mug of beer twice a day, dispensed at a specified area. Drawing beer for consumption from the aging tanks was a privilege reserved strictly for the brewmaster. Management soon became suspicious that more than Gehring's test draws were being removed when it was noted that the ring left inside the Special Export tank was down five feet from full!

Heileman announced plans to start canning beer for the first time on August 13, 1935. One of the first breweries in the United States to use a "metal bottle," Heileman called it the Cap-Sealed Cone Top. Designed by Continental Can Company, the new container's main advantage was that the brewery could use existing bottling lines to fill the cone-top cans. The first cone-top cans were closed with a regular bottle crown and lined with a waxy substance that did not hold up well. Also, the cone shape allowed for a substantial amount of air to be trapped within the can, causing premature oxidation and deterioration of the product. Cone tops were eventually replaced with a flat-top can that had a baked synthetic, resinous, plastic lining. Steel kegs also began to replace wooden kegs at this time and were also coated with a heat-polymerized, synthetic resin liner, necessary because beer tends to acquire undesirable flavors from direct contact with metals.

By 1935, Heileman was turning out 1,800 barrels of beer every day and also had an extensive business in half-gallon picnic bottles, daily selling 3,000 cases of four bottles each. Another third of the beer was shipped each day, in quart and pint bottles, to 37 states. (During this time Heileman also introduced an eight-ounce "Junior" bottle.)

Heileman came up with a unique way to advertise and distribute its beer when it built and opened its Bier Stube (beer room), which was modeled after a 16th-century Dutch inn. The Bier Stube was an exact replica of the tavern scene in painter Fritz Wagner's "The Mariner's Return," which depicts three ship owners listening in wonder to tales told by a ship's captain just returned from a voyage to distant ports. Heileman at one time owned the original of the Wagner painting, and during the 1940s proudly displayed it as a tribute to the rich brewing heritage of its own timeless classic, Old Style beer.

World War II years

From 1939 to 1945, beer was shipped only to 18 states because of World War II rationing, and 75 distributors were eliminated. During the war about 15 percent of Heileman's production was sent to the troops, far different from World War I, when the troops were denied the brew. There were severe shortages of tin, and bottle caps were in short supply, but Heileman developed and successfully implemented a bottle cap rebuilding program. The company also experienced a shortage of equipment parts. Due to war rationing, the amount of hops used had

The Bier Stube

Formerly the brewmaster's office, the Bier Stube was used as a guest room for out-of-town distributors visiting the plant. It was reached by old stone steps with a wrought iron railing that led to a heavy oak door whose upper section could be opened for serving.

Furniture was specially constructed of solid oak, the chairs upholstered in red leather and studded with brass-headed nails just as in the painting. On the west side of the room a high window featured antique leaded glass with air bubbles similar to hand blown glass; through it, a painting of a medieval street scene gave the illusion of looking out over old-world shops. A model of an antique Spanish galleon, an iron treasure chest, old paintings on the wall, and a reproduction of a map of the Old World were placed around the room, just as in the Wagner painting.

FROM THE CLEARY-KUMM FOUNDATION

to be cut back by a third, which resulted in a much lighter beer. A return to the original recipe had been planned for when the war was over, but people liked the lighter taste so Heileman kept the new recipe.

During World War II the Selective Service took a totally different attitude toward the brewing industry, compared with the anti-beer prejudice of World War I. It ruled that anyone directly involved in the brewing industry was exempt from military service. The rule did not apply to those who worked in the bottling operation, however, and Paul E. Koeller (father of the co-author of this book) was one of those who went off to serve in the U.S. Army. When he returned to La Crosse he was given his job back and given credit for his time in the military. He continued to work in the bottle house until retiring in March 1982. About 750 breweries had reopened after Prohibition, but by 1945 there were only about 470 still operating in the United States.

At the end of World War II there were more than 450 employees working at Heileman. Company stock was held primarily by residents of La Crosse and the surrounding area. No individuals or institutions held more than five percent of the stock. Three of the Heileman daughters owned stock—Mrs. Otto Miller, Mrs. Ida H. Langenbach, and Mrs. Jennie Zeisler. There also were two granddaughters of the original Heileman family whose husbands were on the board of directors, Mrs. John J. Desmond and Mrs. William Warmington.

The board of directors consisted of: Robert D. Gordon of Winnetka, Illinois, and formerly of La Crosse; F. B. Evans and Charles B. Goes of Chicago; William Warmington of Winona, Minnesota; and

The first group of retiring Heileman workers included front row, left to right—Bill Broese, Paul Gruley, John Platz, Bernhard Schoenfeldt, Matt Schmidt and Bill Netzer; back row, left to right—Rube Poehling, Emil Horn, Gus Sill, Ted Solie, Bob Zeiler, Hal Lehrke, John Mehren, Herman Jahn, Joe Meiner, Otto Goede and Herman Bantle. Picture was taken February 17, 1944.

PHOTO COURTESY OF MURPHY LIBRARY, UNIVERSITY OF WISCONSIN-LA CROSSE

Nordahl Nustad, John Desmond, and Q. H. Hale, all of La Crosse. Company officers were: Nustad, president; Desmond, secretary and treasurer; and Roy E. Kumm, assistant secretary and treasurer. The brewmaster was K.P. Shellhaus, and Paul J. Voelker was the assistant brewmaster.

Company sales continued to be negatively affected by shortages after the war. There also were government restrictions on the use of grain for beer production. To address these concerns, Heileman obtained prize-winning malting barley seeds and distributed them to seven farmers in La Crosse County, who grew more than 1,000 acres of high-quality barley.

A 59-day strike at Heileman lasted from May until July in 1948. Settlement of the strike brought many new benefits for workers, including paid holidays, paid vacations, overtime pay for Saturday work, and

Heileman beer sales from 1950 to 1956

YEAR	BARRELS SOLD
1950	426,538
1951	373,988
1952	377,841
1953	500,475
1954	471,430
1955	495,693
1956	461,734

third-shift premium pay. Workers also received pay raises that increased the average yearly salary from $1,665 in 1940 to $2,846 by 1948.

Later that year, with the strike settled, the company undertook a five-year capital improvement project. Plant improvements included high-speed bottling lines, new conveyor systems, and a completely new oil-burning malt house. The size of the brewhouse was doubled in 1949, and additional storage cellars were constructed. By the end of the modernization in 1950, the brewery in La Crosse had huge storage cellars with a capacity of more than 50,000 barrels, and was one of the most modern and efficient breweries in the world.

In the early 1950s the Korean War hit Heileman sales. Federal excise taxes were once again increased, rationing was back, and there were more shortages of tin. Although a 1953 brewery strike in Milwaukee helped to stimulate Heileman sales, barrel sales during this period were nonetheless stagnant.

At this point, some Heileman directors felt it was time for a change in management, and on October 16, 1956, President R. T. Johanson resigned from his position. Kumm was named president on February 11, 1957, and Trygve N. Nustad replaced Johanson on the board of directors.

Kumm had definite ideas about where he wanted the company to go, including a return to Heileman's original emphasis on quality control. He also recognized the importance of the wholesale distributors and for the first time invited some 150 of them to the General Sales Kickoff Meeting of March 4, 1957, in La Crosse. Here the new packaging for the Old Style brand was unveiled, to be introduced in May 1957. "Lager" was dropped from the name and the 55-year-old label, which had undergone numerous but basically insignificant changes since 1902, was replaced with the red, white and blue Old Style shield.

Roy E. Kumm

PHOTO COURTESY OF CLEARY-KUMM FOUNDATION

However, Mueller's original caricatures of brewing history remained in the background.

The new look was a result of extensive research which, according to the *La Crosse Tribune,* "confirmed the effectiveness of Old Style's 'aged longer' story and also brought to light an unusual brand loyalty among Old Style drinkers."

The new sales pitch of 1957 held that there were two kinds of people in the world, those who thought Old Style was the world's finest beer, and those who had not tasted it yet. This theme was promoted through newspapers, television, radio, and outdoor advertising.

In 1958, a group led by Bernard Decheine and Warren Loveland unsuccessfully attempted to take control of the company though a stockholders' proxy fight, but Kumm maintained control and was about to lead Heileman into an unprecedented period of growth and prosperity.

King Gambrinus Arrives

Early in April 1939, Heileman made a purchase that in later years came to symbolize the brewery in La Crosse. A statue of King Gambrinus, which had originally cost $3,500, was purchased for $100 from a defunct New Orleans brewery. The statue still stands along Third Street on the east side of the brewery.

The 15-foot-tall, 2,000-pound royal figure is clad in a purple suit with a red cape trimmed in white over a blue coat, and sports a glorious golden crown. Teutonic people enthroned King Gambrinus as the patron saint of beer in the latter half of the 13th century. The brewer's guild suggested this hero was the inventor and king of beers.

Wagon promoting war bonds in front of bottle house, from postcard, early 1940s.

PHOTO COURTESY OF MURPHY LIBRARY, UNIVERSITY OF WISCONSIN-LA CROSSE

Chapter 3

Here Kumms Heileman

THE KUMM YEARS AND THE START OF EXPANSION 1957–1971

His inspired leadership lives on in those of us who follow.

—TRIBUTE TO ROY KUMM IN HEILEMAN'S 1971 ANNUAL REPORT

Shortly after joining the accounting department in 1932, Roy E. Kumm began his rise to power at Heileman, and before his career was over he had become one of the most influential men in the history of the company.

He was named chief accountant in 1937, and in 1947 Heileman President Nordahl Nustad promoted Kumm to comptroller. He was named company treasurer and a member of the board just two years later.

In 1957, Kumm became president of Heileman, by then the 39th largest U.S. brewery, although some were referring to it as a "troubled regional brewer." Kumm saw that if Heileman continued what it was doing the company would go broke. The only alternatives seemed to be to sell out to another company or turn the company around from within.

He established a three-pronged attack aimed at surviving and thriving:

1. Expand the network of distributors to gain access to new markets.
2. Add production capacity.
3. Offer a wide variety of brands in different price ranges.

Kumm's biggest fear was getting locked into one geographic market and a price war with a large national brewery. He embarked on two-year strategies, five-year strategies, and 10-year strategies designed to buy troubled regional breweries in order to expand rather than build new, and he favored breweries with a strong network of wholesalers. These strategies served Heileman well for the next 25 years.

The total number of barrels of beer sold in the United States decreased from 87 million in 1947 to 84 million in 1958, and the annual consumption of beer per individual decreased from 18.5 gallons in 1948 to 15.9 in 1956. In the decade before 1959, an industry that had supported 800 breweries declined

Musicians promoting Old Style Lager participate in a parade on La Crosse's Fourth Street about 1935.

PHOTO COURTESY OF MURPHY LIBRARY, UNIVERSITY OF WISCONSIN-LA CROSSE

to slightly more than 200, and profits had significantly decreased for most. Almost half of the remaining breweries were operating at a loss and were on the verge of closing.

The percentage of beer purchases in retail stores grew from 17 percent in 1949 to 52 percent in 1959 and was predicted to increase to 70 percent by the mid-1960s. To capitalize on this trend, Heileman offered completely redesigned cans, labels, and six-pack packaging in the summer of 1957. The company modernized its advertising as well, and sponsored the popular television show *Sea Hunt*.

Meanwhile, national brewers introduced low-cost brands. Heileman, however, was only marketing Old Style, a premium brand, and Special Export, a super premium brand. In December 1959, it purchased 51 percent of the Kingsbury Brewing Company of Sheboygan, Wisconsin, the No. 1 most popular-priced beer in the state, and also introduced a new Special Export Malt Liquor to fill out its product line.

Kingsbury operated breweries in Sheboygan and Manitowoc, Wisconsin, along with the Sioux City (Iowa) brewery, an unprofitable plant that was closed in October 1960.

The steady pace of expansion was interrupted early on December 12, 1959, when Heileman night watchman Robert E. Lee—along with Borge "Bugsy" Knutson (part owner of Walt's restaurant directly across the street) and a passing policeman—called in reports that flames were shooting out of the Heileman corporate office building. Both on-duty and off-duty La Crosse firemen fought the blaze with all available trucks until it was under control at 2:38 A.M. The last flames were put out between 8 and 9 A.M. The building was destroyed.

A storeroom housing all advertising and office supplies was gone, but company records were mostly intact in the main vault and in a smaller safe in Kumm's office. Firemen saved most of the company records from the basement, although those documents were somewhat water damaged. The estimated loss from the fire was $100,000, but it was entirely covered by insurance.

The day after the fire the switchboard was up and operating above the Bier Stube. It was later moved to the yellow brick Mueller House at 915 South Third Street. The advertising department began operating in the old USO building on Fourth Street near King Street, and the sales and purchasing departments found a new home in the brewmaster's office. The shipping and order department was moved to the northwest corner of the company warehouse, and the accounting department took up residence in the rear of the taste and chemistry laboratories.

Rather than rebuild, Kumm felt it was more important to invest the money in continued expansion. Consequently, in 1960, the company purchased Gottlieb Heileman's old brick house at 925 South

This structure, built in traditional German style, was the original Heileman bottle house. It housed corporate offices when it burned on December 12, 1959. Employees posed for this picture about 1910.

PHOTO COURTESY OF MURPHY LIBRARY, UNIVERSITY OF WISCONSIN-LA CROSSE

Third Street for use as offices to replace those destroyed in the fire.

The effects of the fire dealt with, Heileman was ready to again concentrate on expansion and selling more beer. The company saw some of the trends from the previous decade beginning to change. The number of people of drinking age increased as the baby boomers were growing up, and an improved economy was creating more spendable income and leisure time for the average person.

To capitalize on these trends, Heileman began sponsoring professional sports. In 1961 it sponsored the Chicago Cubs baseball broadcasts on WGN television, and signed a contract to make Old Style available at Wrigley Field. It also sponsored both the radio and the initial television broadcasts of Chicago Bears football games.

On July 1, 1962, Heileman purchased the Fox Head Brewing Company in Waukesha, Wisconsin, for $1,351,000 in cash. It had production of 159,000 barrels of beer, including Fox Head Lager, Old Waukesha Ale, Fox Head "400" Dark, Fox Head "400" Light, Fox Deluxe, and Weber. Kingsbury's debt was then paid off, and Heileman and Kingsbury merged into a single entity on December 21, 1962.

On October 1, 1963, Heileman purchased the brewing rights and some assets of the Independent Milwaukee Brewery. That added Braumeister to its stable of beers, which by now included Old Style, Special Export, Special Export Malt Liquor, Fox Head 400, Fox de Luxe, Braumeister, Wisconsin Premium Kingsbury, Weber, Heidelbrau, and two near beers, Kingsbury Brew and Kingsbury Zing. Kingsbury had a large market in northern Wisconsin and in the Twin Cities, Fox Head was strong in New Jersey and New York, while Braumeister added markets in the Eastern Midwest.

In 1963, the company introduced a new corporate trademark to represent its holdings, a black Maltese eagle inscribed with the words "House of Heileman." Sales were up 20 percent over 1962, and total capacity at the plants in La Crosse and Sheboygan

The Tradition of Oktoberfest Begins

A suggestion, which vastly increased the consumption of Heileman beers over many years without the need for any further acquisitions, was made in 1961 by two malt house employees of German descent.

Why not put on an autumn festival similar to Germany's Oktoberfest?

Heileman and the Greater La Crosse Area Chamber of Commerce launched the first festival, which ran October 13–15, 1961. The term "Oktoberfest" was registered with the State of Wisconsin in 1962, and "Oktoberfest USA" was registered with the federal government in 1963. The company established a $1,000 scholarship in 1966 for an outstanding student from Munich, Germany, to study in the Midwest, to promote friendship between the two cities.

was about a million barrels. The company declared a 30-cent dividend, up 5 cents from the previous year. Earnings were $639,259, which was $1.41 a share on sales of $20,316,000.

Now Heileman added the malt house from Duluth Brewing and Malting and kept its warehouses for distribution into northern Wisconsin and Minnesota. Later on Heileman bought the rest of the assets of Duluth Brewing and Malting and obtained the Karlsbrau and Royal 58 brands. Within six months of the purchase, those two brands had been discontinued. The malt house was vacated by July 1, 1966, to make way for the new I-35 route into Duluth.

More important to the long-term growth and prosperity of the House of Heileman was Kumm's hiring of his son-in-law, Russell G. Cleary, in 1960. Cleary, a lawyer, went on to play the largest role of any individual in the history of the G. Heileman Brewing Company.

Cleary was promoted to vice president of Heileman and then named general counsel in 1964. He was in charge of negotiations, acquisitions, integration of acquired firms, labor relations, general supervision of legal matters, divisional advertising management, and company-owned real estate.

Under Cleary, Heileman purchased the Gluek Brewery of Minneapolis in December 1964, acquiring the Stite Malt Liquor brand, which it continued to produce for many years. Heileman closed the Minneapolis brewing operation shortly after the purchase. Cleary was named to the Heileman board of directors in 1967.

Under his direction the company generated additional cash by selling unused property in Manitowoc, Minneapolis, and Sioux City. The proceeds were used to invest in the improvement and expansion of the breweries in La Crosse and Sheboygan, which saw the installation of additional storage tanks, warehouses, and bottling and canning lines.

Roy Kumm celebrates the 1964 Oktoberfest with his granddaughters, Kristine Cleary, left, and Sandra Cleary.
PHOTO COURTESY OF CLEARY-KUMM FOUNDATION

Aerial view of Heileman operations in La Crosse about 1965.
PHOTO COURTESY OF MURPHY LIBRARY, UNIVERSITY OF WISCONSIN-LA CROSSE

In June 1967, Kumm made his boldest geographic move yet, purchasing the George Wiedemann Brewery of Newport, Kentucky, for about $5 million. Wiedemann, founded in 1870, was privately held, and had a capacity of 900,000 barrels and sales that exceeded $20 million in 1966.

Wiedemann Fine Beer and Wiedemann Genuine Draft were being marketed in Kentucky, Ohio, Tennessee, Indiana, Virginia, West Virginia, Alabama, Michigan and Illinois. In addition to the brewery in Newport, it had sales branches in Cincinnati, Ohio, and Louisville, Kentucky. Heileman decided to operate the brewery as an independent division, expanding production in Newport and extending distribution of the Wiedemann brands. Former Wiedemann President Richard E. Wagner became president of the Wiedemann division of Heileman.

The purchase increased Heileman sales to more than $52 million, and brewing capacity exceeded two million barrels. In a much smaller move, in December 1967, Heileman purchased a small brewery, the Oertel Brewing Company in Louisville. By then, the number of operating breweries in the United States had dwindled to 118.

Heileman expanded outside of brewing for the first time in September 1967 when it purchased Machine Products of La Crosse, a manufacturer of precision parts for the aviation, space, and defense industries.

Despite a one-week labor strike in 1966, Heileman continued to roll up record sales and profits. It used 600 distributors and $2.5 million of advertising to dramatically increase sales, and profits were maximized by the fact that 75 percent of the product line was made up of higher-margin brands. However, the company warned that labor costs had risen 110 percent since 1950, while the cost of living had only risen 42 percent. This trend couldn't continue without long-term negative impacts. Nonetheless, the company's 1967 annual report took an optimistic view of the future.

That report included brewing association research that showed current beer consumption of 107 million barrels could be increased to 200 million by 1975. It declared that the key was a sound advertising investment by the brewing industry. Increased beer consumption, unlike that of wine, whiskey, LSD, marijuana, and narcotics, was benefiting society, it asserted, noting that where the beer drinking age had been lowered to 18 in the country, there was less crime and delinquency. It even made the sweeping claim that there were fewer police problems, highway and job accidents, and firmer family relationships in these areas. The report called for the beer industry to awaken to its own beneficence and increase beer sales for the good of society.

The 1968 annual report continued in this theme, reporting that beer is a healthful, relaxing beverage, enriched with vitamins and minerals, and nonfattening since the only calories in beer are from the alcohol itself, as in other alcoholic beverages.

By 1968, Kumm had accomplished much of what he set out to do. Through the acquisition of smaller breweries he had put together a lineup of more than 40 brands ranging from near beers to malt liquors. He had established a large network of distributors, many of which carried Heileman products exclusively, because of the company's wide range of brands. Furthermore, some products were growing at an impressive rate without much advertising expenditure, such as Special Export, which had a compound growth rate of more than 20 percent.

That year, the company announced a new five-point strategic plan. First, the company intended to build a wider and stronger marketing area with more diversified brands. Second, it would develop a stronger set of distributors by giving them more volume without raising their overhead. Third, it was to rely less on a single brand (Old Style), a single brewery (La Crosse), and a single product (beer). Fourth, skilled management would fully utilize the new computer technology in its research and marketing to reduce costs. And fifth, less efficient plants were to be closed and production concentrated in larger, more modern plants in order to reduce costs, provide greater employment stability, and increase profits.

An August 1968 *Dow Digest* article on Heileman noted a 32 percent increase in sales in 1967, making it one of the fastest-growing breweries in the country, and now the 19th largest. Kumm's goal was to be in the top 10 by 1970, with the growth to come from massive advertising campaigns, a greater acceptance of beer as a social drink and, of course, the purchase of other breweries.

Kumm now declared his intention to expand the company into the East, South, and West. He also decided to expand the company into other industries, such as beverage bottling and snack foods. He foresaw these investments as a way to diversify and reduce overall production costs, and to finance this expansion the company authorized another million shares of stock. Stock analysts strongly recommended Heileman to their clients, and continued strong business resulted in a 2-for-1 Heileman stock split in 1968 and a 4-for-1 split in 1969.

That year, 1969, was an important time in the history of Heileman.

Pabst Brewing had acquired the Blatz Brewery on July 30, 1958, but a federal court order had prevented Pabst from operating it, so the Blatz Brewery had to be closed. Then, in July 1969, the federal government ruled that Pabst must sell the Blatz brand to avoid creating a monopoly. Six different firms—including four breweries, a black citizens' group, and a non-brewing firm—submitted bids for the Blatz brand: Heileman, Associated Brewing, Stroh, Grain Belt, United Black Enterprises, and Bankit Industries Limited. Associated Brewery made an offer of $11.5 million, chopped it to $10.5 million, and then suddenly withdrew its bid completely.

Moments later, attorneys for Pabst accepted Heileman's bid of $10.75 million. Cleary was elated, but cautious, as he awaited the judge's final decision, which came on September 2, 1969, allowing the buyout. The combined breweries could produce 3.5 million barrels, and Heileman became the 17th largest brewery in the United States, up from 39th place less than 10 years earlier. After the purchase, Heileman announced it was prepared to double the number of employees and brewing capacity in both La Crosse and Sheboygan.

Shortly thereafter, Heileman moved into 15th place nationally, but Kumm wasn't satisfied yet. He announced a goal to be No. 5 by 1975, recognizing that if Heileman wasn't in the top five by then, it probably was not going to survive. Kumm set out on a strategy to make Blatz a national label, taking Old Style and Special Export along with it.

Employment in La Crosse included 450 full-time employees, more than 300 regular production employees, and another 200 on temporary basis. The first 150 cases of Blatz produced in La Crosse were ready in time for Oktoberfest. About 150 Blatz employees were offered jobs if they would move to La Crosse or Sheboygan, but the trucking, distribution, and sales organization in Milwaukee were retained. Ironically, to meet demand for Blatz, 300,000 barrels had to be brewed by Pabst.

At midnight on March 31, 1969, Brewery Workers Local 81 went on strike again, with a settlement reached 29 days later. It came after a nonstop 9.5-hour negotiating session and was announced by Cleary and Erwin Schlicht, business agent for Local 81. The contract raised brewery workers' wages from

Heileman aging tanks in La Crosse became known as the world's largest six-pack.
PHOTO COURTESY OF MURPHY LIBRARY, UNIVERSITY OF WISCONSIN-LA CROSSE

$3.38 to $4.08 an hour over its three-year term, increased vacation and health benefits, and added a seventh week of vacation after 25 years of service. The settlement also included a 10-cent-an-hour raise for temporary employees.

A year later, a strike hit the Newport brewery, and in 1971 a strike idled the brewery in Sheboygan. The company was beginning to feel that younger union workers had come to accept strikes as a way of life. While wages at the Heileman breweries were already higher than those paid by most other employers in the cities where they operated, union workers were more interested in comparisons with brewery workers at the large national breweries in Milwaukee and Saint Louis.

The brewing industry continued to shrink dramatically, and by 1969 there were only 86 breweries still operating in the United States. Of those, only about 25 were actually operating at a profit. During the previous decade actual brewing capacity had grown by 500 percent, but most of the growth was at the five largest brewers at the expense of smaller breweries.

In 1969, Heileman's built what would become a tourist attraction for many years, the "World's Largest Six-Pack" on Third Street in La Crosse across from the brewery. In 1970, six storage tanks, each 53 feet tall, were painted to look like a six-pack of Heileman Old Style. It took 160 gallons of white paint for the background and 12 gallons for the graphic label design. The tanks were repainted in the mid-1980s and again in 1995. Each held 22,000 barrels of beer. If you were to drink a 12-ounce can of beer every hour, 24 hours a day, 365 days a year, it would take you 120 years to drink all of the beer in just one of the storage tanks. Don't try to drive home afterwards.

Heileman expanded into the baking industry in March 1970, purchasing the Erickson Bakery in La Crosse and the Federated Bakery in Winona, Minnesota, plus a number of additional bakeries elsewhere in the Upper Midwest. In August 1970, Heileman acquired the Nesco Sign Company of La Crosse, and Machine Products was expanded with the purchase of the assets of Rheem Manufacturing of Los Angeles, California.

Heileman's strategy of purchasing, at bargain prices, small regional breweries pushed to bankruptcy by large national brands, was paying huge dividends. It was estimated the company was able to expand capacity at a cost of $3 to $4 a barrel this way, as opposed to $35 to $40 a barrel if it had built new breweries. As a result, Heileman had its first $100 million sales year in 1970.

That year, company management was reorganized. Kumm became chairman of the board and chairman of the executive committee, while Cleary was named president. Russell L. Smith was made executive vice president, Howard L. Aiken was named marketing director, and Robert Jornayvaz became general advertising manager.

Kumm became ill and in the fall of 1970 he underwent surgery for a stomach ulcer but, sadly, doctors found invasive stomach cancer. He died in March 1971. The 1971 Heileman annual report was dedicated to him: "His contribution to the survival and growth of the House of Heileman is beyond measure. His inspired leadership lives on in those of us who follow."

There was only one person who could replace Kumm. His son-in-law, Cleary, took over as head of Heileman and proved eventually to be a powerful leader. When he took over Heileman it was the 15th largest brewery in the United States with annual sales of $104 million and a profit of $5.4 million. Cleary believed his company was capable of becoming the third major brewery in the United States, behind Anheuser-Busch and Schlitz.

Chapter 4

Go West, Young Man

THE EARLY CLEARY YEARS AND RAPID EXPANSION 1971–1977

Heileman has taken the friendly first-name atmosphere of La Crosse. I find the people in La Crosse to be different. They like to be your friend. I think Heileman has taken that attitude and spread it out.

—WHOLESALER DESCRIBING HEILEMAN'S FRIENDLY APPROACH

When Russell G. Cleary took over as president of Heileman in 1971, the brewing industry and G. Heileman Brewing Company were very different from what Roy Kumm had inherited back in 1957.

In the middle of a massive contraction, the five largest brewers in the United States controlled 53 percent of the beer sales. Small regional breweries were unable to compete against these large national breweries, and many of them had been forced to close or had been bought out by larger breweries. Kumm successfully used these forces to his advantage. He had taken Heileman from being one of those small regional breweries, ranked 39th, to a competitive and thriving brewery, America's 15th largest.

Cleary felt he had been swept into the leadership role at age 38 by the circumstance of his father-in-law's untimely death. But Kumm had been a good teacher and Cleary intended to continue to follow those strategies.

Shortly before Cleary assumed the presidency at Heileman, the Philip Morris Company bought Miller Brewing of Milwaukee with the intention of diversifying beyond the cigarette market. Miller was the seventh-largest brewery in the United States, but it was going nowhere. However, Philip Morris had clever marketing strategies and large coffers to support advertising. Within a few short years Miller had grown to become the second-largest brewery in America and was challenging the nation's largest, Anheuser-Busch.

Philip Morris dramatically altered the beer industry by applying its knowledge of cigarette marketing to it. Prior to that time most beer marketing featured the product. Philip Morris changed Miller's advertising from a theme of "The Champagne of Bottle Beers" to "If You've Got the Time, We've Got the Beer." The ads featured factory workers, welders, and cowboys, people who represented the targeted market.

Cleary made his first major move in 1972, when he bid on Associated Brewing Company of Detroit. The U.S. Justice Department filed suit to block the inclusion of Associated's breweries in South Bend, Indiana, and Saint Paul, Minnesota, arguing that would eliminate competition in the Midwest. Cleary could not understand why the government would waste its time on this issue, considering the much larger market shares of the dominant national breweries.

In June 1972, the government relented and allowed Heileman to purchase all of Associated Brewing for about $17.5 million, but stipulated that Heileman not buy any other breweries for the next 10 years within a 12-state Midwest region.

With the purchase, Heileman took over Jacob Schmidt in Saint Paul, Sterling in Evansville, Indiana, and Drewrys in South Bend, whose brands included Schmidt, Pfeiffer, Drewrys, and Sterling.

The brewery in South Bend was closed shortly after the purchase, but Heileman hired John Pedace from Associated. Pedace had been in the beer business since 1951, starting at Piel's Beer in New York. Cleary offered him the job of director of advertising for the Associated brands, which turned out to be a brilliant decision. Within a few years, Pedace had become a senior vice president in charge of all marketing and a member of the Heileman board of directors.

Heileman now was the nation's eighth-largest brewer and accounted for about 3 percent of all beer sales. Cleary had his sights set on being No. 5 or No. 6 to ensure survival in the brutal brewing industry. Heileman's success was shared with its stockholders; the stock dividend was increased from 10 cents a share to 15 cents.

In 1972, Heileman had 537 employees at its La Crosse plant with an annual payroll of $7.5 million; 181 at Erickson Bakeries with a payroll of $1.7 million; 134 at Machine Products at $1.45 million; and 12 at Nesco Signs at $110,000. It also supported several local suppliers such as Continental Can Company with 75 employees and a payroll of $725,000, and Hoerner Waldorf Container Division with 22 people at $150,000. The company purchased nearly $7.5 million in supplies and utilities for the first 10 months of 1972 and paid $345,167 in real estate and personal property taxes. During that year, 38,000 people toured Heileman, bringing valuable tourist dollars to the city of La Crosse.

At the same time, Heileman announced plans to double its brewing capacity in La Crosse during the next two years by adding thirty 31,000-gallon aging tanks at Third and Winnebago streets and adding on to the brewhouse. Capacity was increased from 1.5 million barrels to 2 million barrels in early 1973. Capacity was at 2.5 million barrels by the end of 1973, and had reached 3 million barrels by 1974. The company also purchased a brewhouse in Cleveland from Christian Schmidt Brewing Company of Philadelphia and transferred the equipment to La Crosse, as well as a new high-speed bottling line from the firm's recently closed plant in South Bend.

In April 1972 a bitter seven-week-long strike took place at the La Crosse brewery. At first, management personnel operated the brewery, but after about three weeks the company took out a half-page advertisement for replacement workers and hired about 230. Strike tensions led to acts of vandalism such as the throwing of eggs and rocks, spray painting of replace-

On May 23, 1973, Russ and Gail Cleary (center) celebrated the first day that Heileman stock was traded on the New York Stock Exchange.
PHOTO COURTESY OF CLEARY-KUMM FOUNDATION

ment workers' cars, and reports of Heileman trucks being forced off the road. Heileman brought a $1 million lawsuit against the union.

Cleary and Dale Conrad, president of Local 81, announced the end of the strike on May 21, 1972, and the lawsuit was dropped. The workers received a 78-cent-an-hour raise over three years up to an average pay rate of more than $5 an hour. Workers' other concerns regarding the pension plan and grievance procedures were addressed, and Cleary vowed to improve labor relations. This was, in fact, the last strike during his tenure, and in 1973 the 275 members of Heileman AFL-CIO Local 81 Brewery and Soft Drink Workers Union became Teamsters Local 1081.

Heileman stock was first listed on the New York Stock Exchange on May 23, 1973, after previously being sold only on the Chicago Stock Exchange. But the market, especially brewing stock, was in a period of decline, and Heileman stock declined accordingly. However, over time the dividends increased, the stock split several times, and the price began a steady rise.

In these years the Heileman board saw many changes, with William Warmington retiring and Ralf H. Owen, William A. Barney, and Bernard C. Reese coming on, along with Pedace in 1975 and Arthur N. Trausch Jr. in 1977.

At the end of 1973, Heileman was operating breweries in La Crosse and Sheboygan, Wisconsin; Newport, Kentucky; Evansville, Indiana; and Saint Paul, Minnesota. Primary brands marketed were Old Style, Special Export, Blatz, Wiedemann, Schmidt, Sterling, and Drewrys.

Heileman, for the first time, had to deal with the problems of producing small amounts of numerous other brands. Consequently it sold the Fox Head, Fox Deluxe, and Weber labels to Pickett Brewing Company of Dubuque, Iowa, and closed the Kingsbury plant in Sheboygan. That brewery had originally opened in 1847. About 100 Kingsbury employees lost their jobs when production was transferred to the breweries in Saint Paul, Evansville, and La Crosse.

On June 13, 1974, the U.S. Justice Department announced a consent decree settlement with Heileman. That settlement required the company to divest itself of 400,000 barrels in sales. It also prevented the company from acquiring any more brands or breweries in Wisconsin, Minnesota, Iowa, Illinois, Indiana, Michigan, Ohio, or Kentucky without the prior approval of the Justice Department for a 10-year period.

During the early 1970s, Schlitz and Anheuser-Busch each had about 20 percent of the market in Chicago. Heileman was a distant third with less than 10 percent. However, in 1974 Heileman announced that two Chicago distributors, Julius Jensen of Southwest Beer Distributors Incorporated, and Robert Terry of Sheriden Beverage Company, had become the first two members of the "Old Style One Million Case Club."

In 1975, August "Augie" Busch III took over Anheuser-Busch from his father, August "Gussie" Busch Jr., and vowed to increase Budweiser's market share to compete with rapidly rising Miller. But, in 1976, Anheuser-Busch suffered a lengthy labor strike, which led to its product disappearing from many retailers' shelves.

Then Schlitz decided to shortcut its traditional brewing practice. Schlitz drinkers complained about the look and taste of the beer and switched to other brands. For years after Prohibition it was the largest brewery in the United States, but Schlitz now slipped to fourth place. It tried to undo the damage by hiring a new brewmaster and promising a return to the old formulas, but the brand never recovered.

Heileman seized the opportunity in the Chicago market, taking a 30-percent share and moving into first place. The Old Style brand, in particular, saw a 41-percent increase in sales. By the late 1970s, a common sight along I-90 from La Crosse to Chicago was a steady stream of semis loaded with Heileman's Old Style.

With its purchases and success in Chicago, Heileman sales topped $200 million for the first time. Sales for 1975 were up 18 percent over 1974, earnings had increased in 14 of the last 15 years, and in 1976 the company had the largest single-year sales gain in its history. Flush with success and cash, Heileman considered purchasing the Christian Schmidt Brewing Company of Philadelphia, but an agreement couldn't be reached.

In 1974 beer sales throughout the nation soared as consumption reached a record 21 gallons per capita. *Financial World* noted that Heileman had grown faster than any brewery in the United States over the previous decade, at an average rate of 13.9 percent. *Business Week* reported Heileman had found the secret to hard-sell beer marketing.

The top five breweries in 1976, Anheuser-Busch, Schlitz, Miller, Pabst, and Coors, controlled 70 percent of the American beer market, and industry analysts predicted that by 1980 the top five would control 90 percent. A 1976 article in *Value Line* predicted that during the next three to five years there would be room for the larger brewers to continue to grow rapidly, at the expense of smaller competitors, and that Heileman would join the winners. By this time there were only 63 companies operating about 100 breweries.

In 1976 Heileman bought the Grain Belt Brewery of Minneapolis for $1.6 million from investor Irwin Jacobs. Despite the 1972 government decree that Heileman not purchase more breweries in the Midwest, this purchase was seen as a hardship case. Jacobs would reappear five years later to play a large role in the events of the early 1980s.

Early in December 1976, Heileman celebrated five million barrels of production in a single year,

Kraeusening—The Most Costly Process of Brewing Fine Beers

At Heileman, as at other breweries across the United States, barley malt, rice, and corn were cooked for several hours with water at approximately 165 degrees to convert the grains' starch into a fermentable mash. The solid grains were filtered out and the remaining liquid put into large brewing kettles. Further boiling then took place, and at the right moment, hops were added to the brew. The liquid was then cooled and put in large open fermenting tanks. Cultured yeast was added and fermentation took place.

At this point, other breweries collected and stored the carbon dioxide gas as it escaped from the fermenting tanks and returned it to the flat beer after a few days of storage. The entire beer-making process at other breweries took no more than a couple of weeks.

Heileman, however, continued the brewing process by "kraeusening" (sometimes called "double brewing")—refermenting an active beer in which the fermentable solids are still being split into alcohol and carbon dioxide so that the carbon dioxide is absorbed and literally locked into the beer. This process takes place over a period of several weeks and creates flavor and carbonation purely by nature.

including more than three million produced in La Crosse. Heileman now had 2,500 employees, (1,000 in La Crosse), and was selling beer in 43 of the 50 states. The La Crosse plant was operating four bottling lines and three canning lines, and Heileman also had built two new million-gallon aging cellars on Fourth Street, just north of the storage buildings. Sales soared 26 percent and earnings were up 33 percent.

Heileman next added 26 new aging tanks on Third and Fourth streets north of Mississippi Street that held 1.25 million gallons, raising the total storage capacity to about three million. The tanks were used to "kraeusen" the beer by storing it for 45 days at a temperature of 32 degrees. Initially used for just Old Style and Special Export, long-term plans included a new low-calorie light brand, which would also be kraeusened.

During this period the brewing industry was experimenting with new markets. Heileman sold malt liquors, fruit flavored beers, Special Export in 7-ounce bottles known as "X-7," packaged in the form of a handy basket carrier, and a set of Kentucky Derby Winner commemorative cans for the Sterling brand.

Then came the introduction of light beers.

Miller introduced the concept with its "Lite" brand—"Less filling, tastes great"—and soon Heileman began to test-market Heileman Premium Light. The new Heileman Premium Light was marketed with the slogan "We took our time and got it right."

Miller brought suits against Heileman and eight other brewers in November 1976, asking for an injunction to prevent them from selling a "Light" beer, and was granted a temporary injunction in January 1977 by Judge James Doyle.

Eventually the U.S. Circuit Court of Appeals in Chicago ruled in Heileman's favor, allowing Heileman to market a low-calorie beer using the term "light," based on the fact the term "light" was a generic or common descriptive word when applied to beer. It also ruled that neither the word nor its phonetic equivalent "lite" could appropriately be used as a trademark for beer. In January 1978, the U.S. Supreme Court rejected a request by Miller to review the decision of the Appellate Court.

Anti-Takeover Tactics Enacted in 1977

In a move that showed great foresight, the Heileman board in 1977 passed amendments to the company's articles of incorporation to make it more difficult for someone else to acquire the company. That action was prompted by an increasing number of hostile takeovers in the brewing industry.

Specifically, the amendments said 75 percent of the stockholders were required to vote in support of a takeover, not the previously stated 66 percent. Furthermore, the board was split into three groups, with rotating renewal dates for re-election, requiring at least a three-year period before a majority of the board could be replaced.

Heileman made a dramatic move in the brewing wars in November 1976 when it announced the purchase of Rainier Brewing Company of Seattle for about $8 million. That sale was completed on December 31, 1976. Rainier, the No. 1 seller in the state of Washington, had sales of about one million barrels for more than $42 million for the previous 12 months, along with 375 employees and a payroll of $5 million. With this move, instead of spending $50 million for a new West Coast brewery, Heileman got a brewery, 199 wholesalers in Washington, Oregon, California, Idaho, Montana, Wyoming, and Hawaii, and a lucrative market for its other brands.

Following the purchase, Cleary was quoted as saying: "We think we have a chance to become one of the ultimate survivors in the savage struggle going on in the industry. We have no way to go but up."

After the purchase of Rainier, Heileman was marketing 20 brands of beer in 46 states, but none nationally. The closest thing Heileman had to a national brand was Blatz, sold in 35 states, with sales going up due to an aggressive advertising campaign touting the idea that a regional beer could be as good as a national brand.

Heileman's primary market was still in a 20-state territory where 90 percent of its beer was sold, from Pennsylvania to the Dakotas and down to Missouri. The good news was this area had a large German and Scandinavian heritage and consumed half of the beer sold in the United States.

Heileman passed Schlitz in 1977 to become the No. 2 beer seller in Wisconsin, behind Pabst. Special Export was the No. 1 super-premium beer in Milwaukee, Schmidt was the best-selling beer in Minnesota, Rainier continued to be the top-selling beer in Washington, and Wiedemann was popular in Ohio, Tennessee, and Kentucky. Sterling sold well in southern Indiana and Kentucky and was No. 1 in Louisville. Total barrels sold that year were 6.2 million.

Also by 1977, Heileman had the most wholesalers in the industry, with 1,100, and took a friendly and personal approach with them. They responded by being dedicated to the company. One was quoted as saying: "Heileman has taken the friendly first-name atmosphere of La Crosse. I find the people in La Crosse to be different. They like to be your friend. I think Heileman has taken that attitude and spread it out."

A 1977 article in *Dun's Review* highlighted Heileman as thriving in the beer industry, with earnings up 98 percent in the previous five years when most regional breweries had been crushed by the rising costs of grains, aluminum and glass, and the inability to negotiate bulk discounts. The large national brands were taking a new aggressive pricing strategy, with Miller holding its price increases to 1 percent despite the fact that costs were rising much faster. *Forbes* magazine declared: "Heileman seems to have learned to walk among the elephants without getting trampled."

With the purchase of Rainier, Heileman had completed its transition from Midwest regional brewery to major player in the lucrative West Coast market. But two major markets still eluded Cleary and Heileman, the East Coast and the South. Cleary knew that to continue to compete he needed access to the entire United States. Heileman was the seventh-largest brewery in America, but Cleary was within striking distance of a position in the top five. He knew what needed to be done, and he was ready.

Meanwhile, in Golden, Colorado, Coors experienced a setback on December 31, 1976, when its union contract expired. The union went on strike, and the company took a hard line against it. Eventually the union was broken and Coors became the only nonunion brewery in the United States. But the company's victory came at a cost. Union members started a nationwide boycott of Coors beer that was joined by African Americans, Hispanics, and gays. That boycott lasted until the mid-1980s.

Recognizing the importance of Cleary to Heileman, in 1976 the board of directors rewarded him with an annual salary exceeding $100,000, and he signed a contract preventing him from working for a competing brewery if he ever left Heileman. In return, the contract guaranteed Cleary or his estate four years of his current salary if the company terminated him for any reason.

Chapter 5

Looking East

CARLING AND OTHERS 1978–1979

Brewing is a savagely competitive industry.

—RUSSELL CLEARY IN 1978

As Russ Cleary led Heileman into 1978, he had a clear idea of where he wanted to take the company and how to proceed there.

Heileman products were sold in 46 states, but the company needed better access to the lucrative East Coast and the South. Heileman did have brands in those markets, but not with a cost-effective structure. Its existing breweries were too far away and shipping costs made it difficult to compete effectively. In order to expand into the huge potential market in the large cities along the East Coast, Cleary had to find a brewery there.

By now the company was swimming in $31 million of working capital, plenty to finance both acquisitions and expansion without borrowing. In April 1978 Cleary refused to confirm rumors that Heileman was considering the purchase of either Christian Schmidt Brewing of Philadelphia or Genesee in Rochester, New York, but said the company was always looking for ways to expand in both the brewery and bakery industries. In the next few months, Heileman purchased the Dick Brothers Bakery of Manitowoc, Wisconsin, and Emrich Baking Company in Minneapolis.

Pabst Brewing was also looking to expand by purchasing struggling breweries, and in 1978 attempted to merge with Carling National Brewing of Baltimore, Maryland, the 10th-largest brewery in the United States with sales of 4.35 million barrels. Lately, though, it had fallen on hard times and had lost $10.5 million in the previous nine months. Nevertheless, the U.S. Justice Department blocked the merger of Pabst and Carling, and Heileman let it be known in late July 1978 that it was negotiating to purchase Carling. News of the announcement caused an hour halt to the trading of Heileman stock.

Then Cleary announced in August that Heileman was dropping plans to acquire Carling, citing a mutual decision to terminate the acquisition talks. He said the deal didn't make sense financially and indicated his unwillingness to make any acquisition that wouldn't strengthen Heileman. Carling issued a press release declaring that it intended to remain an independent, viable player in the U.S. brewing industry.

Cleary had not given up on his plan to acquire a brewery within a 300-mile radius of New York City. He knew that whoever moved into this lucrative market to replace the rapidly failing regional brands would own it in the future.

By this time there were only 45 breweries still operating in the United States, primarily the big nationals such as Anheuser-Busch, Miller, Schlitz, Pabst and some smaller regional breweries. Heileman didn't really fit either of these models. By purchasing other breweries, it had obtained a variety of strong regional products, but it had no single brand nationwide. Heileman had a $15 million advertising budget, but no cost-effective way to spend it on a nationwide ad, a huge competitive advantage enjoyed by the national brands.

Despite those problems, Heileman had rapidly grown its business in the previous seven years, second only to Miller, by increasing production 20 percent, sales 25 percent, and earnings 25 percent. Pabst and Schlitz, both larger than Heileman, had lost sales in the previous year, and Heileman stock, rated the best brewing stock buy by analysts, was listed on both the New York and Midwest Stock Exchanges with about 8,000 shareholders. In August, the company announced its second 3-for-2 stock split that year. It also raised the stock dividend to 25 cents per share, up from 20 cents, the ninth dividend increase in 10 years.

In September 1978, Heileman announced an interest in acquiring Falls City Brewery of Louisville, Kentucky, which produced Drummond Brothers, Falls City, and Billy Beer brands. Billy Beer was a recent addition to the lineup and was named for Billy Carter, roguish brother of President Jimmy Carter. Falls City Brewery had a capacity of about a million barrels.

In October 1978, the deal was finalized for $940,000. Shortly after the purchase, Heileman announced the brewery would be closed in Louisville because it already had adequate capacity at the nearby Newport, Kentucky, brewery. Heileman didn't eliminate local brands when it bought a brewery, because Cleary realized that if Heileman rushed in and ripped out the hometown signs on the buildings, local people would resent it. Instead, it continued to sell the local brands and gradually encouraged wholesalers to fill out their product line with other Heileman high-profit brands. Falls City Brewing gave the company access to new markets in the South, but the closest brewery it had to New York City was in Evansville, Indiana.

Some Falls City employees were offered jobs at other Heileman breweries, but many lost their employment. Falls City's 180 wholesalers—in Kentucky, Tennessee, North Carolina, West Virginia, Virginia, and Indiana—brought Heileman's total to 1,300. Anheuser-Busch had about 950 wholesalers, and Miller around 800. Independent wholesalers distributed 95 percent of Heileman's beer and Cleary believed in establishing relationships with them, regularly holding gripe sessions to address their problems and concerns. Cleary attended many of these meetings personally and knew almost all of his distributors on a first-name basis.

Heileman was operating five breweries in December 1978: La Crosse, Saint Paul, Newport, Evansville, and Seattle. The La Crosse brewery was the largest with a 3.2-million-barrel capacity, and plans were in place to expand it to 4 million barrels. The Saint Paul and Newport plants had each been expanded from 900,000 barrels to 1.5 million barrels in the previous two years, the Seattle plant was growing from 1 million to 1.5 million barrels, and the Evansville plant had a million-barrel capacity for a grand total of about 8 million. All of the Heileman plants were operating at or near capacity with further plans to expand to 10 million within two years.

As 1978 came to a close, sales stood at just short of $400 million. On December 20, Heileman issued a commemorative glass recognizing the production of 7 million barrels of beer that year. Heileman moved into sixth place, leapfrogging over Olympia Brewing Company of Tumwater, Washington.

With Olympia behind him, Cleary set his sights on fifth-ranked Coors, which was sold only in 16 states. Cleary also had plans to expand into the East Coast market and increase capacity to 12 million barrels, but he knew he still needed several more big acquisitions over the next few years if he were to continue to compete in what he called a "savagely competitive industry." Late in 1978, Heileman again started negotiations to take over Carling. The sticking point was licensing rights for domestic production of the Danish beer, Tuborg. This issue was finally resolved in March 1979, and an agreement was signed in Copenhagen, Denmark.

Celebrating a brewing milestone, reaching the 7 million annual production level, are, from left: union leader Bill Akright, Russell Cleary, John Pedace, and Patrick Zielke, mayor of La Crosse.

PHOTO COURTESY OF MURPHY LIBRARY, UNIVERSITY OF WISCONSIN-LA CROSSE

With the agreement in place, Heileman purchased Carling National Breweries Incorporated of Baltimore, for $35.25 million. The purchase was made from C&N Holding Limited, a member of the Rothman Group of London, England, which had bought Carling in December 1977 for $28 million. The company had lost $27 million in the previous six years, but buying a brewery that was losing money didn't bother Cleary, who noted that Rainier was the only brewery Heileman had ever bought that was making money when acquired.

The Carling purchase gave Heileman its long-sought entry into the heavily populated East Coast market. The brewery in Baltimore was only 18 years old and had between 800 and 900 wholesalers, including between 500 and 600 who weren't selling any Heileman products at the time of the sale.

The purchase of Carling also finally brought Heileman two national brands, Colt 45 malt liquor and Tuborg. Carling Black Label was almost a national brand, and the other brands were Heidelberg, Stag, National Bohemian, National Premium, Red Grape Malt Duck, and Apple Malt Duck. Carling was the exclusive importer of Carlsberg Beer from Denmark, but Rupert Interests retained those rights as part of the agreement, and also imported Carling Red Cap Ale, O'Keefe Ale, and Old Vienna Beer from Canada.

Carling had breweries in Frankenmuth, Michigan, Belleville, Illinois, Baltimore, Phoenix, and Tacoma, all of which Heileman obtained in the deal. Baltimore was the largest brewery, with 1.8 million barrels capacity. The other breweries were significantly smaller. The purchase of Carling added about 4 million barrels to Heileman's capacity, bringing the company's annual production to within striking distance of Coors' 12.5 million barrels. Cleary was elated, and admitted that while Heileman probably wouldn't catch Coors in 1979, the years of 1980 and 1981 looked interesting.

The relatively new plant in Baltimore was by far the most beneficial to Heileman, and the Phoenix plant gave it new inroads into the Southwest. Frankenmuth was important because of Michigan's mandatory bottle and can deposit law. Prior to obtaining this brewery, Heileman had to ship returnable bottles to Detroit and the rest of Michigan from its plant in Newport, Kentucky.

On March 28, 1979, Heileman officially took control of the Carling breweries in Belleville and Tacoma. On the first day as owner, Heileman posted notices to the workers that both of those breweries were for sale and if no owner were found the breweries would be closed, since they were losing money and Heileman already owned breweries there. Two months later, the workers at both of these plants collected their last paychecks. At the time, the Stag brewery in Belleville had about 300 employees and a payroll of about $4.5 million.

In August 1979, Heileman reconsidered its decision and announced plans to reopen the Stag brewery, since the plant's 1.2-million-barrel capacity was required to meet increased demand for Heileman's other brands. Heileman negotiated some concessions from the city of Belleville, which approved $2 million in industrial revenue bonds and vacated some streets to make room for expansion. Plans were put in place to refurbish the plant before it was reopened in November.

The Carling purchase triggered the reorganization of Heileman into three divisions: East, Central, and West.

The Central division had its headquarters in La Crosse and was headed by Ronald Drout. Other executives were: Edward Dolan, director of sales for Old Style, Special Export, and Heileman Light; William Bloom, director of sales for Blatz, Blatz Light, Blatz Cream Ale, and Mickey's Malt Liquor; Poley LaPage, director of sales for Schmidt, Grain Belt, Pfeiffer, and Hauenstein; Raymond Flower, director of sales for Carling; and Larry Thomas, director of sales for Wiedemann, Falls City, Sterling, Drewrys, and Kingsbury.

The East Coast division, which included everything from Maine to Florida, was based in Baltimore. Tom Myers was vice president of sales, and Sid Marcus was vice president of advertising.

The West region was based in Seattle and covered all of the states west of North Dakota, South Dakota, Kansas, and Texas. It was headed by James Martin, vice president of marketing.

At the 1979 annual meeting, Cleary told stockholders he thought Heileman had a chance to have sales of more than $500 million in 1979. He announced that brewing capacity in La Crosse would increase from 3.5 million to 4 million barrels, and in Seattle from 1.1 million to 1.6 million barrels, giving the company a total capacity of about 13 million barrels.

Once again, Cleary took time to credit Heileman's success to its employees, who worked harder and longer and made decisions rapidly in marketing and production. Stockholders re-elected to three-year terms on the Heileman board were 85-year-old La Crosse lawyer Quincy H. Hale and 87-year-old C.B. Goes Jr., chairman of the board for Goes Lithography in Chicago. Hale had joined the board in 1933 and Goes in 1935. The number of shares of stock was doubled from 6 million to 12 million, to be used for more acquisitions and future stock splits.

John Pedace, executive vice president, reported to stockholders that only three U.S. breweries—Anheuser-Busch, Miller, and Heileman—had increased market share in 1978. He went on to show the latest advertising, which stressed the quality of the beer and Heileman's superior methods of production, featuring the "fully kraeusened" and "pure Wisconsin spring water" themes. He claimed that these advertisements proved multi-brand regional marketing could work.

By now, Heileman's progress was attracting attention from the larger breweries. About this same time, Miller Brewing Company asked the federal Bureau of Alcohol, Tobacco, and Firearms (BATF) to prohibit the use of the terms "light" and "lite" for any beer that contained more than 100 calories. It also asked that the term "natural" be prohibited in beer advertising. These actions were primarily aimed at Anheuser-Busch, which was marketing Michelob Light at 134 calories.

Heileman had three light beers, Heileman Light, Blatz Light, and Rainier Light, all with 96 calories. The reduction in calories was accomplished by reducing the alcohol content to 2 percent. Cleary called Miller's requests "legal folderol" and specifically pointed out that Miller didn't want to talk about how beer was processed because other breweries took a longer time and greater pains with their brewing processes.

In April 1979, the president of Pabst complained that the U.S. Justice Department had given Heileman preferential treatment when it allowed it to acquire Carling National. Cleary responded that Heileman, ranked sixth, was smaller than fourth-ranked Pabst and also pointed out that Pabst already had two plants on the East Coast while Heileman had none. Finally, Cleary accused Pabst management of still being bitter because Pabst had lost Blatz to Heileman back in 1969.

By now, Heileman's bakery division was playing an increasingly important role in the company and Cleary had a long-term goal that eventually the bakery division would produce the same revenue as brewing. Bakery division sales were a record $48.69 million in 1978, and Heileman announced an agreement in April 1979 to buy Our Own Bakeries of Marquette, Michigan.

In May 1979, Heileman announced an agreement to act as a distributor of Beck Beer of Bremen, Germany. Beck was sold in 140 countries and was the No. 1 German import in the U.S. The agreement made Heileman sole distributor in 21 states. It shared distribution rights in Pennsylvania, Illinois, Mississippi, Colorado, and Nevada. Sales of Beck were already strong on the East and West coasts. With this agreement, Cleary expected dramatic sales increases in the Central states. Heileman was selected because it had the strongest overall market penetration of any American brewery.

In June 1979, Heileman stock jumped 10 percent after a favorable article was published in *Fortune* magazine, and it was now ranked 535th among all U.S. corporations. Record sales and earnings were again reported for the first six months of 1979. Heileman had 1,400 employees in La Crosse in June 1979, and brewery executives predicted employment would increase by 135 to 180 more workers.

Work was begun in June on a $12 million to $14 million expansion in La Crosse, which increased brewing capacity by about 40 percent and was required to meet demand for Old Style and Special Export in Wisconsin and Chicago. The expansion included 10 cellars, each holding 26,000 barrels, where the beer was metered for tax purposes. Also included in the project were 10 Uni-tanks at Fourth and Winnebago streets. A new 45,000-square-foot warehouse also was included. The cost of these expansions was estimated to be about $2 million.

Plans were made at this time for a new brewhouse bounded by Third, Jackson, and Mississippi streets. It was estimated the brewhouse would cost between $8 million and $10 million and would increase capacity from 3 million or 4 million barrels up to 4.5 million, and eventually up to 5.5 million to 6 million barrels. Some of the equipment used in the new brewhouse was new and some was salvaged from a brewery in Massachusetts closed three years earlier by Carling. During this time, 98 percent of the production in La Crosse was Old Style and Special Export. The other 2 percent was Blatz, which because of its wide distribution was brewed in all Heileman plants.

In August 1979, the company completed a $2.5 million expansion of the Schmidt Brewery in Saint Paul by adding 1.7 million barrels of capacity in its aging tanks. Saint Paul brewed Schmidt, Grain Belt, Blatz, and Heileman Light. In Kentucky, capacity at the Newport brewery was doubled, and a $5 million expansion was made to the plant in Seattle.

Late in 1979, Heileman announced plans to enter yet another industry, to bottle water from the Cold Spring Brewery of Cold Spring, Minnesota, as a competitor of Perrier.

With the purchase of Carling and the increased capacity, Heileman celebrated its achievement of the goal of 11 million barrels of production in 1979.

Growth, however, brought headaches over the next few years.

The city of La Crosse was beginning to have concerns about the amount of wastewater generated by Heileman, and had considered charging $1 million a year for wastewater treatments. Environmentalists across the country were pushing breweries to use only returnable bottles, but the cost and amount of water required to wash bottles were prohibitive. Heileman did announce the commitment of $1 million annually to reduce the amount of waste generated by the brewery, recycling 75 percent of its spent grain for sale to farmers as a high-protein cattle feed and recovering yeast for a company in Milwaukee that used it in bakery operations and as a diet supplement.

In December 1979, Heileman announced plans to build a $15 million pretreatment plant to recover and reuse waste from the brewing process. It hired Biospheres Incorporated of Rockville, Maryland, to build a miniature prototype of its system to prove its viability. The goal was to recapture the waste, compress it, and sell it as a high-protein food supplement for dairy cows. This new system was similar to an existing $3

Heileman Makes a Big Move in 1979

Labor Day 1979 was a big day for Heileman in La Crosse. Cleary was named parade marshal for the Labor Day Parade, and was honored for excellence in leadership and making La Crosse a better place to live. While Cleary participated in the parade, the legal, marketing, and advertising divisions moved into the recently completed corporate headquarters in Harborview, and all remaining departments moved into the new building over the next few weekends.

George Smith, Heileman treasurer, was in charge of the move to the new corporate headquarters. Except for favorite pieces that employees wanted to move, all furnishings were also new. Fittingly, employees were given beer cases in which to move their personal belongings.

Future Heileman office site in La Crosse.
PHOTO COURTESY OF CLEARY-KUMM FOUNDATION

million system used to recover yeast and grains from the brewing process.

The need for this plant came about as the result of a study that showed the city of La Crosse would need to spend $14.39 million in the next 20 years to improve its treatment plant. But the city would have to spend just $10.13 million if Heileman processed its own waste, which was 12 percent of the total flow through the city plant.

As the year came to a close, Heileman became involved in a fight over mandatory deposits on beverage containers. The proposed Wisconsin law was a showdown between environmentalists and big business, the breweries, and national labor organizations such as the AFL-CIO, which opposed the legislation.

Heileman argued the bill would increase the cost of beer and hurt the company. Cleary even argued that passing the law could result in layoffs and less beer production in La Crosse. He said similar legislation in Michigan and Iowa had increased the price of beer in those states, resulting in decreased sales as consumers crossed state lines to buy cheaper beer.

Robert W. Davis, community development manager at Heileman, argued for recycling as a better alternative, pointing out that Heileman had recycled 8 million cans since the opening of its Alumi-Ca$h Recycling Center in 1976. He related further that the program had paid out $92,381 for recycled cans and $46,272 in proceeds to various civic groups.

At year-end, Heileman operated nine breweries: La Crosse, Saint Paul, Phoenix, Seattle, Baltimore, Belleville, Evansville, Frankenmuth, and Newport. It announced record sales of $657.28 million, up 67 percent over 1978, with earnings of $27.3 million, up 52 percent. Heileman now marketed 34 brands of beer, led by strong sales of Old Style and Special Export. The Blatz, Rainier, Schmidt, and Wiedemann labels also continued to do well.

At 11 million barrels, Heileman remained in sixth place nationally, and several analysts, including those at *Value Line,* predicted the company would rank third behind Anheuser-Bush and Miller by 1982 to 1984. Cleary wasn't quite as positive, as that forecast would require passing both the faltering Schlitz and Pabst, although Heileman's sales were rapidly gaining on Pabst in Wisconsin.

Chapter 6

The Sunshine State

FLORIDA AND LA CROSSE EXPANSION 1980

Heileman's advertising featured "on-target, no-nonsense marketing."

—RUSS CLEARY, 1980

Cruising into 1980, it seemed that Russell Cleary and Heileman could do no wrong. Cleary was getting recognition for being a brilliant leader, Heileman stockholders were being handsomely rewarded for their investment in the fastest-growing beer company in the United States, and the company's relationship with its employees and the city of La Crosse was good.

But there were clouds on the horizon. Some industry analysts predicted Heileman had seen its best days and the growth couldn't continue, and that aggressive pricing and increased advertising by the big national breweries would diminish Heileman's sales.

In January 1980, *Corporate Report*, an Upper Midwest business magazine, named Cleary executive of the year, based on business success and aggressive management style. Cleary credited the work ethic and dedication of the employees for making the small company succeed. However, Heileman wasn't such a small company anymore. Sales for 1979 were $657 million, with a $27.3 million profit. Nationwide, Heileman had about 5,600 employees, including 3,600 in brewing, 1,600 in baking, and 350 in other businesses.

Beer industry analysts said Cleary was too modest, pointing out that he had consistently discovered opportunities that increased both sales and earnings. He also had steered clear of acquisitions that might have sent Heileman zooming up the industry rankings at the expense of long-term stability, and stayed away from market situations which would have mired the company in losing battles. Heileman stock had soared 737 percent in the previous five years, and several industry analysts predicted Heileman would pass the struggling Pabst and Schlitz breweries by 1984.

But analysts also noted that Anheuser-Busch, Miller, and Coors had all announced plans to invade Heileman's rich markets in the Upper Midwest and were spending incredible amounts of money. Cleary's response was that Heileman intended to concentrate on "on-target, no-nonsense marketing." He said the company would continue to expand products into vacuums created by the erosion of regional and national breweries as it struggled against the two giants.

By April 1980, two stock analysts, C. James Walker and Arnold P. Robinson, were predicting little or no continued growth for Heileman. At the annual stockholders meeting worried wholesalers and stockholders were looking for answers. An obviously irritated Cleary told the 600 attendees that the two analysts did not know the first thing about Heileman operations and had made no attempt to talk to company representatives.

At the same meeting, Heileman announced a 65 percent increase in sales and a 30 percent increase in earnings for the first quarter, mostly the result of acquiring Carling. Earnings were up, but were adversely affected by startup costs at the Belleville brewery that had reopened late in 1979. Wholesalers also were paying high interest rates—close to 20 percent—on their inventory. That April, Heileman moved into the Fortune 500 with a rank of 418, sales were up 69 percent, (sixth best in the nation), and it ranked 10th in the country on money returned to investors, with a 140 percent increase over 1978. During the previous 10 years the company's average return to investors was almost 15 percent.

Heileman then announced plans to acquire Duncan Brewing Company of Auburndale, Florida, which produced several brands of beer for Florida supermarket chains and was a major producer of Malta, a nonalcoholic beverage marketed in Florida and the Caribbean. The Florida brewery was producing about 150,000 barrels a year, but had the potential for 400,000. At the time of the purchase, Heileman was selling about 200,000 barrels a year in Florida, which it had to ship from plants in Evansville or Baltimore. With this purchase, it was hoped that sales in Florida would follow a pattern similar to those in Arizona, which had increased 500 percent after Heileman took over a similarly sized Carling brewery in Phoenix.

Expansion was also taking place at the breweries in Seattle and Saint Paul and brought the company's capacity to 15 million barrels for all breweries. It was too early to tell if they would reach 15 million barrels for the year, but all of Heileman's facilities were running at or near full capacity. In October 1980, the company announced plans to acquire Bake-Rite Baking Company of Plover, Wisconsin, from Mor-America Financial Corporation of Cedar Rapids, Iowa.

In December, Robert Korkowski, vice president of finance for Heileman, announced plans to use the Baltimore and Seattle breweries to produce straight alcohol for use in making gasoline. The plan was to be financed by $8.1 million from the U.S. Department of Energy—$5.3 million going to Baltimore and $2.8 million to Seattle.

During these years of rapid expansion the company's legal department was occupied on several fronts, filing five lawsuits in La Crosse Circuit Court against the city and county to try to recover taxes paid in 1974 through 1977. Heileman argued that 10 tanks and a malt elevator classed as real estate subject to property taxes should have been called manufacturing equipment, and not subject to taxes. The company sought a refund of about $400,000 in overpayment of taxes, but the court ruled against Heileman because the company hadn't disputed the taxes at the time they were paid. Following an appeal, the brewery equipment and tanks were ruled to be exempt from property taxation

In May 1980, the Illinois House delayed a bill that would result in a $350,000 tax break to Heileman for its Belleville brewery. The existing law dated to the 1940s when Illinois had 61 breweries, but by 1980 there were only two breweries still operating in the state. Heileman lawyer Randy Smith admitted it was doubtful the company would leave the state if the new law didn't pass, as had previously been threatened, but he pointed out that Heileman would always be looking for a favorable business climate when making future investment decisions. His argument apparently resonated with the members of the Illinois House, for the bill passed and Heileman's 300 employees kept their jobs there, at an annual payroll of $4.5 million.

In Wisconsin Heileman was doing battle with Pabst for the No. 1 ranking, which it attained with 1980 first quarter sales of 348,000 barrels, compared with Pabst's 320,000. In 1975, Pabst had sold 2.1 million barrels compared with Heileman's 568,973, but by 1979 Heileman's sales were up to 1.7 million compared with Pabst's 1.9 million. Most of Heileman's gain came in the Kenosha, Racine, and Milwaukee area, a traditional stronghold of Pabst, which was going through a management shake-up.

Meanwhile, Heileman was No. 1 in Minnesota and growing. In the Northwest, Rainier was still No. 1 in the state of Washington and growing in popularity in Montana and Oregon. In the East, things were looking promising with the former Carling brewery in Baltimore running at capacity. Old Style remained the foremost brand in Chicago and was widening its lead. Blatz was doing much better since introducing its "taste test" advertisements. Eight brands accounted for 80 percent of Heileman's sales: Old Style, Special Export, Blatz, Rainier, Schmidt, Wiedemann, Black Label, and Colt 45.

The brewing, baking, and metal product divisions were also experiencing record sales and earnings. Rapid growth moved Heileman's sales and earnings ahead of La Crosse's Trane Company, a large heating and air-conditioning manufacturer, to become the city's largest company.

By the end of 1980, Heileman was operating 10 breweries and eight bakeries in the Upper Midwest. Employment in La Crosse was about 1,600. Production for 1980 company-wide was 13.27 million barrels, compared with 11.52 in 1979. Heileman ended 1980 as the 376th largest corporation in the United States with sales of $722 million. The new corporate headquarters in Harborview was already jammed, primarily due to the purchase of Carling. The main office of the bakery division was moved to the old Ellickson Building in the 400 block of Cass Street, and Heileman was contemplating adding space to the new corporate headquarters or more room elsewhere.

As the year came to a close, competition in the brewing industry was again described as brutal —there were rumors that both Schlitz and Olympia were in trouble. One bright spot was that the remaining small regional breweries seemed to be doing better. In Wisconsin those included the Huber Brewery of Monroe, Leinenkugel Brewery of Chippewa Falls, and the Point Brewery in Stevens Point.

Cleary was pleased with this trend and said Heileman was glad to give these smaller breweries a chance. Anheuser-Busch led the large breweries, followed by Miller, Schlitz, Pabst, and Coors. Heileman was the sixth-largest brewer, but only a few million barrels separated Schlitz from Heileman, and Cleary was already busy brewing up his next big deal.

Chapter 7

The Beer That Almost Made La Crosse Famous

THE SCHLITZ TAKEOVER ATTEMPT 1981

A Schlitz-Heileman combination would be a perfect "hand-in-glove" fit.

—ANALYST DESCRIBING THE MERGER PROPOSAL THAT WAS DOOMED BY THE U.S. JUSTICE DEPARTMENT

Russ Cleary's moves in 1981 were his boldest yet. Heileman entered the year as the sixth-largest brewery in the United States, and the fastest growing. Third place was only 2 million barrels away, and Pabst and Schlitz were both in trouble with declining sales.

Forbes magazine named Heileman the No. 1 stock in overall performance in the beverage industry for growth and return on investment. The company ranked 44th out of 1,041 in profitability, 85th in growth, and 36th in stock performance. Stock dividends had increased 283 percent in five years, and sales had ballooned from $80 million to $700 million in 10 years. The news sent Heileman stock soaring nearly 10 percent in one week and 20.8 percent overall in 1980.

Heileman was selling more than 30 brands of beer in all 50 states. There were now seven light beers being marketed by the major breweries, five of them Heileman products. However, the competition wasn't standing still. Anheuser-Busch was stepping up capacity and had set its sights on controlling 40 percent of the market by 1990. Miller also wanted a bigger market share.

Industry analysts warned that if Heileman wanted to compete against the big two it needed to liven up its stodgy ads. Heileman's strategy was to sell beer at competitive prices by holding down its advertising budgets. Its ads didn't feature entertainers or sports stars, but emphasized the quality of the beer. Cleary referred to it as making the beer the hero. In comparison, Anheuser-Busch and Miller used expensive national advertising campaigns, especially during sporting events.

Cleary recognized the fight he was in with the big guys and was searching for ideas to motivate Heileman distributors. Heileman Credit Manager Walter Baltz provided Cleary with the idea he was looking for. Baltz, who had an interest in guns, came up with his idea after Heileman obtained the Colt 45 brand, suggesting the company give gold, silver, or blue 45-caliber Colt pistols to its top wholesalers.

The idea soon mushroomed. Baltz suggested that at the annual sales convention, the "top gunner" salesman be given a violin case with a semiautomatic version of the Thompson submachine gun made famous by mobsters in the Roaring '20s. Cleary loved the idea and even joined the National Rifle Association. He had Baltz obtain a federal firearms license so he could buy the guns in quantity at a discount. All through the 1980s, the company vault contained not only the financial records, but also Heileman's own little arsenal of Thompsons.

In March, the Falstaff Brewery in Omaha was looking for a buyer, but Heileman was not interested since that market was already covered by the breweries in La Crosse, Belleville, and Saint Paul. Cleary wanted breweries in California and Texas, but acquisition opportunities appeared slim there because of the scarcity of independent brewers.

At the April 1981 stockholders meeting, Cleary told 750 in attendance that while the brewing industry as a whole was down 1 percent, Heileman

"Top gunner" salesmen Harold "Dutch" Beckman, left, John Wasmund, center, and Len Morrison, far right, "protect" Russ Cleary and John Pedace, second from right, in this early 1980s photo in front of the Heileman Corporate Center.

PHOTO COURTESY OF CLEARY-KUMM FOUNDATION

sales were up 12 percent for the first quarter. That rewarded investors with yet another 3-for-2 stock split and a quarterly dividend raise to 24 cents. News of the split and dividend increase caused a temporary halt to trading of the stock on the New York Stock Exchange, and when trading resumed the stock was up. Later in the month, Heileman stock hit a high of $40 a share after the company denied rumors it was considering a merger with Schlitz.

Heileman was making sales gains in Kansas, Florida, Alabama, Arizona, and Texas, was ranked first in sales in Wisconsin, Minnesota, Illinois, and Washington, and was widening its lead in Chicago. In a swipe at Anheuser-Busch, Cleary summarized these announcements as "more bad news for Augie Busch."

At the same meeting he also announced the tentative purchase of Barrel O' Fun, a Minnesota-based maker of snack foods, viewed as a hedge against the beer industry's slowing growth rate. Plans were put in place to increase sales by distributing the snacks through Heileman's network of 1,900 beer distributors. Heileman also announced plans to purchase Walt's Restaurant, located across from the La Crosse brewery at 310 Mississippi Street, a deal that was completed in June 1981 for $350,000.

In May 1981 Heileman denied a rumor it was going to purchase the Ross Furniture building in La Crosse to solve overcrowding at the new Harborview Corporate Headquarters. At the end of October, however, the company purchased the Riverfront Activity Center building, 27 Market Street, for $400,000, but without announcing any immediate plans for it. Heileman made the purchase not only to acquire available nearby property for future expansion, but also to be a good neighbor. The Riverfront Activity Center, a learning and jobs center for adults with disabilities, was able to use the money from the purchase to move to a better facility.

During 1981, Wisconsin Governor Lee S. Dreyfus toured Heileman's La Crosse brewery and corporate headquarters, commenting that he enjoyed Becks, a beer imported from Germany by Heileman. At the time, Wisconsin was having budget problems, and he jokingly thanked Heileman for its profitability and for its tax payments.

Preliminary results for the first half of the year showed Heileman in fourth place in beer sales, moving past Pabst and Coors. Pabst had recorded a loss in 1980 and had suffered recently from several management changes and increased competition from Heileman and others. Coors had suffered a large decline in sales in the first quarter due to a strike. But despite its problems, the Adolph Coors Company of Golden, Colorado, was another cash-rich company looking to expand.

Sales for third-place Schlitz fell 61 percent, while Heileman sales were up 15. Leading brewer Anheuser-Busch had huge gains in the first quarter, and in an eerie foreshadowing of future events, Stroh Brewing, a family-owned brewery in Detroit, implemented a strategy of purchasing other breweries.

The continuing problem of brewing capacity was being addressed by a major expansion in La Crosse, but unfortunately, in May 1981, a strike by bricklayers and cement masons put a halt to work on the new brewhouse, putting it nearly eight weeks behind schedule. The new wastewater treatment plant was already a month behind schedule, costing the city of La Crosse an extra several thousand dollars a month for processing Heileman's wastewater. Finally, in July, the new 900-gallon tanks were installed in the new brewhouse.

But offsetting these problems were some positive events. In June, *Wall Street Transcript,* a small financial publication, named Cleary the best corporate executive officer in the brewing industry. In June, the stock dividend was raised for the 12th time in five years and another 3-for-2 stock split was approved. Record sales for the first half of 1981 were announced; earnings were up 19 percent, and sales were up 15 percent. In July, Heileman was ranked among the top 10 corporations in Wisconsin in a variety of categories —second for stockholder return on investment, fifth in growth rate, and ninth in sales volume.

In late July 1981, Cleary made by far the biggest and boldest move in the history of the company when he announced a $494 million offer to merge with the Joseph Schlitz Brewing Company. The Schlitz purchase dwarfed the purchase of Carling for $37 million. Cleary and Frank J. Sellinger, the vice chairman who had been hired from Anheuser-Busch in 1977 to try to turn Schlitz around, made the announcement jointly.

In the 1950s, Schlitz had been the largest brewery in the United States, recognized worldwide, but its fortunes turned sour in the '70s, and in 1979 it recorded a $50.6 million loss. Its stock plummeted from a high of $64 a share to $5. Schlitz's downfall could be traced to a disastrous 1975 change in its brewing recipe. That change had been rejected by loyal drinkers, and the company was never able to recover. Adding to its woes was a series of ill-advised and unprofitable foreign acquisitions, including a Pakistani glass factory and fishing fleets in Chile and Panama.

News of the Heileman and Schlitz merger caused a suspension of the trade of both stocks on the New York Stock Exchange. When it resumed, the price of both stocks went up. At the time of the announcement, Heileman, Pabst, and Schlitz were all in the race to be America's third-largest brewery, but Heileman sales were increasing, while sales for Pabst and Schlitz were decreasing. The merger would give Heileman brewing capacity in the southern states that Cleary had been seeking. Schlitz owned breweries in: Milwaukee; Longview, Texas; Winston-Salem, North Carolina; Tampa, Florida; and Memphis, Tennessee. But those plants were only running at about 60 percent capacity overall. Its brands were Schlitz, Schlitz Light, Schlitz Malt Liquor, Old Milwaukee, Old Milwaukee Light, and Erlanger.

Schlitz also owned: five aluminum can plants with a combined capacity of 5 billion cans; two Spanish breweries; Geyser Peak Wineries of California; C&D Foods, a Wisconsin-based producer and processor of ducks; and Murphy Products Company, a Wisconsin producer of animal foods and feed concentrates. It also possessed valuable real estate, particularly around the brewery in Tampa, and a beachfront brewery it had closed in Hawaii. A bonus in the deal was an estimated $180 million in cash, securities, and receivables.

About 720 members of Brewery Workers Union 9 had been on strike at the Schlitz Brewery in Milwaukee since June 1, and rumor had it that if Heileman were not interested in the Milwaukee brewery it would be closed. Coors also was thought to be interested in purchasing that brewery if Schlitz closed it.

On July 31, 1981, Schlitz shut down the Milwaukee brewery, laying off about 700 workers, with the rest taking early retirement. This reduced the brewer's production capacity from 25.6 million barrels to 18.8 million, a number more in line with 1980 sales of 14.9 million barrels. Schlitz announced it intended to keep open the Milwaukee headquarters and a container plant in Oak Creek, Wisconsin.

The proposed Heileman and Schlitz merger was the largest business deal in the history of the state of Wisconsin. The merged company would have sales of almost $2 billion and assets of $900 million, making it the second-largest or third-largest company in Wisconsin behind the Kimberly-Clark paper company in Neenah, and possibly Allis-Chalmers, a manufacturer of farm implements in Milwaukee. Noting that only Anheuser-Busch, Miller, or Heileman had the wherewithal to join forces with Schlitz, analysts called the merger a perfect "hand-in-glove" fit.

Stock analysts predicted the merged company would have about 16 percent of the market and be strong competition for No. 1-ranked Anheuser-Busch and No. 2 Miller. Analysts also forecast future merger announcements involving Stroh, Olympia, and Pabst. James Horn, of Smith Barney, predicted that antitrust laws wouldn't be a problem for the merger because of Anheuser-Busch's 28 percent and Miller's 21 percent market share.

Other industry observers noted that while the purchase price seemed high, it was well worth it for Heileman to obtain brewing capacity and markets in the South and Southwest. Cleary noted that these breweries would allow Heileman to take advantage of the population shift to the South.

Now it was felt that Schlitz's problems would be solved by the merger and improved management and marketing. Old Style, Special Export, Rainier, and some malt liquor products could move into the southern markets where Heileman had only 10 percent of its sales, but Schlitz had 57 percent. Pabst and Coors would be hard-pressed to make gains against Heileman if the merger went through, but even with it, a Heileman challenge of Anheuser-Busch or Miller wouldn't be an easy thing.

In early August, Pabst responded to Heileman's $494 million bid for Schlitz with a bid of $588 million. However, the Pabst bid involved only $200 million in cash and $388 in debentures or loans. Stock analysts called the bid a desperate move on the part of Pabst, tracing it primarily to Minneapolis investor Irwin Jacobs, who owned 9.6 percent of the Pabst stock and had recently threatened a proxy fight to take over control of Pabst. Jacobs was the owner of Watkins Products of Winona, Minnesota, among other enterprises.

It didn't appear that a Schlitz and Pabst merger made sense for several reasons. First, both companies were already losing money and suffering from overcapacity. Second, Pabst already operated breweries in Milwaukee, Newark, Georgia, and Portland, not a good fit with the locations of the Schlitz breweries.

Cleary was also critical of the Pabst offer, saying it didn't make sense for Schlitz stockholders. He questioned whether Pabst could afford to make the estimated $60 million in principal and interest payments on the loans that would be required to finance the deal. Cleary also argued that a Heileman merger would not hurt smaller breweries, but would allow the company to compete against the two market leaders. With the addition of the Schlitz plants in Texas, Florida, and a recently closed brewery in California, he felt Heileman could compete with Anheuser-Busch and Miller.

Henry Maier, mayor of Milwaukee since 1960, came out in support of Pabst's purchase of Schlitz rather than the Heileman proposal, saying he wanted to preserve strong local ownership of the brewery to ensure economic success for Milwaukee. Days later, Schlitz announced it had rejected Pabst's offer and had agreed to the Heileman proposal. A Schlitz stockholder vote on the Heileman offer was tentatively scheduled for October 28, 1981, after the U.S. Justice Department had ruled on the merger.

Pabst issued a press release saying it was frustrated and disappointed by the action of the Schlitz board. Jacobs urged other members of the Pabst board of directors to continue to bid on Schlitz despite the fact it had announced acceptance of Heileman's offer. He refused to speculate on the fate of the Schlitz brewery in Milwaukee if Pabst bought Schlitz, but did say that in his opinion there would be more jobs in Milwaukee if Pabst merged with Schlitz.

In mid-August, Cleary speculated that some headquarters jobs would remain in Milwaukee, noting that data processing facilities were better there, and also there was better access by air for suppliers and wholesalers than in La Crosse. He indicated Heileman would probably follow a model similar to the Carling and Rainier arrangements, having branch headquarters in those locations.

Cleary denied rumors that Heileman was considering moving all headquarters operations to Milwaukee, saying Heileman had been in La Crosse since 1858 and moving would be difficult, if not impossible. He also noted that Schlitz had 1,000 people working in Milwaukee, and it would be impossible to move all those jobs to La Crosse.

Late in August, Pabst announced it had hired a Washington, D.C., law firm to persuade the Justice Department to block the Heileman and Schlitz merger.

The company motto, "Schlitz, the beer that made Milwaukee famous," became a trademark in 1894. The story was that the slogan was adopted when Schlitz provided beer to Chicago as a result of a water shortage there following the fire of 1871. By August 1981, the joke around Wisconsin was that Schlitz would need to change it to "Schlitz, the Beer That Made La Crosse Famous."

In September, Heileman and Schlitz announced that the stockholder meeting to vote on the merger had been moved to November 13 to allow time for the Justice Department to rule. Schlitz had about 16,200 stockholders and Heileman about 10,000. This was the first time in history Heileman stockholders had to vote on a purchase, since this one involved Heileman stock rather than just cash. Previously, all Heileman purchases had been made with cash only, which didn't require stockholder approval.

Later that month, Jacobs resigned from the board of Pabst, declaring his dissatisfaction with the Pabst chairman and other members of the board for failing to act on the takeover of Schlitz. He had been named to the board earlier in the year after threatening a proxy fight for control of Pabst. Jacobs had tried to persuade the Pabst board of directors to bid

$600 million in cash for Schlitz, but they couldn't accomplish the funding so the offer was never made.

In October, Schlitz Brewery Workers Union Local No. 9 filed a lawsuit against Heileman, asserting it had intentionally and improperly induced Schlitz to close the brewery in Milwaukee. Cited was a 1973 Justice Department ruling that Heileman could not purchase any more breweries in the Midwest. The suit argued that if the Milwaukee plant wasn't closed, Heileman could not have been merged with Schlitz. The union sought recovery of benefits lost by more than 700 members. Cleary called the lawsuit frivolous and grossly untrue.

Meanwhile, Heileman announced record sales and earnings for the third quarter. Sales were up 13 percent for the first nine months and earnings were up 17 percent from the year before. It also announced a 16-cent-a-share dividend and a second 8-cent-a-share bonus dividend to be paid in December.

Rumors were spreading of possible problems with the merger. A brewing industry analyst wrote that, by textbook definition, the deal violated antitrust laws. Anthony Nanni, a member of the Justice Department's antitrust division, referred to the Herfindahl Index, used by the department to determine when a given merger would or wouldn't be allowed within an industry. He noted the decision involved things such as the rate of technological change and growth of the industry, the amount of capital required for a new firm to enter the market, and the stability of the firm's market share over time. One other important factor considered was comparative strengths of the two breweries in regional markets.

On October 21, 1981, Assistant Attorney General William F. Baxter announced the U.S. Justice Department would file suit if Heileman proceeded with the Schlitz merger, which immediately canceled the stockholder vote scheduled for November 13. As the deal fell apart, Schlitz announced a third quarter loss of $36.1 million and confirmed that the ruling would not change the decision to close the brewery in Milwaukee.

Cleary was obviously disappointed and couldn't believe the government wouldn't allow the merger to proceed. He again pointed to the domination of the industry by Anheuser-Busch and Miller, and declared that the ruling put the future of the entire beer industry in jeopardy.

This was the first denial of a corporate merger during President Ronald Reagan's administration. Industry analysts were shocked by it, one pointing out that the ruling handed over the entire Sunbelt to Anheuser-Busch and Miller. Anheuser-Busch stock reacted immediately by achieving a new high for the year. The analyst also noted that Schlitz was a sick company and in desperate need of a merger, and that the denial clouded the long-term outlook of Heileman.

In November, a number of groups announced support for Heileman to appeal the decision. Wisconsin Governor Lee Dreyfus met with the Justice Department and asked it to reconsider the decision, and members of La Crosse Area Industrial and Economic Development Incorporated voted to ask elected officials to lobby to reverse the decision.

Wisconsin Senators William Proxmire and Robert Kasten, and U.S. Representatives Steve Gunderson,

James Sensenbrenner, Thomas Petri, and Robert Kastenmeier all signed a letter asking for a reversal. Their request came after Heileman informed the federal government of important changes in the structure of its original merger proposal.

Cleary, in an address to the Harvard Business Club of Milwaukee, which presented him with the Wisconsin Business Leader of the Year award, remained hopeful that the Justice Department would rethink the issue.

An article in the London-based *Economist* said blocking the Heileman and Schlitz merger was inexplicable, and possibly politically motivated, noting that the combined Heileman and Schlitz company would control 16 percent of the beer market, while Anheuser-Busch controlled 28 percent and Miller had 21 percent.

The Justice Department might have allowed the Heileman and Schlitz merger if Heileman would have agreed to give up the Blatz label, but Cleary was not willing to do so. One industry observer speculated most companies would have taken Schlitz over Blatz, but Cleary wouldn't betray Heileman wholesalers who had built up the Blatz brand.

The bad news continued for Heileman with the announcement that it would not get the La Crosse property tax refund it had sought. The courts ruled that Heileman was entitled to the refund, but the impact would be too great on the governmental units that would have to pay the refunds, even though Cleary had vowed to hold the liability down to $300,000. The company announced it did not intend to appeal the ruling.

Cleary ended the year frustrated and angry over the Justice Department's decision. He wanted to fight it, but said it wasn't an option because Schlitz management wouldn't allow it. Now Heileman was rapidly reaching a capacity crisis and still needed better access to the southern markets. And it was becoming increasingly difficult for Heileman to compete because of its older, smaller, and less efficient breweries.

But Cleary and Heileman weren't ready to go down without a fight. The Schlitz ruling behind him, Cleary looked for alternatives, setting his sights on another competitor—the Pabst Brewing Company.

With each passing year, the deals seemed to be getting bigger and more complex.

Chapter 8

Blue Ribbon Victory

THE PABST AND OLYMPIA MERGER 1982

Someone in Washington just didn't like Heileman.

—ANALYST REACTING TO U.S. JUSTICE DEPARMTMENT BLOCKING HEILEMAN ATTEMPT TO ACQUIRE SOME PABST ASSETS

Heileman finished 1981 as the fourth-largest brewery in America, the only brewery besides Anheuser-Busch and Miller to gain market share. The latter two controlled 54 percent of the beer sales in the United States and were widening the gap between them and the other breweries.

Cleary had hoped the U.S. Justice Department would take a more realistic look at the industry in view of the rapid growth of the two largest breweries.

Heileman's earnings had increased in 19 of the last 20 years despite unprecedented competition, but sales were slowing, up only 1 percent in 1981, which was blamed on a cool summer and recession gripping the country.

Schlitz, Pabst, Stroh, and Olympia were all having financial problems and were desperate for potential mergers in order to survive. Heileman also was looking for a merger, but it was financially strong, with cash available to purchase another brewery. All of the others would have difficulty initiating a merger and all, including Heileman, needed one in order to compete with Anheuser-Busch and Miller. The big two, as they were called, were taking market share by spending massive amounts on advertising and by cutting price. However, medium-sized breweries feared competition from a Heileman merger as much if not more than they feared a battle with the big two.

Before giving up on the merger of Heileman and Schlitz, there was one final attempt to reverse the decision. In February 1982, Murray L. Weidenbaum, one of President Ronald Reagan's top aides, rejected a request from U.S. Representative Henry Reuss of Wisconsin that asked the president to personally intervene in the matter. With the Schlitz merger out of the question, Cleary was considering Pabst Brewing Company as an alternative.

There was a merger mania in the brewing industry, and it was getting more confusing every week. At the time, Pabst, Schlitz, and Stroh were all essentially one-brand companies, susceptible to advertising assaults by Anheuser-Busch and Miller. Stroh, like Heileman, was attempting to move into the Sunbelt states and needed a brewery in the South.

Heileman had had discussions in 1981 about the possibility of buying Pabst, which was asking a $370 million purchase price. Cleary offered only $200 million. In late January 1982, William Smith, president of Pabst, was struggling to pull out of a sales slump that had forced him to close a brewery in Peoria Heights, Illinois. Pabst was also involved in lawsuits and had countersued investor Irwin Jacobs, who was himself suing to gain control of Pabst after it failed to acquire Schlitz. In addition to Jacobs, other parties also were attempting to take over Pabst. A small Philadelphia brewer, Christian Schmidt Brewing, had come in with a low offer of $128 million, $20 per share in cash and $5 in secured debt. Pabst rejected the bid, demanding 100 percent cash.

Rather than pursue Pabst, Heileman instead made the 1981 offer on Schlitz. After the Heileman takeover of Schlitz was prevented in late 1981, Schlitz failed in an attempt to take over Stroh, of Detroit. Stroh then took over Schaefer Brewing Company, resulting in a $4 million loss for Stroh in 1981. Then, in April 1982, Stroh made an attempt to take over Schlitz, and the U.S. Justice Department ruled Stroh and Schlitz could merge, on the condition that the Schlitz plant in Winston-Salem or Memphis be sold to someone other than Anheuser-Busch or Miller.

Cleary was vigorously opposed to the ruling and vowed to fight it in court. He said it didn't make sense for Heileman to buy either of the Schlitz breweries without getting one of the Schlitz brands also. The breweries were large modern facilities that Heileman couldn't run profitably if they were to produce only existing labels.

For the first time, Cleary was worried this ruling would affect his company's ability to compete. Heileman was still in an extremely strong financial position, with plenty of working capital to fund additional purchases, and Cleary still wanted to buy. He also doubted that Stroh could afford the $500 million debt required to purchase Schlitz.

William F. Baxter, head of the Justice Department's antitrust division, in explaining why he disallowed the Heileman and Schlitz merger but permitted Stroh and Schlitz to merge, said that Heileman didn't need Schlitz to survive and Schlitz was financially healthy on its own. Strangely, one of the reasons Heileman wasn't allowed to merge with Schlitz was that this would give it too much marketing power in the Midwest. Yet less than a year later Stroh, another Midwestern company, was allowed to take over Schlitz, giving it a 13 percent share. In 1981, Heileman had 7.5 percent and Schlitz 8.5 percent, so a merger would have resulted in a share of 16 percent.

Now Anheuser-Busch had just over 30 percent of the market, Miller almost 23, Stroh 13, Heileman a distant fourth at 7.9, and Pabst fifth at 7.6 percent. Five breweries now controlled 82 percent of all the beer sales in the United States, while in 1970 the top five breweries controlled less than half the total sales.

Following the merger, Stroh laid off a large number of Schlitz management people in Milwaukee, leaving only Pabst as a locally owned brewery. Many felt it was only a matter of time before Pabst fell too, leaving the once thriving Milwaukee brewery scene with no local ownership.

Heileman filed a lawsuit against the merger of Stroh and Schlitz in April. Cleary felt the ruling would benefit Anheuser-Busch and Miller and eventually lead to those two companies essentially taking over the entire industry. He feared Stroh would have too much debt after the Schlitz takeover and would not have enough money to advertise. He also worried that assets from Stroh and Schlitz would need to be sold to reduce debt, and Anheuser-Busch would be able to purchase those assets. In 1981, after Heileman attempted to purchase Schlitz, August Busch III had flown to La Crosse to persuade Heileman to sell the Schlitz plant in Memphis to Anheuser-Busch.

Heileman's chief financial officer, Robert Korkowski, estimated the breweries in Memphis and Winston-Salem would probably each sell for about $80 million, a price Heileman could not afford for a single brewery. Pabst had a big new plant in Georgia that would be helpful to Heileman, but this still wouldn't give the company plants in the critical markets of California or Texas. Cleary said his previous description of the state of the beer industry as all-out war was now an understatement.

Heileman made its next big move in May, offering to buy Pabst's 88.2 million shares at $24 a share for a cash purchase of about $196.4 million. At the time Pabst stock was selling for $21 a share. Just days later, instead of accepting the offer, Pabst bid $70.2 million for Olympia, under the assumption that the Justice Department would not allow a merger between Heileman and Pabst. The deal would have given Heileman a 16.5 percent share, moving it ahead of the recently merged Stroh and Schlitz breweries with their 13 percent market share.

Pabst was correct, and in mid-June the Justice Department ruled against the Heileman and Pabst merger. It cited the 1973 consent decree that prevented Heileman from purchasing any brewery in an eight-state area of the Upper Midwest. Heileman issued a statement in opposition to the ruling, saying it would give Anheuser-Busch and Miller an even larger market share.

The Justice Department also announced a change in the policy that had been in effect since 1968. In the future it would allow slightly more concentration of market share through mergers in a given region, and would look more favorably on a merger if one of the companies involved was failing or had a failing division, or if the merger would result in operating efficiencies. Many stock analysts noted that the Herfindahl Index, used by the Justice Department to determine if a merger would be allowed, had suffocated the brewing industry for the previous two decades.

The situation becomes more confusing

Jacobs put together a group named JMSL Acquiring Corporation and made a $196.5 million offer to take over Pabst. As part of the deal he offered to sell Heileman the Pabst breweries near Perry, Georgia, and Newark, New Jersey. The modern Georgia brewery and its 5.5-million-barrel capacity was exactly what Cleary needed, and the New Jersey brewery, with its 1.3-million-barrel capacity, would also be useful since Heileman's only East Coast brewery, in Baltimore, was already running at capacity.

Jacobs also offered Heileman the rights to sell the Pabst brands in a 27-state area for $135 million. Pabst would continue to operate breweries in Milwaukee and Portland. Cleary considered this offer less desirable than an outright purchase of Pabst, but at least it gave him access to the long-sought Southern market.

At the same time, a small New Orleans brewer, Coy International, made a competing offer. It proposed that Heileman purchase Pabst for $196.5 million, but included a complex set of conditions, including one calling for Heileman to sell 4.7 million barrels of production back to Coy and give it marketing rights to the Pabst brands in four Midwestern states, including Wisconsin. Coy also was to be given nationwide rights to Pabst's Red White and Blue brand and Heileman's Grain Belt and Hauenstein brands. Cleary favored the simpler Jacobs deal.

Meanwhile, Pabst had still been negotiating for the purchase of Pittsburgh Brewing Company and Olympia Brewing in Tumwater, Washington. With the announcement of a potential deal between Pabst and Heileman, however, Pabst withdrew its offer for Pittsburgh Brewing.

By the end of June, Jacobs announced he had obtained loans of $196.5 million for the purchase of Pabst, and Heileman announced it had obtained a $150 million loan from the same three banks to purchase some of the Pabst assets. All three lenders said they would pull out of the deal if the Justice Department blocked the sale of the Pabst breweries in Georgia and New Jersey to Heileman.

Behind the numbers it was clear Heileman was providing almost 75 percent of the funding for Jacobs in his Pabst takeover attempt. A deadline of December 1, 1982, was set for completion of the deal, which required that Heileman first purchase the two breweries.

Now Pabst filed a lawsuit against Heileman and Jacobs to try to prevent Jacobs from taking over the company. The suit contended that the deal would leave Pabst, with only a 23-state market, no longer able to compete. It also accused Heileman and Jacobs of violating antitrust laws.

Cleary could not believe it.

Less than two months earlier, Pabst had been ready to merge with Heileman if the Justice Department would allow it. Now it claimed the acquisition by Heileman of two of its breweries would amount to its total destruction. Cleary called the lawsuit frivolous and said that Heileman attorneys would attempt to have it dismissed.

Pabst formally rejected Jacobs' offer, and to further fight the takeover decided to essentially merge with Olympia, agreeing to purchase 49 percent of its stock. Olympia Brewing then created a subsidiary, OBC Acquisitions Incorporated, which in turn purchased 49 percent of the Pabst stock.

Days later Jacobs brought a $600 million lawsuit against Pabst and Olympia, arguing that their merger was a betrayal of shareholder interests. He accused Pabst management of illegally funding the creation of Olympia's OBC Acquisitions, and argued that the entire deal was financed by and organized by Pabst management for its own benefit. Finally, he accused Pabst management of falsely leading shareholders to believe the purchase of Pabst by Jacob's JMSL Acquisitions would never happen.

Within a week, the Justice Department's Baxter struck another blow to Cleary and Heileman. He announced the department would block Jacobs' attempt to purchase Pabst. In the ruling, he indicated the sale of some of the Pabst assets to Heileman would increase Heileman's dominance in the Midwestern and mid-Atlantic areas above a level set forth in the department's merger guidelines. Stock analysts reacted by calling the decision incredible and ludicrous. One, referring to this decision and the previous year's Schlitz ruling, speculated that someone in Washington just didn't like Heileman.

Cleary considered his options, which mainly were to bring another lawsuit to try to reverse the decision, or look for other alternatives, including a bid for Coors. This wasn't considered the best option, because Coors had a unique brewing process that avoided pasteurizing its beer. Duplicating this process at Heileman's existing breweries would have been very difficult, and shipping costs from Coors' Colorado plant were prohibitive.

He also considered buying other smaller regional breweries, including: Pearl Brewery in San Antonio, Genesee in Rochester, New York, Christian Schmidt in Philadelphia, and Pittsburgh Brewing, but these were just too small to solve any long-term problems.

Yet another alternative was to buy one of the two Schlitz breweries in either Memphis or Winston-Salem, now owned by Stroh because of its merger with Schlitz. But both of these breweries were very large and costly, and Heileman didn't immediately have need for that much capacity.

To make use of extra production capacity, Heileman could undertake an expensive advertising plan to increase sales of Carling Black Label, already popular in the East, or it could close either the Belleville or Newport brewery and possibly move that production to the brewery now owned by Stroh. Cleary was reluctant to do the latter, because he felt it would have a negative effect on Heileman's image, which had been built by working hard to win the loyalty of those cities by keeping their breweries open.

Stroh's merger with Schlitz had left it in debt, and Cleary felt Stroh might be forced to consider selling off brands or breweries. On the other hand, he thought the Pabst and Olympia deal might force a sale of the plant near Perry, Georgia, or Olympia's Lone Star Brewery in San Antonio.

With all these options before him, one thing was certain. Cleary would do something, and he was probably going to do it soon. Cleary's office featured a collection of the cans and bottles of Heileman brands, and a framed copy of his favorite poem on the wall:

> *On the plains of hesitation*
> *Bleach the bones of countless millions,*
> *Who at the dawn of decision,*
> *Sat down to wait,*
> *And waiting, died.*
>
> —GEORGE W. CECIL, *1923*

In July, Heileman announced record earnings for the 30th consecutive quarter. Earnings were up 13 percent and sales were up 6 percent.

Manny Goldman of Sanford C. Bernstein Company gave Heileman a buy rating on a nationally broadcast stock program, saying it was exceptionally strong and predicting it would eventually figure out a way to obtain a Southern brewery from Schlitz, Stroh, or Pabst. Once it obtained a brewery he felt it would rapidly expand into the Southern market. Two other brokerage firms also came out with strong-buy ratings on Heileman stock.

In Saint Paul, Heileman spent $3 million to expand the brewhouse, packaging lines, and aging tanks, and to build a new warehouse. That brewery was primarily producing Schmidt, but also was brewing for the Blatz, Grain Belt, Wiedemann, Kingsbury, Schmidt Light, and near beer labels. In Seattle, a $6 million project included enlargement of the warehouse, packaging lines, and aging tanks. Rainier was the biggest product, but Heidelberg, Mickey's Malt Liquor, Rainier Light, and Rainier Ale brands were produced there as well.

Even as the U.S. economy worsened, Heileman announced record earnings for the third quarter.

But Anheuser-Busch also was thriving. In late 1982, Anheuser-Busch mounted a major counterattack into the Chicago market. During the mid-1970s, Anheuser-Busch and Schlitz each held about 30 percent of Chicago's market share, but in the summer of 1976, Anheuser-Busch had suffered a devastating strike. Heileman took advantage by moving into first with about 40 percent of the market, and Anheuser-Busch slipped to 10 percent.

To regain sales, Anheuser-Busch opened the corporate coffers and started pouring $20 million to $25 million annually into Chicago, sponsoring almost every sporting, ethnic, or city event. Anheuser-Busch sponsored the Chicago Cubs for the 1983 season, bought the rights to Chicago Bears preseason games, Chicago White Sox radio broadcasts, and various sponsorships of the Chicago Sting, the Chicago Black Hawks, and the Chicago Bulls. Comiskey Park and Soldiers Field sported huge Budweiser ads on new scoreboards, and Anheuser-Busch also sponsored college events at Northwestern University, the University of Illinois, and DePaul University. It even went into amateur sporting events such as boat races, trap shooting, and bowling tournaments. At Arlington racetrack, Anheuser-Busch created the world's richest horse race with a $1 million purse.

Analysts presumed that Anheuser-Busch was taking all of its profits from California, Texas, and New York and pouring them into the battle to win back Chicago. The stakes were high for Heileman, since Chicago represented 35 percent to 40 percent of all Old Style sales. Cleary compared trying to outspend Anheuser-Busch with playing poker with an oil sheik. Many industry insiders were disgusted by the tactics Anheuser-Busch was using to buy the beer business, likening them to George Steinbrenner attempting to buy the World Series every year for his New York Yankees.

Heileman fought back with a "Chicago You've Got Style" advertising campaign and introduced an Old Style beer stein series. It still had a very strong Chicagoland wholesaler base.

Meanwhile, Cleary was considering his options, among them the acquisition of either the Falstaff Brewing Company in California or the Pearl Brewing Company in Texas. Ironically, Heileman's success was also its worst enemy. It was running at capacity at most breweries, but still was unable to meet demand. Its smaller, older, and less efficient breweries around the country were stunting its growth.

The Justice Department had ruled against Heileman in the previous two years because it didn't see the need for mergers to make it successful. Also, some industry insiders felt Cleary hadn't been flexible enough in his dealings with the Justice Department, unwilling to give up any of his existing brands to complete some of the mergers.

On November 6, Cleary made one more attempt at a complicated merger between Heileman, Pabst, and Olympia. He offered Pabst about $150 million for 6 million of the outstanding 8.17 million shares at $25 a share. As part of the deal Heileman would get the Pabst brewery in Perry, Georgia, the Lone Star Brewery in San Antonio, and the Blitz Weinhard Brewery in Portland, Oregon. Thus, Heileman would be acquiring the Lone Star, Lone Star Light, Buckhorn, Red White and Blue, Blitz, Henry Weinhard Private Reserve, Bohemian, and Burgermeister brands. Heileman would also brew Pabst brands on a five-year contract.

Pabst would spin off a new company, retaining the Pabst Blue Ribbon, Hamm's, Olde English 800, Olympia, and other Pabst and Olympia brands. It would keep its breweries in Milwaukee and Newark and the Olympia breweries in Tumwater and Saint Paul. Unlike previous merger attempts, Cleary and Pabst president Smith had discussed the deal ahead of time with the Justice Department and didn't foresee any problems.

The one problem still facing the merger was Jacobs who, in recent months, had teamed up with 77-year-old multimillionaire Paul Kalmanovitz in yet another attempt to take control of Pabst. Kalmanovitz already owned a major interest in three smaller breweries, Falstaff, General, and Pearl, and had a history of taking over a brewery and initially increasing profits by reducing or eliminating advertising. To fight off Jacobs and Kalmanovitz, Pabst initiated a lawsuit charging them with violating federal security laws.

Days later, Heileman upped its bid to $27.50 per share in an attempt to get Pabst stockholders to sell their shares. The total cost to Heileman still remained about $150 million because it would purchase 5.5 million shares rather than 6.0 million.

Things get ugly

Jacobs reacted by asking Wisconsin Governor Lee S. Dreyfus to investigate the conduct of Securities Commissioner Richard R. Malmgren, charging that Malmgren was unfairly siding with Heileman in the Pabst controversy. The matter was referred to the state Ethics Board.

Jacobs then filed suit in U.S. District Court to block the deal between Pabst and Heileman, saying it violated antitrust laws and, at the same time, upped his bid from $24 a share to $30. Industry analysts speculated Heileman could afford to raise its bid to $37 and still buy enough shares to take control. Even at those prices, Heileman would be getting added capacity at about $20 a barrel versus $50 a barrel for a new brewery.

The Justice Department approved the Heileman merger with Pabst, and now Jacobs raised his bid from $30 to $35. His JMSL Corporation needed only 3 million shares, while Heileman needed 3.9 million to gain control. Pabst stockholders faced a deadline of early December to decide which deal to accept.

Cleary said Heileman intended to do whatever it took to complete the deal, and with just days to go, he had enough shares on deposit to acquire Pabst. However, stockholders could still withdraw their shares. Heileman announced it would keep the depository open for four hours on Thanksgiving Day so people could deposit their stock in Heileman's account. Jacobs was only 200,000 shares short of what he needed, so the deal would come down to the wire.

As the clock ticked, Heileman and Jacobs cut a final deal. Heileman agreed to raise its price to $29 per share, and since Jacobs and his group owned 1.1 million shares of Pabst stock that they had purchased at $13 per share, they walked away with about $18 million in profit. Heileman also agreed to pay Jacobs an additional $7.5 million for lawsuits and legal costs resulting from his fight to acquire Pabst. Heileman's cost for the purchase of Pabst went from $151 million to about $160 million, but in return, Jacobs agreed to withdraw his offer on Pabst and stop acquiring more shares of Pabst before the deal was completed.

Most considered the deal a win-win situation. Industry insiders and analysts felt Heileman was more interested in making beer and seeing Pabst thrive, while Jacobs and Kalmanovitz were more interested in making money. With a Heileman and Pabst merger it appeared that more Pabst employees would be able to keep their jobs, Heileman would finally get the Southern brewery it so desperately needed, and Jacobs would pocket the profit he wanted. Surely everyone was a winner, except for one.

Kalmanovitz wasn't happy with the deal and decided to fight it. He was worth $250 million at the time and had been the money behind Jacobs' efforts. He argued he had given Jacobs a $33 million loan that would have allowed him to raise his bid up to $35 per share. Kalmanovitz said he was prepared to offer up to $42 a share to obtain Pabst on his own, was no longer involved with Jacobs and his group, and threatened legal action against Heileman, Pabst, and Jacobs.

But the Justice Department told Kalmanovitz it already had approved the deal, and had no antitrust concerns. Heileman tried to appease Kalmanovitz by offering him a $5 million settlement, but he wasn't interested and went ahead with his own offer of $32 a share for Pabst. However, he faced an uphill battle since Heileman already owned a good share of the Pabst stock.

Heileman and Pabst then filed a lawsuit against Kalmanovitz charging him with federal securities law violations, and Kalmanovitz countered with a $90 million lawsuit against Cleary and Smith for conspiring to defraud Pabst shareholders. Interestingly, he did not bring similar charges against Jacobs.

As the battles dragged on, Heileman marked record-breaking sales of 14 million barrels for 1982. At the celebration, Cleary lamented that if Heileman had better friends in Washington it might be celebrating 20 million barrels rather than 14 million. But he was reasonably sure the whole Pabst matter would be resolved by the end of the year.

With the Pabst deal offering access to Southern markets, Cleary indicated his next target would be expansion on the East Coast. Stroh, Pabst, Coors, and Olympia all had suffered sharp sales declines during 1982, and the beer industry had a 1 percent drop, the first in more than 30 years.

With Christmas approaching, a deadline of December 22 was set for Pabst stockholders to deposit their

Russ and Gail Cleary celebrate 14 million barrels in 1982.
COURTESY OF CLEARY-KUMM FOUNDATION

shares with Heileman. But a group of 10 professional stock investors had gotten control of 7 million shares of Pabst stock, and were willing to sell large blocks of it to the highest bidder on a moment's notice.

The only interest of these arbitrageurs was to make money. Korkowski announced that Heileman was upping its bid to $32 per share in order to match Kalmanovitz, raising Heileman's total cost to $179.2 million. At that, Standard & Poor's immediately added Heileman to its credit watch based on the new amount. It felt Heileman's traditionally conservative balance sheet could be weakened and its financial flexibility reduced by the purchase.

Kalmanovitz's lawyer, former San Francisco mayor Joseph L. Alioto, announced that his client had 12 percent of the Pabst stock and would continue to obtain more. But, with just three days remaining before the deadline, industry analysts felt certain Heileman had the shares it needed to seal the deal.

On the day of the deadline, Kalmanovitz raised his bid one last time, to $40 a share, in a desperate attempt to sway the professional arbitrageurs to him. But it was too late. At the end of the day, Heileman had the shares it needed and won the battle for Pabst, but the victory came at a cost. The final purchase price was $179.2 million, and Heileman required loans to meet it. However, in addition to the breweries and brands, Heileman also obtained 30 acres of valuable land surrounding the Lone Star plant in downtown San Antonio, and 500 new wholesalers.

At year-end, the entire brewing industry was in a state of confusion. Seven of the 11 largest U.S. breweries had been involved in one or more acquisitions, and there were rumors of more. With Christmas approaching, Cleary and the rest of the Heileman team had been totally consumed by the Pabst deals.

Cleary had spent his entire brewing career at Heileman, and was known for his understanding of the beer industry and his ability to capitalize on opportunities. He was considered a tenacious and single-minded workaholic who personally ran the company. Outside of work, Cleary's main interests were his wife, Gail, and their two daughters, Kristine and Sandra. He looked forward to a well-deserved Christmas break with his family.

As the year came to a close, Heileman had fought and won a long, hard, expensive battle for access to the Southern states. For the first time the company had been forced to borrow money to finance a merger and was now on a credit watch because of this debt. It had a variety of legal problems in La Crosse and elsewhere, and the country was in a recession with public sentiment turning against beer drinking. Worse yet, another huge battle loomed on the horizon in Chicago with Anheuser-Busch. While Cleary and Heileman were winning battles at the end of 1982, there were questions as to whether they could win the war.

And halfway around the world, an Australian named Alan Bond decided to get into the beer business by acquiring his first brewery, the Swan Brewery in Perth.

Chapter 9

Thrust and Perry

THE PABST BREWERY IN PERRY, GEORGIA 1982–1983

Heileman was gobbling up brands and competitors like Pac-Man

—ANALYSTS COMPARING THE LA CROSSE BREWERY'S ACQUISITIVE WAYS TO A POPULAR VIDEO GAME

Russ Cleary returned from Christmas confident and smiling, and Pabst president William F. Smith celebrated at the brewery with a brass band, certain that the Heileman merger was the best possible Christmas present for the company and its employees. Smith felt strongly that if Irwin Jacobs and Paul Kalmanovitz had won control of Pabst they would have eventually closed the brewery in Milwaukee.

Most people agreed, though, that many Pabst stockholders were the big losers, since Pabst stock, which had sold for $100 a share, dropped to $10. They also worried that the new Pabst Corporation, formed from the assets of Pabst and Olympia, could not survive. Both companies had decreasing sales, and the new one would have almost $95 million in debt.

Some speculated that Irwin Jacobs was the big winner, with large stock gains plus money Heileman had paid him for legal costs. On the other hand, Pabst employees, who had feared for their jobs, were delighted to be rid of Jacobs, and Heileman was a big winner with the new breweries. Apparently Wall Street agreed, for Heileman stock went up to $52.50 a share, from $31.50 going into the fourth quarter of 1982.

The Heileman and Pabst deal was named the Wisconsin news story of the year for 1982. For the first time ever, annual sales topped $1 billion, and Heileman finished 1982 as the fourth-largest brewery in the United States behind Anheuser-Busch, Miller, and Stroh. Total barrels for 1982 were 14,518,000 and recent acquisitions had added capacity for 8 million more barrels. It was the 33rd most profitable company in the United States.

Cleary went to work integrating the Pabst acquisitions into the House of Heileman. The brewery in Perry, Georgia, was located on 700 acres and had a can manufacturing facility. Perry, which had been running at about 60 percent capacity, began to produce Wiedemann, Sterling, Colt 45, and Red White and Blue, plus the 3 million barrels of Pabst products under contract to the new Pabst Corporation. Heileman estimated the additional capacity cost about $12 per barrel versus an estimated $50 per barrel to build a new brewery. With the additional capacity the company had a total of almost 25 million barrels.

The Lone Star Brewery sat on 37 acres of prime real estate in downtown San Antonio, but the brand had been neglected and would require lots of advertising and wholesaling help. Heileman moved all of the production for beer it sold in Texas to Lone Star, and moved some of the Pabst Blue Ribbon contract production there. This took the pressure off Baltimore and Evansville, which were running at capacity, and reduced shipping costs.

The Henry Weinhard brewery in Portland, Oregon, was very efficient, and the brand had a cult-like following in California. Portland would be used to reduce pressure on the brewery in Seattle, which had been unable to meet demand. It also allowed Heileman to make a push into the California market.

Cleary announced the company would probably develop or sell some of the Milwaukee real estate it had obtained in the deal, and plans were discussed to lease some office space back to Pabst. Twenty-one salaried Pabst employees had been laid off when accounting and billing functions from Georgia were moved to corporate headquarters in La Crosse; at one time, the brewery in Georgia had 600 employees but that number had been reduced to 400 because of decreased sales by Pabst. Heileman expected to hire additional production employees as it increased capacity there. It closed the Newport, Kentucky, brewery, the least efficient of the 13 operating plants.

Now Cleary contemplated introducing the Old Style brand into Texas and the southeast United States. In Arizona, Heileman had been able to double its market share with Old Style, which was particularly saleable given the number of people from the Midwest who wintered there. Old Style, however, wasn't as well known in the other areas and would require expensive advertising to build up a following.

Instead, Cleary felt it might be more effective to use the extra capacity to increase market share for the Carling, Colt 45, Tuborg, and Sterling brands, which were already marketed in those states. Either way, he was willing to fight the battle by waging a price war, but Heileman still couldn't afford to spend the massive amounts on advertising that Anheuser-Busch and Miller did.

Miller Brewing was able to pass Heileman in Wisconsin sales for the first two months of 1983 when its ad program began to kick in. Heileman retook the lead from Miller the next month, but Cleary now knew that Miller was going to be a tough competitor in the future.

On April 22, 1983, 1,200 Heileman stockholders came to the 50th annual meeting since its reorganization after Prohibition. The meeting was held in the newly opened Heileman Hall and Visitor Center in the former Walt's Restaurant building.

Cleary had nothing but good news for the stockholders, announcing that sales were up for the 33rd consecutive quarter, a 2-for-1 stock split, and an increase in the dividend. He also revealed expansion plans in Baltimore and Frankenmuth, Michigan, and possibly Phoenix.

He proposed a change in the company charter to make a two-tier takeover of Heileman more difficult. (In a two-tier takeover, a higher price is offered for the first amount of the company stock needed, and a lower price for the remainder.) Its approval raised the percentage of stock required from 75 percent to 89.3 percent. The newly formed Pabst Corporation also modified its articles of incorporation to head off further disruptive takeover attempts. That change required 80 percent of the stockholders to vote in favor before a company director could be removed.

The purchase of the Pabst breweries had left Heileman with a long-term debt of $170 million, which resulted in a lower credit rating by Standard and Poor's, and the drop of its stock price from $52.50 a share to $45. Heileman argued Standard and Poor's had incorrectly attributed to it an extra $60 million in debt which really belonged to Pabst, and besides, its debt was backed by over $500 million in assets in the breweries, equipment, and inventory. Analysts also estimated Heileman had about $100 million in cash it could use to retire the debt. Record profits in 1983 quickly put to rest any doubts about Heileman's creditworthiness.

Heileman again expanded its bakery division, purchasing Red Seal Quality Foods of Denver, Colorado, in May 1983. The 72-year-old company had sales of $12 million in potato chips and corn chips, primarily in Colorado, Montana, Wyoming, and New Mexico. Sales of Barrel O' Fun snacks had surged from $5 million to $15 million since Heileman had purchased the company; for 1982, the bakery division had total sales of $87.4 million. Heileman announced it intended to look for additional bakeries to purchase somewhere in the South, near the new breweries it had purchased.

Just when things seemed to be going well, more legal problems surfaced in June when Heileman was fined $900,000 by the Securities and Exchange Commission for alleged illegal use of inside information in the purchase of Olympia stock. Cleary, the suit charged, had met with Pabst officials prior to purchasing Olympia stock and knew Pabst intended to purchase 49 percent of Olympia stock. Cleary neither admitted nor denied wrongdoing, but paid the fine. He felt Heileman couldn't afford to fight the government.

Even with the legal problems, analysts remained positive about Heileman and the future. Alluding to a popular video game at the time, they said Heileman was gobbling up brands and competitors like Pac-Man.

In July 1983, *Consumer Reports* magazine featured an article rating beers. The report gave Blatz and Old Style only fair ratings, near the bottom of their respective categories. Cleary blasted the report and said the magazine should stick to testing toasters. An official from an independent lab that tested beers for all the major brewers called the report laughable and questioned the validity of the test and the qualifications of the experts involved in it. Heileman didn't really think the report would impact sales.

Record earnings, up 32 percent, were again announced for the second quarter of 1983. This gain allowed Heileman to make a $55 million payment against the money it had borrowed to finance the

Pabst deal. All Heileman breweries except those in Portland and San Antonio were running at capacity, and Cleary predicted that Heileman could well catch Stroh for third place in 1984.

In early December, Heileman held a celebration marking the production of 17 million barrels and annual sales that exceeded $1 billion. Sales for 1983 increased to $1.32 billion and earnings were $56.9 million. Cleary took pride in the fact that just since 1979 both of these figures had doubled. At the ceremony, he also discussed that year's drop in Heileman's stock price, from a high earlier in the year of just over $50 a share down to $28.50. Cleary blamed this on Anheuser-Busch, which had issued a less-than-optimistic earnings prediction, making Heileman guilty by association. In addition, he said, many stockholders were selling toward the end of the year, and industry analysts were down on beer stocks in general based on the economy and the public's increasingly negative attitude toward alcohol. However, *Value Line* still had a favorable recommendation on Heileman stock.

Chapter 10

Blue Ribbon Defeat

ANOTHER PABST TAKEOVER ATTEMPT 1984–1985

Pabst employees were told Heileman was not the enemy; the enemy was in Saint Louis. Russ Cleary promised to send the first case of Pabst to Augie Busch III along with a note telling him the beer wars were on.

As 1984 dawned, industry analysts speculated about a Heileman buyout of the rest of Pabst.

Heileman's continued success in 1983 had allowed it to pay off part of its debt from the previous Pabst deal, and *Forbes* ranked Heileman No. 1 in the beverage industry. The magazine praised Heileman's sales increases of close to 30 percent in each of the previous five years, better than Anheuser-Busch and Miller in a beer industry that was essentially flat.

Pabst was in trouble going into 1984, with only $5 million in earnings on sales of $800 million. Worse yet, sales for a combined Pabst and Olympia had decreased by a million barrels. The brewery in Milwaukee would have to be shut down for a week in late January and possibly again later in the spring.

Meanwhile, Stroh declared war on Heileman in Minnesota, where Schmidt was No. 1. Then Coors announced plans to move into the Minnesota market, despite high shipping costs. Not to be left out, Anheuser-Busch and Miller also joined the battle, figuring they could compete on price. Heileman was No. 1 in sales in Wisconsin for 1983, but Miller jumped out to an early lead for 1984 and Heileman President Russ Cleary knew he was in for a dogfight. Miller was pushing Meister Brau and had recently introduced Milwaukee's Best, a new low-cost brand. And despite attempts by Heileman and the other major brewers, Miller was leading the light beer market with Miller Lite.

Cleary rolled out a new program he called "Heileman's March to the Sea." He would introduce Old Style and Old Style Light in Georgia, South Carolina, Oklahoma, Houston, Texas, and Las Vegas, Nevada, using the "God's Country" advertising theme. This was not an effort to overtake the big two brewers, but just to remain competitive.

At this point, Old Style was Heileman's most popular brand, responsible for 35 percent of Heileman sales. John Pedace, vice president of marketing, described the new campaign as guerrilla warfare. Along with Old Style, Heileman would bring its low-cost beers, malt liquors, and near beers into those markets.

Old Style was shipped from La Crosse to Houston, Las Vegas, and Oklahoma, purposely limiting its initial assault so it wouldn't run into production problems. It preceded the move into Houston with $5 million in advertising.

Old Style was a premium beer and could afford to make up the higher cost of shipping from La Crosse, but the company hoped to start producing it at the Perry, Georgia, plant and eventually in San Antonio to reduce that expense. In anticipation of increased sales, Heileman had completed a $10 million expansion at the San Antonio brewery. In the Midwest, sales soared during the summer months and then dropped off during the cold winter months. In the South, demand for Old Style could be year-round.

After the first quarter, Heileman moved up 55 places to become the 268th largest company in the United States. About 1,000 stockholders were in La Crosse for the annual meeting, where the news was that Miller's new Milwaukee Best brand was being sold for about $1.50 a six-pack, which was below cost. Stroh also was selling its beer below cost in an effort to take market share. Cleary vowed to selectively match prices where necessary to avoid losing customers.

Progress was being made in the Southern markets. In Missouri, Anheuser-Busch's home state, Heileman went from 6.9 percent to 10.3 percent market share. It was still No. 1 in Wisconsin, Illinois, Minnesota, and Washington, and was strong in Iowa, Missouri, and Tennessee. Markets where it was gaining were Virginia, Arizona, and South Carolina.

Cleary told the stockholders that within three months the last $30 million in debt from the Pabst merger would be paid off, and they voted for another increase in the number of shares of stock—from 28 million to 70 million. They planned for future stock splits and possible acquisitions, and yet another dividend was granted.

Cleary blamed the recently declining stock price on a pessimistic report by Anheuser-Busch on the future of the brewing and baking industries, which were being adversely affected by increased costs and price cutting.

Cleary also fielded tough questions on problems Heileman suffered in Chicago. During 1984, it had raised prices in Chicago, hoping the other competitors would follow suit, which they didn't. The result was a loss of market share in Chicago, but Cleary vowed there would be blood on the streets before Heileman would let anyone else take over Chicago.

First quarter sales were up for the 37th consecutive quarter, and in addition to the expansion of Old Style into Southern markets, Heileman started a campaign to expand Rainier, Lone Star, and other brands into Eastern markets.

The falling price of Heileman stock prompted the E.F. Hutton brokerage firm to issue a pessimistic stock report that Heileman would be hurt by rising material and advertising costs, increased price pressure from competitors, and mounting public concerns over alcohol abuse. Hutton suggested, ominously, that Heileman could eventually be chewed up by larger competitors.

Cleary responded that the report put too much emphasis on the pricing wars among the economy brands, which only accounted for about 35 percent of Heileman sales. Heileman had always faced such tough competition.

Days later, E.F. Hutton issued another report on Heileman, this one naming it perhaps the best publicly traded brewing company. However, it still considered the Heileman stock price to be generous and expressed doubt the company could maintain its recent growth rates.

In June, Heileman stock suffered a devastating blow when it was announced that sales would decrease 7 percent after 37 consecutive quarters of gains. The share price fell immediately to 40 percent below the start of the year. Although the entire stock market was down 10 percent for the first half of 1984, Heileman's performance was among the worst in Wisconsin.

Miller was on the attack in Wisconsin, and both Coors and Stroh were attacking in Minnesota, Washington, and Wisconsin. Miller was selling its Milwaukee's Best for as low as 99 cents per six-pack or $2.93 a case. The good news was it had not yet introduced this brand into Wisconsin.

Industry analysts forecast that Heileman, Pabst, C. Schmidt, Falstaff, and Pearl would be victims in this latest price war. Stroh, they said, could afford to compete on price because it didn't have to worry about turning a profit for stockholders, its only financial obligation being to the Stroh family. Miller, which was owned by tobacco giant Philip Morris, could afford to finance the price wars with its cigarette profits.

Analysts speculated there might be changes at Heileman headquarters and sales staff in La Crosse, but Cleary was optimistic. The new Heileman low-alcohol brands were doing better than expected, and he was confident that sales declines were only temporary, to be blamed on poor weather, especially during the Memorial Day weekend. He predicted sales would bounce back, as Heileman always did best when the brewing market was in turmoil.

Stock analysts weren't as confident as Cleary. E.F. Hutton analysts felt the problem was long-term and recommended its clients switch from Heileman stock to Coca Cola, stressing growing concerns over alcohol abuse and drunken driving plus massive price cutting in the industry. Despite the decrease in sales, Heileman was still financially strong, with low debt and strong earnings. There were other breweries in worse shape, and Heileman might once again be interested in acquiring a weakened rival.

Late in the year, Cleary made a $63 million offer to buy troubled Pabst. The deal would give Heileman four more breweries—in Milwaukee, Newark, Tampa, and the Olympia plant in Tumwater, Washington. It would also acquire the Pabst Blue Ribbon, Olympia, and Hamm's labels, along with several other brands. The move would increase the over-capacity problems Heileman and the rest of the industry were experiencing because of decreasing sales, but Cleary considered the capacity too good a bargain to pass up. He considered it to be an investment in the future.

The industry was surprised by this move, but reacted with praise for Cleary and Heileman, noting their 25-year history of successful acquisitions. Heileman was still thought to be the best-managed company in the entire brewing industry.

But now an old foe, Paul Kalmanovitz, showed up again. His S&P Holding Company announced that it, too, was making a bid for Pabst. Kalmanovitz even announced that he had reached a binding agreement with Pabst, despite the latter's denials.

Given the $100 million in debt, decreasing sales, and over-capacity problems at Pabst, analysts considered these bids to be very generous. Both were offering $10 per share, but differed significantly in terms. William Smith, president of Pabst, knew drastic action was required, and he referred to this latest move as selling off the crown jewels to save the company. It was difficult to determine which offer was really more attractive to stockholders.

The answer was clear to most, but not all, of the 800 Pabst employees and directors in Milwaukee. Some Pabst employees still harbored bitter feelings for Heileman, but most favored it over Kalmanovitz. Pabst and Heileman had been bitter competitors in Wisconsin, but they knew Heileman had a history of reviving failing breweries while Kalmanovitz favored aggressive cost cutting and the sale of assets.

Antitrust concerns resurfaced over Heileman market share in the Midwest and West Coast given a takeover of Pabst, but the industry had completely changed in the last two years, and speculation was that this time the Justice Department would look more favorably on the deal. It had already ruled it had no antitrust concerns with Kalmanovitz's proposal to Pabst.

In a replay of 1982, Pabst brought a lawsuit against Kalmanovitz, claiming it never signed a binding agreement with him and that a document dated November 9, 1984, was not a contract, but nothing more than a letter documenting the Kalmanovitz proposal.

Heileman waited for the Justice Department decision and industry analysts pondered the fate of the Pabst breweries after the merger. They speculated Heileman would close Newark and move production to the Heileman brewery in Baltimore, and the Pabst brewery in Tampa would be closed in favor of Perry, Georgia.

The Northwest scenario wasn't as clear. There the Pabst plant, previously owned by Olympia, was a very modern facility but too close to Heileman's Rainier plant in Seattle. Finally, they felt Heileman would probably keep the Milwaukee plant open to produce Pabst products for the Midwest, but for the fourth time that year Pabst was forced to close the Milwaukee brewery for a week to save money.

The Justice Department announced its decision on the takeover in November, another complicated solution. It had concerns about competition in the West and Northwest, and ruled that Heileman could have the breweries in Milwaukee, Newark, and Tampa, but not in Tumwater. It also gave Heileman the Pabst Blue Ribbon, Andeker, and Jacob Best brands, but not Olympia, Hamm's, and Olde English.

Cleary was elated. He felt that finally the Justice Department was beginning to recognize the need for competition against Anheuser-Busch and Miller. Now Heileman was ready to go head to head with Kalmanovitz for control of Pabst, and everyone expected a replay of the previous battle back in 1982 and 1983, with neither side giving in without a desperate struggle.

Heileman announced that if it prevailed, it had a potential buyer for the brewery and brands the Justice Department disallowed—Stroh, which was interested in the Tumwater brewery and brands. However, it wasn't to be. Kalmanovitz wanted those same assets and negotiated hard to obtain them.

Within days, a three-way agreement was announced between Heileman, Pabst, and Kalmanovitz. Heileman officials flew to San Francisco and cut a deal with Kalmanovitz in which they upped their offer to $11 a share, or $68 million, for Pabst. In turn, Kalmanovitz agreed to drop his bid for Pabst, but would pay Heileman $54 million for the brewery in Tumwater and the Olympia, Hamm's, and Olde English brands. In the deal Heileman received the breweries in Milwaukee and Newark, and was given an option to buy the brewery and a can plant in Tampa for $25 million. Analysts speculated Heileman would also receive contracts from Kalmanovitz to brew his brands for sale in the Midwest.

Once the agreement was made, Heileman still had to actually obtain the stock from the Pabst stockholders to complete the deal. The offer was officially announced in the *Wall Street Journal* with a January 8, 1985, deadline for stockholders to sell to Heileman.

Pabst employees in Milwaukee still feared for their jobs. Milwaukee Mayor Henry Maier urged Cleary to keep Pabst in Milwaukee open and threatened that if Heileman attempted to close the brewery, the city of Milwaukee would join the Christian Schmidt Brewing Company in its previously threatened antitrust lawsuit. At the same time, though, he pledged to help in any way possible to keep the brewery operating.

Hysteria grew in Milwaukee. Cleary responded with a personal call to the *Milwaukee Journal* vowing to do everything possible to keep the brewery open and Pabst headquarters in Milwaukee. He agreed to meet with representatives of Pabst's Brewery Workers Local No. 9 in Milwaukee to discuss Heileman's plans and told them that for the first time in almost 20 years Blatz beer would once again be brewed in Milwaukee. He also said he would honor the union's current contract.

Cleary told the Pabst employees Heileman was not the enemy; the enemy was in Saint Louis. He promised to send the first case of Pabst to Augie Busch III along with a note telling him the beer wars were on. He called Heileman the home team and reminded them Heileman was a Wisconsin company and that positive attitudes from both the city of Milwaukee and union employees were needed to make the deal work.

Employees at the brewery in La Crosse feared that if Heileman closed the Milwaukee brewery, sales for both Heileman and Pabst products would decline in the Milwaukee area. Still, few people believed Heileman would keep all of the Pabst headquarters employees in Milwaukee, since Heileman had a reputation for running plants very efficiently.

Pabst had struggled with whether to market Blue Ribbon as a popular-priced or premium beer. Cleary said he intended to promote Blue Ribbon with national advertising, sell it in all 50 states, and come out with guns blazing. Most analysts felt that no matter what Heileman did, it had to be an improvement over Pabst's efforts.

They also felt Heileman should have no trouble financing the purchase of Pabst, one calling Heileman healthy as a hog, having already been able to repay the entire cost of its previous purchase of Pabst assets. In addition to the purchase price of $68 million, Heileman would take on an estimated $80 million to $85 million in debt from Pabst, which would be partially offset by the $54 million that Kalmanovitz had agreed to pay for the Tumwater brewery.

As the fight for Pabst dragged on during November, Heileman announced the closing of its brewery in Phoenix. Jack Isherwood, vice president of operations, cited shortcomings in capacity and packaging that affected the brewery's efficiency. Production of Carling Black Label, Blatz, Mickey's Malt Liquor, and Colt 45 was moved to Portland and 92 employees were laid off. Heileman held out the possibility of future expansion and reopening of the plant.

Then Stroh and C. Schmidt Brewing of Philadelphia brought a lawsuit to block the merger, arguing it violated a 12-state midwestern market guideline. Furthermore, they claimed Heileman would exert too much power with distributors and prevent them from carrying Stroh and Schmidt products.

Cleary called the suit a futile gesture from jilted suitors. Pabst said it had entertained, but not accepted, offers from both Stroh and C. Schmidt and indicated that C. Schmidt didn't have the resources to purchase Pabst.

Pabst union employees also filed a request with the federal court, asking it to allow Heileman to proceed with the purchase. Each week that passed made Pabst much weaker and brought irreparable damage to the hundreds of Pabst employees, they pointed out.

A federal judge issued a temporary restraining order at the end of December that halted Heileman's purchase of more Pabst stock and ordered a trial at the end of March 1985. Heileman immediately appealed the ruling and asked the trial be moved to at least February. Industry analysts still speculated that Heileman would ultimately prevail, since the Justice Department had already approved it.

As 1984 came to a close, five major players controlled 88 percent of the market. Anheuser-Busch was still first, followed by Miller, Stroh, Heileman, and Coors. All of the breweries were fighting a declining beer market that had peaked in 1981. Recent social developments such as increased health concerns, higher legal drinking ages, and grassroots movements against drinking were all working against them.

For the first time since 1957, Heileman production declined for the year. Sales were up slightly, to $1.34 billion from $1.32 billion, but earnings declined to $45.8 million from $57 million. Cleary blamed pricing pressures and heavy competition. However, Heileman also had been hurt by the cost of introducing several new brands and its less than successful push into the Southern market.

Miller, realizing profit margins were larger on the premium brands, announced plans to focus on Miller High Life rather than the low end of the market, which was welcome news for Heileman. Facing the Pabst takeover, Heileman needed a respite from the relentless price cutting in the economy brands that Miller had forced on the entire industry during 1984.

Early in January 1985, a panel of three judges ruled against Heileman in the lawsuit brought by Stroh and C. Schmidt, finding sufficient evidence for the lawsuit to go to trial in late March. They said the merger could have a negative impact on distributors and have an adverse impact on C. Schmidt and other smaller brewers.

Heileman was twice forced to extend its deadline for the purchase of the Pabst stock because of the ruling. Then, a judge ruled Kalmanovitz could make a counter-offer to buy all of Pabst. Kalmanovitz went ahead with a $10-per-share bid for Pabst, saying he would sell some of the assets to Heileman, which he claimed would result in the same outcome as if Heileman bought Pabst. Then just days later he withdrew all statements about any deals with Heileman.

Meanwhile, Heileman lawyers claimed its future as a national brewer would be at stake if it were unable to purchase Pabst. Analysts knew if Heileman wasn't allowed to purchase Pabst, certainly Stroh wouldn't be, and it was doubtful Stroh had the necessary assets anyway. Pabst finally asked the U.S. Supreme Court to consider the question of its takeover by Heileman.

In early February, Kalmanovitz filed a lawsuit against Stroh accusing it of predatory pricing, and continued to bid for Pabst at $10 a share. Like the last time Heileman tried to acquire Pabst, professional investors whose only concern was to make money held the majority of the stock.

With the Kalmanovitz deal seeming inevitable, morale among Pabst employees and wholesalers declined quickly. Some analysts speculated Kalmanovitz might still turn around and sell Pabst to Heileman for its $11 per share, a quick $7 million profit. But Heileman was unable to continue the bid due to Securities and Exchange Commission rules, and let the deadline to acquire Pabst stock pass. Kalmanovitz had successfully taken control of Pabst, and Heileman immediately asked the Justice Department to quash the lawsuit by Stroh and C. Schmidt, since it was now pointless.

In an interview in March, Cleary said Heileman was still interested in obtaining some of the Pabst assets, but he wasn't sure Kalmanovitz still wanted to sell, nor was he sure the Justice Department would allow Heileman to purchase them.

Kalmanovitz did exactly what industry analysts had predicted. Desiring to quickly recoup his $65 million investment, he immediately fired almost all of the 100-member Pabst sales force and within months raised prices twice, ordered additional layoffs of white-collar workers in Milwaukee, and even canceled tours of the plant. Pabst wholesalers tried to deal with the price increases by not passing them on to their retailers, but they were fighting a losing battle. Smith left the company and later in the year bought the Huber Brewing Company in Monroe, Wisconsin.

Cleary was outraged over the lost jobs, and said that had Heileman purchased Pabst those jobs would likely still be in Wisconsin. Now the Pabst market was up for grabs, and he would go after it. Unfortunately, so did both Anheuser-Busch and Miller.

At the annual stockholder meeting in April, Cleary promised business would improve, but Miller overtook Heileman in Wisconsin. Still, Cleary wasn't worried. He felt Heileman was in a better position to capture more of the Pabst market, whose distributors also carried Blatz, which they would push as a Wisconsin product.

Heileman might purchase additional snack food companies and bakeries, but there were only a few candidates left for brewery acquisitions, such as Genesee Brewing in New York and the Pittsburgh Brewing Company.

Standard and Poor's once again placed Heileman on its credit watch list, citing a decline in earnings and the uncertainties surrounding the Pabst deal. But Heileman's debt-to-equity ratio was the lowest it had been in more than 10 years, and it had recently completed major expansions at many of the breweries.

Industry analysts weren't nearly as concerned about the drop. In 1984 the first quarter had been a particularly strong one and thus a difficult comparison, and had included a large gain from the sale of real estate in Milwaukee. Furthermore, the previous year had included large pushes into the new Southern markets and stockpiling of Heileman products by wholesalers in anticipation of a strike in La Crosse that never materialized.

In September 1985, Heileman brought a lawsuit against Pabst for reducing the number of barrels it was to produce for Pabst under contract. The five-year agreement was part of the original purchase of Pabst assets back in 1983, and even with the contract the Perry, Georgia, plant was only running at 80 percent capacity. The suit claimed that without the original contract, the Perry plant might be closed.

Furthermore, it argued loss of the contract brewing would hurt its ability to compete in the South. A judge issued a temporary order requiring Pabst to honor its contract, which covered the next week and was intended to keep the brewery operating. A few days later, Pabst agreed to honor the contract, and the lawsuit was dropped.

Back in 1983, it had seemed that Heileman had won a blue ribbon victory when it purchased half of the Pabst assets. But now those same breweries were part of a serious overcapacity problem. With Kalmanovitz in control of the rest of Pabst in 1985, it appeared that Heileman had suffered a major setback.

Chapter 11

Stock Prices and Poison Pills

TAKEOVER RUMORS WERE NUMEROUS 1985–1986

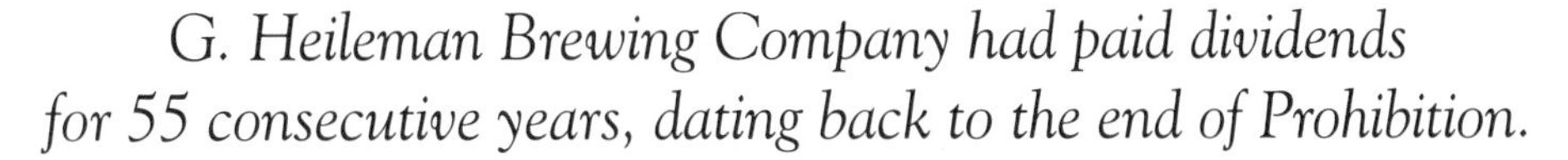

G. Heileman Brewing Company had paid dividends for 55 consecutive years, dating back to the end of Prohibition.

—NOTATION AFTER THE COMPANY DECLARED YET ANOTHER DIVIDEND PAYMENT FOR 1986

Heileman stock suddenly and unexpectedly began a rapid rise in April 1985, going from $14.38 to $21. Rumors ran rampant as investors, La Crosse residents, and industry analysts tried to explain the cause.

According to one rumor, PepsiCo Incorporated was considering buying Heileman to head off its own rumored takeover by Philip Morris. Another had Heileman considering a merger with Miller. Yet another was that the Heileman management team planned its own buyout of the company from the stockholders. And many stockbrokers and investors simply saw Heileman as a bargain and a good long-term investment.

More than 1,000 stockholders showed up in La Crosse for the annual meeting that month. In his address to them, Heileman President Russ Cleary didn't mention the recent rise, but stockholders questioned him extensively about it and recent earning declines. Cleary said he had been unable to detect a pattern that would indicate someone was attempting a takeover. He attributed the rise to analysts seeing Heileman stock as a good buy, or recognizing that it was stronger than its competitors, which put it in a good position to benefit from brewing industry turmoil. Plus, Heileman's bakery and Machine Products divisions were still performing well.

Cleary admitted the push into the South had not been as successful as hoped, running into a storm of new low-cost competing brands. He promised stockholders things were improving and new advertising campaigns were in the works for Old Style, Blatz, Colt 45, and Schmidt.

Rumors continued of a leveraged buyout by Heileman management for $26 to $27 a share, but industry analysts doubted the rumor, noting any buyout would require the company to first reduce its debt. They speculated a buyer would be forced to sell off many of the assets, such as the bakeries and Machine Products Company.

Cleary denied the rumors in an interview with *Forbes* magazine. However, he didn't rule them out for all time, as he expected an even greater shakeout in the industry. He also continued sniping at Stroh, describing its merger with Schlitz as a classic blunder that would inevitably cause financial problems. Stroh management, however, thought it would be making money by the following year, partly by saving $50 million annually by closing the Detroit brewery.

The second quarter of 1985, sales were up 10 percent. New wine cooler and water products were well accepted, although still a very small part of sales. Volume was also up in some of the Southern markets, and Cleary vowed the company would continue its push there.

Now, a new battle was on the horizon as Coors announced a major expansion into the Heileman stronghold of Chicago. In the past few years, Heileman's market share there had dropped from almost 40 percent down to about 25 percent at the hands of Anheuser-Busch.

Heileman announced plans to raise $75 million by selling zero-coupon bonds to finance future acquisitions. While no specific targets were named, Heileman had frequently indicated its desire to obtain additional bakeries and consumer product companies. In August it sold $83 million in bonds.

When third-quarter results were released, sales were down slightly, but earnings were up slightly over 1984. The loss was blamed on a 13-week strike at the Baltimore brewery and decreased production at the Perry, Georgia, brewery.

Heileman was a different company in 1985, having introduced numerous new products in an effort to increase sales in an ever-changing market. The price pressures of earlier years had decreased, but strong competition continued in most markets. The most notable battle was taking place in Chicago, where Heileman was weathering concentrated attacks from Anheuser-Busch and Coors. In response to this competition, Heileman had rolled out a whole new advertising campaign.

Heileman ended the year with $122 million in cash and securities, including the $83 million in notes it sold in August. Analysts speculated Cleary might once again go out looking for acquisitions, but there were fewer and fewer breweries to acquire and not many would furnish any strategic gain for Heileman. Stroh and Pabst were vulnerable and might be candidates, but many thought Cleary might direct his attention to large acquisitions in bakeries and consumer products instead.

Across the globe in Australia, aggressive financier Alan Bond purchased the Castlemaine Toohey Brewery in Brisbane. He now controlled 42 percent of the Australian beer market.

The entire brewing industry made a recovery in the first quarter of 1986. Four of the six largest breweries, including Heileman, had sales gains. Troubles for Stroh and Pabst continued, however, with Pabst sales down almost 16 percent.

Early in January, Cleary met with reporters to update them on the progress of the company. He discounted reports of dramatic sales drops for Old Style, attributing the losses to Old Style Light and Old Style L.A. He told them Heileman was regaining market share in Chicago previously lost to Anheuser-Busch, Miller, and Stroh, recouping about 2 percent each month, and was back up to 35 percent. He attributed the gains to aggressive new distributors in Chicago and an enhanced reputation within the black community because of Heileman's increasing number of black distributors.

Heileman was still No. 1 in Minnesota and Washington and had made good gains in Iowa and Montana. Cleary used the term "halo markets" to describe the sales increases in states that surrounded those where Heileman was ranked No. 1. In Wisconsin, Heileman was ranked second behind Miller, but had gained on it during 1985. Nationwide, Heileman was first in sales of malt liquors. But even though sales were good, total barrels in 1985 had declined from 1984.

Heileman was slowly gaining back business in its Northern markets, which had been invaded by Stroh, Coors, and Miller, and was still trying to make inroads in the South, avoiding head-to-head competition against Anheuser-Busch and Miller in those areas. The price wars of recent years had taken a toll.

Early in 1986, Heileman passed up an opportunity to purchase Pittsburgh Brewing, which provided the Australian, Bond, his entry into the U.S. brewing industry.

Across the globe in Australia, aggressive financier Alan Bond purchased the Castlemaine Toohey Brewery in Brisbane. He now controlled 42 percent of the Australian beer market.

In March Heileman stock once again started to rise, but this time without any accompanying rumors. Instead, stock analysts were citing a strong comeback by Heileman, which was regaining ground it had lost to Coors, Stroh, and Miller. Coors had moved much of its attack away from Heileman strongholds in Minnesota and Chicago, concentrating on New England. Heileman had made good gains in Florida, too, where some of its competitors had halted expansion plans. Analysts speculated 1986 would be a good year for Heileman, and the company could see gains in the 15 percent to 20 percent range in earnings. They considered Heileman to be the best-managed company in the entire brewing industry.

Cleary was pleased by his stock performance, but even more by the opinions of analysts, with some 75 large pension funds and insurance companies investing in large blocks of Heileman stock. When first-quarter sales were announced, Heileman delivered on predictions. Sales were up 36 percent and Cleary was elated. Competition remained intense, but Heileman was regaining lost market share, the price wars were letting up, and costs were coming down.

Cleary told stockholders that sales for no-alcohol brands were up 50 percent, with low-alcohol brands up 17 percent. He said he refused to pursue the strategy of chasing barrels of low-priced beer just to pass

Stroh for third place. Heileman sales problems in 1985 were short-term, Cleary said, yet the press had depicted them as long-term.

He also complained about proposals to eliminate deductions of federal excise taxes for breweries, pointing out that beer was already taxed at three times the rate of other consumer products. If these laws were passed, he predicted there would be massive price increases for beer that would devastate the industry. He also questioned the recent proposal in Wisconsin to raise the drinking age to 21. Cleary didn't think it would have a significant impact on Heileman's business, but questioned how the new law could be enforced.

Problems beset the company in the second and third quarters. In June, the New York attorney general charged Heileman, Anheuser-Bush, Miller, and Stroh with causing an artificial price increase in New York. The suit charged that starting back in late 1982 those four brewers had carved out exclusive territories for their distributors, eliminating competition and resulting in at least a $1 price increase for a six-pack of beer.

The New York Beer Wholesalers Association denied the claims and said it was nothing more than harassment and political intimidation, attributing the price increases to New York's mandatory bottle deposit laws. Randy Smith, Heileman vice president and counsel, concurred and said the lawsuit was primarily politically motivated. The New York attorney general was critical of the laws governing the liquor distributors and was trying to get legislative changes made.

On August 30, 1986, the contract expired with the union at the Perry plant, which was operating below capacity because of declining production contracts for Pabst products. Heileman management was seeking concessions in wages, holidays, and sick days. The union, however, wanted wage increases. A bitter strike resulted when the sides were unable to come to agreement, and there were reports of rocks and vegetables tossed at management cars. Heileman obtained a temporary injunction to limit the number of pickets and things quieted down.

The strike was finally settled in mid-November with workers agreeing to cuts in wages, holidays, sick days, and the length of the lunch break. The union wasn't thrilled with the settlement, but there was some consolation. Without it, some 200 employees would have lost their jobs. With the settlement, only 30 employees would be laid off.

When third quarter results were announced, there was good news. Earnings were up, and Heileman was the third-largest company in Wisconsin with sales of $1.3 billion. Stockholders were rewarded with a 25-cent dividend.

The bad news, however, was sales were down, which Cleary attributed to renewed price pressure on low-end brands. Sales were also negatively affected by the reduced contract brewing for Pabst in Perry, as well as the strike there. Heileman announced it would close down most of the breweries for the last two weeks of the year, which Cleary attributed to the way the holidays fell, with only three work days between Christmas and New Year's. He asked wholesalers to stock up prior to year-end to ensure adequate stock over the holidays.

Heileman finished 1986 with a strong fourth quarter and an 11.5 percent gain in earnings for the year. For the 17th consecutive year, Heileman stockholders were rewarded with an extra fourth-quarter dividend in addition to the regular dividend. The company had paid dividends for 55 consecutive years, dating back to the end of Prohibition.

However, for the third year in a row, sales were essentially unchanged from the previous year. Cleary, cautiously optimistic about prospects for 1987, pointed to tax law changes and the fact that earnings were being helped by a trend toward the Heileman premium and super-premium brands. At the low end it continued to be hurt by competitive pricing pressures, and the bakeries were facing severe price cuts on snack foods and escalating costs in new markets. He speculated that the new Val Blatz microbrewery in Milwaukee could be used for additional joint ventures with foreign breweries.

As the year came to a close, the board of directors announced a new "poison pill" plan meant to discourage a two-tier, or hostile, takeover. The plan allowed stockholders the right to purchase one share of Series A preferred stock for every 100 shares of common stock they held. The plan would only become operational if someone purchased a large stake in the company or announced a tender offer to purchase part of the company.

Company officials assured stockholders the plan was in no way a response to any announced effort to gain control of the company.

Brewery portrait dated 1975 was painted by local artist Yvonne Spreiter.

COURTESY OF CLEARY-KUMM FOUNDATION

ANNUAL SALES FROM 1935 TO 1985

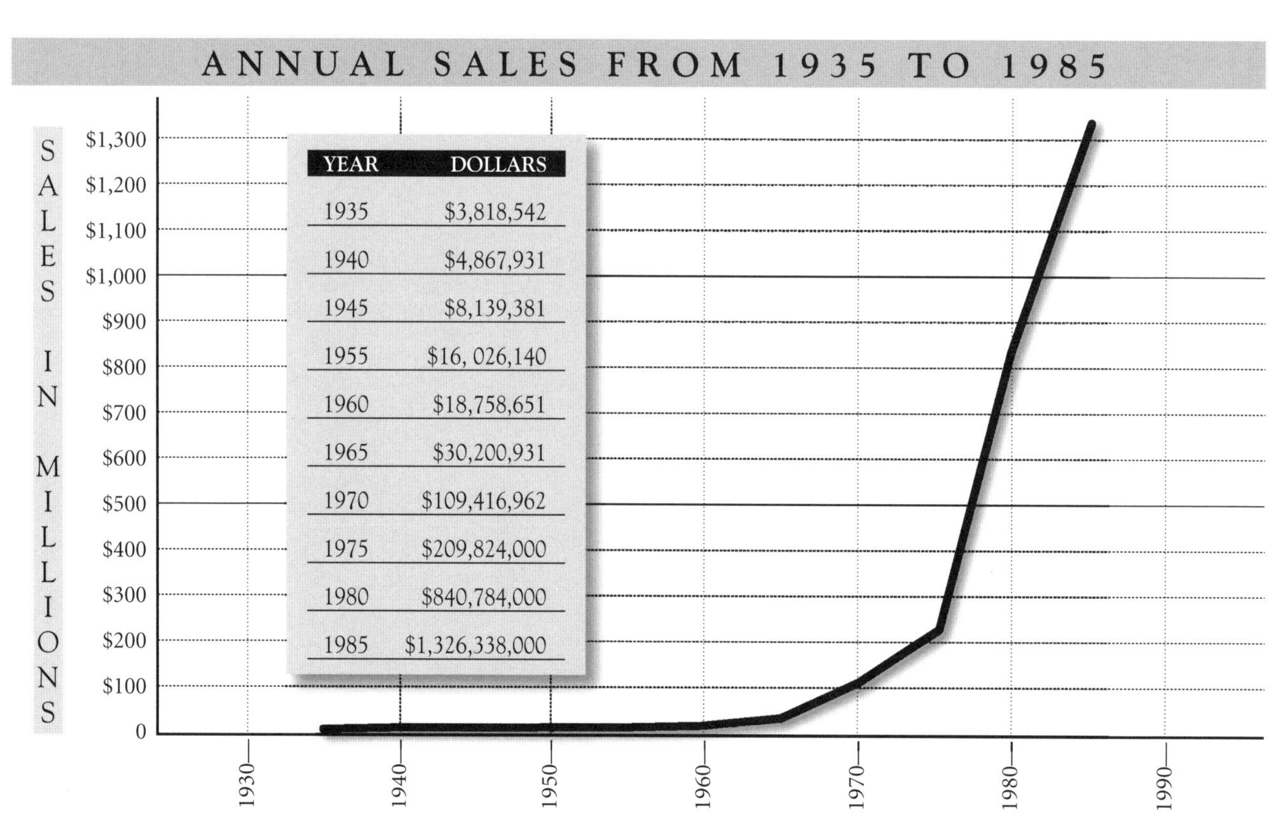

YEAR	DOLLARS
1935	$3,818,542
1940	$4,867,931
1945	$8,139,381
1955	$16, 026,140
1960	$18,758,651
1965	$30,200,931
1970	$109,416,962
1975	$209,824,000
1980	$840,784,000
1985	$1,326,338,000

Chapter 12

I'll Have Another Schmidt, Please

THE TAKEOVER OF CHRISTIAN SCHMIDT 1987

Besides being a leading brewer, Heileman also is the fifth-largest bakery company in the United States.

Heileman stock began to rise rapidly again in March 1987. Institutional buyers, insurance companies, and pension funds were purchasing large blocks of stock, analysts speculated.

But as the stock continued its rise, an article in *Barron's* magazine theorized that Heileman might be the target of a takeover attempt, possibly by Elders IXL, an Australian brewing, wool, and financial services company. It had recently made an offer to purchase the Carling brewery in Canada for $294 million, and rumor had it the company also wanted to expand into the United States.

Analysts again touted Heileman stock, reporting the company had built up $159 million in cash to use for acquisitions and expansion, and was poised to benefit from its diversification into baking, snack foods, wine coolers, malt coolers, mineral waters, bottled water, specialty beers, and imported beers. They attributed much of the success to Heileman president Russ Cleary, whom they described as a wonderful manager and marketer. If Cleary were to leave the company, they felt the value of Heileman would be greatly reduced.

Some brokers recommended that if Heileman stock rose above $30, holders should sell. They believed Anheuser-Busch was firmly in control of the market, and it was going to be difficult for anyone to compete against the nation's largest brewer. But other brokers continued to recommend that their clients hold onto Heileman stock.

At the annual stockholder meeting, Cleary laid out the Heileman battle plan for the coming year. Stroh and Miller were continuing to sell beer below cost in a brutal price war of economy brands, but Heileman wouldn't match price. Cleary said the company would benefit from recent plant modernization and lower labor costs because of the settlement in Perry, Georgia, which had reduced the cost of producing a case of beer by 50 cents. There was another increase in dividends, the seventh in the past 11 years. Heileman's Rainier products were being exported to Canada and Taiwan.

First quarter sales were down 4 percent, but earnings were up 6 percent, which Cleary attributed to the continued price wars in the economy brands and increased sales of the higher-priced Old Style and Special Export. He also cited the fact that contract brewing for Pabst was continuing to decline, especially at the Perry plant.

Pabst was facing financial problems again. Pabst's principal owner, Paul Kalmanovitz, had died earlier in the year, but his family still controlled the company, which Cleary was still interested in pursuing. If the company went up for sale, he promised Heileman would bid. Pabst chairman Lutz Issleib, who had taken over after Kalmanovitz's death and was working to revive Pabst, quickly denied it was for sale. He had increased advertising budgets, implemented a $20 million plant modernization in Milwaukee, and reinstated tours of the Milwaukee brewery.

Heileman was once again in the acquisition market. Plans were announced to make a bid for Christian Schmidt of Philadelphia, the eighth-largest brewery in the United States. Rumors were that both Pabst and Stroh were also in the bidding for the brewery, which had reported sharply declining sales in recent years. Employment at the Philadelphia brewery had plunged from 1,400 in 1984 to about 250, and its largest creditor, Crown Cork & Seal, called in loans of $20 million.

Rumors were becoming rampant about a takeover attempt of Heileman, and the market reacted with a 7 percent increase in its stock price. . . . In a three-day period, more than 8 percent of the Heileman stock changed hands.

In early April, reports were that Heileman was the leading bidder. Perhaps a factor in the bid was the news that the number of barrels produced annually by Heileman was declining, and that No. 5 Coors would soon be in fourth place.

A tentative agreement with Heileman was announced to the employees at the Philadelphia brewery, the last remaining brewery in that city. Schmidt owner William H. "Billy" Pflaummer negotiated the terms of the sale, which allowed him to retain control of two distributing operations, one in Philadelphia and another in New York.

With the company came its brands—Schmidt's, Schmidt's Light, Bavarian, Erie, Coqui, Knickerbocker, Classic, Reading, Rheingold, Ortlieb's, Kohler, Valley Forge, Duquesne, and McSorley's—plus 200 distributors in the lucrative East Coast market. The brewery's largest markets were in Pennsylvania and New York, but it sold as far west

The Colt 45 Trio

Heileman executives Randy Smith, Dan Schmid and David DeLano, co-author of this book, all learned to play the trumpet in their formative years. In fact, all three were pretty decent trumpet players in their high school and college days.

In the early 1980s, after learning of each other's similar backgrounds, the three brushed the dust off their trumpets and started to practice together after work in Schmid's basement. Soon a portfolio of three-part harmony tunes was accumulated. The group became known as the Colt 45 Trio at the suggestion of salesman Larry Thomas, who said the musicians had lots of "power," just like Colt 45.

The group first performed in the Corporate Center beer stube for a Christmas celebration. A rendition of "Jingle Bells" brought down the house. Other performances were requested and soon the group had quite a reputation.

On one occasion the trio strolled the halls of the Corporate Center playing Christmas songs for the office staff. In addition to their appearances in the Corporate Center, the musicians donated Christmas season performances at a local mall, a church, several nursing homes, and the Chileda Institute (an organization that seeks to further the development and care for children and young adults with severe mental disabilities).

Perhaps the trio's performance highlight occurred at the retirement party for Heileman executive John Pedace in the Heileman Hospitality Center in 1985. On that occasion the group was joined by keyboardist Ken Bernstein. The group's rendition of "The Lonely Bull" featured a trumpet fanfare that many talked about for some time. Smith claimed he nearly fainted during the height of the fanfare.

After the show, Russ Cleary said he was amazed by the group's performance and suggested that we consider becoming professional musicians. That never happened, but the Colt 45 Trio had a lot of fun and brought joy to lots of folks.

—David DeLano

as Ohio. Heileman did not purchase the brewery in Philadelphia, only the brands and trademarks. The agreement included royalty payments over a period of time, and an advance royalty payment at the time of the purchase.

Once Heileman had taken over the Christian Schmidt brands, it immediately set about reviving its new brands, using Doner & Company of Baltimore to handle advertising. Doner already had the advertising contract for Heileman's successful malt liquor products, which had an industry-leading 40 percent market share. Production was moved to its brewery in Baltimore, where the company embarked upon a $6 million investment in a new warehouse and keg-racking operation, as well as expansion of the shipping operation.

In July, Heileman purchased Dressel's Frozen Cakes in Chicago, and the Taystee Division group of midwestern bakeries from American Bakeries Company of New York. The bakeries were located in Minneapolis, Duluth, Detroit, and Kansas City. Michael Moon, president of Heileman Baking, was particularly pleased with the addition of the Kansas City bakery, which provided a snack cake plant and allowed Heileman to compete against the Hostess Company in that market. The purchase made Heileman the fifth-largest bakery company in the United States.

But beer shipments fell almost 10 percent over the previous year in the first six months of 1987, while earnings and sales declines relegated Heileman to fifth place behind Coors, which had recently expanded into the New York City market with good results. Cleary remained confident though, and promised Heileman would reclaim fourth place. He cited the fact Heileman was now selling the Carling Black Label brand at a wholesale price of $3.20 a case, and competing effectively on price in the economy brands. It had also increased advertising budgets and was profiting from stabilized manufacturing costs. To motivate the wholesalers to sell more beer, Heileman awarded top sellers trips to Stockholm, Sweden; Copenhagen, Denmark; and Leningrad, Russia.

Rumors were becoming rampant about a takeover attempt of Heileman, and the market reacted with a 7 percent increase in its stock price. Cleary sold 17,000 shares of his Heileman stock to pay his income tax, and donated 8,000 shares to the Cleary Foundation. In a three-day period, more than 8 percent of the Heileman stock changed hands.

Most watchers of the beer industry were continuing to guess that Heileman's suitor was Australian Elders IXL Incorporated, but other names mentioned were John Labatt Limited of Canada and another Australian company, Bond Corporation Holdings Limited.

Still others thought that Heileman management was considering a leveraged buyout. Despite all the rumors, Cleary continued to assert that Heileman was not in contact with anyone attempting a takeover and wanted to remain independent.

Cleary was looking forward to a relaxing Labor Day weekend, away from the swirling rumors.

Chapter 13

No Kangaroos at Oktoberfest

AUSTRALIAN ALAN BOND FIGHTS FOR CONTROL OF HEILEMAN 1987

The offer by Bond was for about $1.3 billion, but included only $200 million in cash. The rest was to be financed.

September 3, 1987, was a fateful day for Russ Cleary, Heileman, and the city of La Crosse.

Cleary had been working late just before start of the long Labor Day weekend when, at about 6 P.M., an Australian named Alan Bond called and announced he was flying in to La Crosse and wished to have a meeting aboard his jet at the airport. Bond arrived discreetly in La Crosse the same day and met with Cleary later that evening.

The rising stock price was now explained.

The flamboyant Bond presented Cleary with a long letter that detailed the takeover attempt. Bond started by saying he hoped Cleary would think the idea was as good as he did, and that the offer represented an opportunity for shareholders, employees, distributors, the areas where Heileman did business, and discriminating beer drinkers around the world.

However, he pointed out that the existence of Heileman's "poison pill" complicated matters. The "poison pill" was put into place to avert just such a takeover attempt, allowing Heileman to issue additional shares of stock that would dilute the value of the stock already owned. Another more recent provision discouraged the company from selling off assets to pay for any acquisition.

Bond promised $38 in cash to shareholders for each share of Heileman stock, and he pledged to keep the current Heileman management team in place. For Heileman employees, the letter promised job security, commitment to the union, and a commitment to future expansion of the company. Distributors were promised increased marketing muscle and access to Bond's existing line of import beers. Finally, for customers it guaranteed continued availability of all their favorite brands.

The letter gave assurances that Bond's company kept its promises, and offered its 1986 purchase of Pittsburgh Brewing as proof. It also contained additional background information on the Bond conglomerate and some of its other holdings.

News of the takeover attempt spread like wildfire around La Crosse, with the news media scrambling to discover more about Bond. The son of a Welsh miner, Bond dropped out of school at age 13 and moved to Australia in the 1950s, where he took up sign painting and studied accounting at night. After a few years, he began buying land with borrowed money, selling it for 1,000 percent profit, and had made his first million by age 29. He was 49 years old in 1987 and had a personal net worth of about $280 million.

Bond in 1969 had established Bond Corporation Holdings Limited, which, during the period of 1983 to 1987, doubled in size each year. It consisted of 38 subsidiaries with estimated sales of $1.8 billion in industries as diversified as television, radio, gold, silver, coal mines, real estate, and British blimps.

He had about 30 percent of the beer business in Australia, owned the Swan Brewery, second largest in Australia, and the Castlemaine-Toohey brewery. He had expanded into the United States with the purchase of Pittsburgh Brewing in 1986.

But Bond's glittering portfolio hid the fact that he didn't have a great track record managing breweries. Following the takeover of Castlemaine-Toohey, he alienated locals by replacing the large Castlemaine sign with one for Bond Brewery, and outraged loyal drinkers by changing the design of the familiar can. In the period of 1985 to 1989, the Castlemaine share of the Australian market went from almost 60 percent down to about 40 percent.

Experts from the University of Wisconsin tried to explain in the media the difference between a takeover and a merger. A takeover occurred when the management of the target company was bypassed. In a friendly takeover the price offered was favorable to the target company. In a hostile takeover, the target company did not consider the deal favorable. In most takeovers, the acquiring company took out an advertisement in the *Wall Street Journal* announcing the price it was willing to pay per share of stock and the procedure for stockholders to sell. In a hostile takeover, the target company typically would take out its own advertisement telling stockholders not to sell their stock and explaining why.

It didn't take long for Heileman to react. Management worked all weekend bringing in lawyers and consultants. Cleary found it inconceivable that any bank would loan Bond money, because the company couldn't service the debt. The Monday morning following Bond's visit, Cleary urged stockholders to hold on to their stock. He promised investors the company would hold emergency meetings of the board of directors to consider Bond's proposal, and he gave a deadline of September 18 for a formal recommendation to stockholders from the board, well in advance of the October 2 deadline Bond had set for stockholders to tender their Heileman stock.

Bond needed to obtain 75 percent of the Heileman stock. If he were able to obtain only 50 percent, Heileman would be able to use its "poison pill" to thwart the takeover. Most analysts felt Heileman would fight to the death against Bond.

Heileman officials flew to New York City to meet with representatives of Merrill Lynch Incorporated. Heileman agreed to pay Merrill Lynch $550,000 plus expenses to help the company avoid the takeover.

Heileman officials also considered requesting a special hearing by the Wisconsin Securities Commissioner, Ulice Payne, who had the authority to delay the takeover bid or even block it by rejecting registration of the plan.

Just two days after the proposal, Wisconsin Governor Tommy Thompson became involved in the controversy, promising to call a special session of the Wisconsin legislature, if Heileman requested it, to consider new legislation to make a takeover more difficult. Thompson said he would not meet with Bond representatives until Heileman had decided on its plans.

Other Wisconsin legislators came to Heileman's aid. U.S. Representative Steve Gunderson of Osseo, Wisconsin, met with both Heileman officials and Bond representatives, who were very positive about the potential benefits to Heileman and La Crosse. But Gunderson was skeptical and issued a press release that said he would help Heileman in any way possible.

After a few days had passed, more details of Bond's proposal emerged.

According to a Bond circular, the takeover had been first proposed to Bond in 1986. After his purchase of Pittsburgh Brewing Company, he had hired Ocean Securities Corporation of New York as an adviser. That firm had done a financial analysis of Heileman and recommended it to Bond as his next purchase. The circular also disclosed that Bond had already begun acquiring Heileman stock and now owned about 5 percent of it.

Additional financial aspects of the deal also were disclosed. The offer by Bond was for about $1.3 billion, but included only $200 million in cash, which was the amount of cash on Heileman's balance sheet. The rest was to be financed. Ocean Securities and Salomon Brothers Bank of New York, both of which had much to gain from a takeover, had arranged for short-term loans for Bond at five banks. The agreement promised Ocean $1 million in fees. Salomon got $1 million at the time of the announcement and another $6.5 million if the takeover were successful.

With the takeover completed, Bond would need long-term financing, and an obvious concern was that he would start selling Heileman assets to pay off the debt. Specifically, there were concerns about the Heileman bakeries and Machine Products in La Crosse. Bond officials said they didn't understand much about those businesses, but wanted to learn more about them.

Standard & Poor's reacted to the proposal by putting Heileman on credit watch, concerned about the financial implications to Heileman if management decided on a leveraged takeover. It also noted the high level of debt Bond would incur if the takeover were accomplished.

Naturally, the battle moved to the courts. Bond officials wanted a list of Heileman stockholders and argued the company's "poison pill" would make the takeover prohibitively expensive for Bond and was unfair to stockholders.

Bond won the first round when he reached an out-of-court agreement with Heileman to release its list of stockholders. As required by law, a 5 percent shareholder could obtain the list. This decision was critical because Wisconsin law governing takeovers applied only if Wisconsin residents owned more than 33 percent of the stock involved. The decision allowed the Bond group to target these stockholders.

However, Heileman won a ruling that the Wisconsin Securities Commissioner could hold a hearing on the takeover attempt, in order to protect Wisconsin stockholders.

Wisconsin's governor called a special session of the legislature at Heileman's request. Governor Thompson was concerned about the long-term effects of passing far-reaching legislation on such short notice, but felt he had no choice but to protect against the possible loss of jobs in Wisconsin.

After a five-hour debate in a hot and crowded room, the special session passed two new laws dealing with the takeover of Wisconsin companies. The first protected the right to create "poison pill" plans, and the second prevented a company from selling off assets in order to retire loans for three years after a takeover, and prevented buyers from merging a target company into another corporation. The new legislation applied only to companies with headquarters in Wisconsin and, in a concession to opponents, would sunset in four years, too late for Heileman but perhaps good for other companies. The bills were signed into law the next day at a ceremony attended by Cleary and Thompson.

Next, U.S. Senator Bill Proxmire of Wisconsin expanded the case to the national level. Proxmire, chairman of the Senate Banking Committee, asked for a hearing on the takeover by the Securities and Exchange Commission. He proposed new federal legislation to aid companies in fighting hostile takeovers. His proposals included requiring a corporate raider to make a public announcement of its intentions once it had obtained 3 percent of a company's stock, and forcing the raider to disclose all previous discussions with anyone working for the targeted company.

Proxmire also wanted to increase the length of time stockholders had to tender their stock from three weeks to five weeks. Finally, he wanted to give states more rights to pass takeover legislation even if it conflicted with federal laws.

Stock analysts were giving a full range of advice to Heileman management and stockholders: hang on for loyalty's sake; do whatever it takes to maximize shareholder interests; or compromise and sell half. Heileman stock continued at a high both locally and nationally, with professional stock speculators, known as arbitrageurs, buying at every opportunity.

Heileman officially recommended that stockholders reject the Bond offer. Cleary announced the Heileman board had decided not to invoke the "poison pill" provisions, to buy more time. He also confirmed he had talked to Pabst and Stroh over the past four to five months about a possible merger, but denied he was currently engaged in those discussions as a way to prevent the takeover.

Cleary still insisted that Heileman wanted to remain independent, but agreed to meet face to face with Bond who, claiming illness, instead sent Peter Beckwith, his chief executive officer. Initial meetings between Cleary and Beckwith, which Cleary described as cordial, were held in Milwaukee. Cleary expressed interest in agreements that would allow Heileman to sell its products in Australia and import Bond's products into America.

Despite these discussions, Amber Acquisitions, a subsidiary of Bond Corporation Holdings Limited, brought a suit challenging the two new Wisconsin laws as unconstitutional, and arguing that Heileman had abandoned its stockholders and wasn't fairly representing them. At the same time, two Minnesota investors, Michael Cottle and Morris Rottman, initiated a class action lawsuit on behalf of stockholders to force Heileman to negotiate with Bond. They also wanted the Heileman "poison pill" provisions to be invalidated.

Amid all the takeover controversy, Heileman announced that sales in the third quarter were up 8 percent. It attributed the increase to a 5 percent gain in beer sales and a large increase in the baking division.

Wisconsin takeover laws applied only if more than 33 percent of the stock was owned by Wisconsin residents, and so much stock had been sold by now that less than 20 percent of it was still owned by residents.

Cleary wanted to fight to the bitter end, but realized that nothing could be done. He then tried to negotiate the best possible deal for employees, stockholders and the city of La Crosse. On September 21, 1987, Cleary announced a preliminary agreement to merge with Bond, and that he no longer considered the takeover to be hostile. Bond had upped the bid from $38 per share to $40.75, and a deadline of October 9, 1987, was set for stockholders to tender shares. Cleary indicated there were still additional details to be worked out to protect the jobs of Heileman's 3,000 Wisconsin employees.

Cleary praised the new Wisconsin laws as being key to forcing Bond to negotiate with Heileman and assured worried employees and La Crosse residents that Bond had no intention of breaking up the company or eliminating jobs.

Governor Thompson praised Cleary for negotiating in favor of the Heileman employees, but reaction from other lawmakers was mixed. La Crosse Mayor Patrick Zielke praised Cleary and said he had fought like a tiger for the Heileman employees. Several local legislators weren't so sure, but indicated all they could now do was trust the Bond people.

Some legislators even wanted to repeal the new laws, but others cautioned they might save jobs in the future. It really didn't matter anymore to Heileman, for once the deal moved from takeover to merger, the laws no longer applied.

When October 9 arrived, Bond owned 91 percent of the Heileman stock and expected to close on the deal by the end of October. In one final detail, Heileman announced it would give each shareholder an additional five cents per share to compensate them for the "poison pill" shares, which were never offered.

Not all stockholders benefited from the Bond purchase. Long-term stockholders made huge gains, in some cases originally paying as little as $2 a share for the stock for which Bond would now give $40.75. The biggest losers were some arbitrageurs, who had speculated Bond would go as high as $45 a share.

News of the merger made headlines in newspapers worldwide. It created the fourth-largest

About Alan Bond

Alan Bond lived in Perth, Australia, in a house with a six-car garage, a swimming pool, and tennis court. He was an avid art collector, with a collection of works done by French Impressionists valued at $70 million. He was best known as a sailor who won the first Australian victory in the America's Cup race in 1983.

After winning the America's Cup race Bond became a national hero in Australia on the magnitude of the American astronauts who had landed on the moon. Arriving home to a hero's welcome parade watched by an estimated 200,000 people, he quickly became heavily involved with the Australian government in a variety of deals to expand his business.

Between the time he won the race and made his bid for Heileman, he had become world famous, having had audiences with Pope John Paul II, President Ronald Reagan, and other world leaders.

Bond's greatest talent was his power of persuasion. When he set his mind on something, whether in business, sailing, or his personal life, he refused to take no for an answer. He had the charm and charisma to convince others that he knew where he was going, and was on the correct course.

brewery in the world, with control of almost half of the Australian market and 9 percent of the U.S. market. Cleary became a member of Bond's board of directors and was given control of all North American beer operations, including Bond's Pittsburgh Brewing Company.

Cleary also negotiated continued charitable contributions by the company and agreements that allowed existing employees and management first opportunity to purchase any assets Bond might decide to sell. Bond agreed to continue to fund existing advertising budgets with future cost-of-living increases. In addition, it was announced that all existing contracts and agreements with unions, distributors, and vendors would be honored.

There also were agreements for Bond to continue funding for improved technology, plant maintenance and expansion, as well as expansion of the corporate headquarters in La Crosse. Finally, Bond agreed to pay one year's salary to any Heileman employee fired without Cleary's consent.

With the agreement reached, analysts began to speculate on the implications for Heileman. Some felt Bond would develop a single national brand and heavily advertise and promote it. Others felt he'd continue to offer the range of regional Heileman brands.

Some observers even predicted this was the break Heileman needed to take on Anheuser-Busch, while others speculated that another Australian company, Elders IXL, might try to take over Anheuser-Busch. Elders IXL was a large, debt-free Australian company best known for its Foster's brand of beer. In the previous year it had purchased the Carling O'Keefe brewery in Canada, and there was even some speculation that if it couldn't get Anheuser-Busch it would attempt to buy Miller Brewing from Philip Morris instead.

Then, on October 19, 1987, the stock market was hit by the worst crash since the famous one of 1929 that caused the Great Depression. Before Bond and his management team had even completed the Heileman merger, they had to rush back to Australia from around the world to try to save not only their own company, but also other stricken Australian banks and corporations.

Cleary joked that there wouldn't be any kangaroos at that year's Oktoberfest, but it was clear that things would never be the same for him, Heileman, or the city of La Crosse.

The Heileman shield, made of flowers and decorative stone, graced the front entrance to the Heileman Corporate Center, which faced west and the Mississippi River along La Crosse's waterfront.

PHOTO COURTESY OF CITY BREWERY

Chapter 14

Going Down Under

RUSS CLEARY RETIRES AND HEILEMAN EXPERIENCES FINANCIAL PROBLEMS UNDER BOND MANAGEMENT 1988–1989

The Bond corporation lost $726.4 million in 1989, the largest loss in Australian corporate history.

La Crosse was a different place after Alan Bond took over G. Heileman Brewing Company.

Australians were around town more often. One story told of a clerk at a La Crosse motel who checked in an Australian who said he wanted to be "knocked up in the morning." The confused clerk was flustered until the Australian explained the phrase was slang for wanting a wake-up call.

As the financial details with Bond were worked out, the Internal Revenue Service ruled that the Pabst assets Heileman had purchased in 1983 were worth more than Heileman had paid, and back taxes were owed on the difference. Heileman said it had paid the market value for the assets.

Heileman also was disappointed by recent free trade agreements that disallowed U.S. beer exports to any Canadian province where the American company didn't operate a brewery. No beer could be exported to Mexico either, even though both Canada and Mexico were exporting beer to the United States.

Late in the year, however, the combined Heileman and Bond company won a tax break in the U.S. Congress. The break was worth up to $50 million if Bond decided to sell any of the assets. Originally the law was set to expire before Bond could legally sell any Heileman assets, but the new legislation extended the tax break until January 1, 1993.

Bond quickly made personnel changes in La Crosse. All existing board members except Russ Cleary were asked to resign. Ian S. Crichton, an Englishman by birth but now from Australia, came to La Crosse as vice president of marketing and sales, reporting directly to Cleary.

A month later, John Thames, vice president of human resources, announced several marketing executives from La Crosse had been sent to jobs at Heileman in major metropolitan markets such as

Chicago, the Twin Cities, Seattle, and San Antonio. If Heileman didn't start doing better in those markets, there would be big problems, it was said. But Thames assured wary La Crosse residents that this was not a corporate gutting.

Heileman entered 1988 in fifth place in domestic beer sales behind rapidly expanding Coors, although Cleary argued that Heileman and Pittsburgh Brewing were now a single entity whose production of 16.25 million barrels put it ahead of Coors. Anheuser-Busch held a 2-to-1 lead over second-place Miller, third-place Stroh had a 5 percent drop in sales, and sixth-place Pabst's sales slid by more than 16 percent.

Cleary announced new aggressive advertising on radio and television. He tried to calm local fears about company executives leaving the city, saying he didn't foresee any significant change in the number of employees in La Crosse. Cleary opposed the concept of moving sales personnel out of La Crosse. He felt the ability to have face-to-face interaction with a salesman was preferable to long-distance management.

Bond's annual report for 1987 made no mention of the Heileman merger, since the deal had been completed so late in the year. The Bond conglomerate had almost $2 billion in long-term and short-term debt before taking over Heileman; with that purchase, the debt would grow to more than $3 billion. Bond sales for 1987 had been $1.9 billion, and with the addition of Heileman were expected to grow to $3.2 billion in 1988.

Undaunted, Bond completed the largest Australian real estate deal ever with a $215 million bid to build a new government center, a 48-story hotel, and other buildings in Sydney's prime central business district. Then, late in 1987, he caused a furor when he purchased a gold mine and the state-owned telephone company in Chile.

Harvey Sanford, president of Pittsburgh Brewing, resigned in January 1988, leaving Cleary as the head of all of Bond's North American brewing operations.

Heileman announced plans to expand production and increase employment by 30 to 50 employees from the current 250 at Pittsburgh Brewing. At the same time, the Evansville, Indiana, brewery was closed, leaving 150 employees jobless. The Evansville operations were moved to Perry, Georgia, putting that plant back at full capacity. The Evansville brewery was purchased and put back in operation by a group of local investors, and by 1994 was producing several regional brands and marketing some internationally.

As had been feared, Bond began to sell off Heileman assets to raise cash to pay off his mounting debt. Barrel O' Fun snack plants in Perham and Willmar, Minnesota, and Denver, Colorado, were sold. By May, Machine Products had been sold to a group of La Crosse managers and investors.

Heileman Baking Company was sold to RT Holding SA, a Belgian sugar company. Initially things looked promising, and headquarters staffing grew in La Crosse. But in July the company was sold a second time, to Metz Baking of Sioux City, Iowa, and Heileman Baking Company President Michael Moon and many members of his staff lost their jobs within days.

As the realities of life under Bond set in, residents, employees, and government officials struggled to put a positive spin on events. The *La Crosse Tribune* published an editorial challenging business leaders and citizens to take inventory of the benefits of doing business in La Crosse. They were told to look to the future, rather than dwell on the past, not an easy message for those who were jobless or worried they soon would be looking for work.

Heileman sales were up 6 percent in the first quarter, attributed to an increased marketing effort in selected target areas such as Chicago, Minneapolis, San Antonio, and Seattle. It also announced shareholders had approved a reverse stock split designed to pay off the last 8 percent of stockholders who hadn't tendered their stock to the Bond corporation.

During the first quarter there was more bad news. In early February 1988, Pabst sued Heileman for $18 million, alleging an overcharge of $6 million for its contract brewing at Perry. Heileman laid off 15 salaried employees at the Perry plant, which was now operating with only 50 employees, down from 200 in the recent past and 460 at peak. The Pabst contracts ended in controversy. The brewmaster at Val Blatz Brewery in Milwaukee resigned over differences with the company.

In June, 180 of the 230 employees at the brewery in Belleville, Illinois, were laid off immediately, and the others were kept on only until 1 P.M. on September 1, 1988, when Terry Galati pushed the final case of Stag beer off the line. The Belleville brewery was sold to Commercial Development Corporation, then was partially demolished and its equipment sold to the newly formed Evansville Brewing Company.

Belleville Mayor Richard Brauer and brewery employees were shocked by the news. Heileman officials pointed out the brewery had been running at only about 65 percent capacity, but the mayor attributed the closing to a recent ruling by the Illinois Environmental Protection Agency that would have required Heileman to build a wastewater treatment plant for the brewery. A few months later the U.S. Environmental Protection Agency brought suit against Heileman trying to levy a $37 million fine for repeated waste discharges.

Increasingly pressed by debt, Bond announced a complicated plan to buy 60 percent of the stock of the Bell Group, which if successful, would allow him to borrow up to $8 billion against the assets he owned. But industry analysts were concerned about Bond's finances, saying his debt burden was already too much to handle.

In September 1988, Bond made his first visit to La Crosse since taking over the company. He told reporters he intended to continue promoting several strong regional brands in selected target markets and saw nothing but growth for Heileman. He said he intended to keep the Heileman headquarters in La Crosse, had no plans to close any additional breweries, and intended to make plant improvements and triple spending on advertising. Investment in the La Crosse operation would include a $200,000 loading dock and receiving area at corporate headquarters.

Bond also told reporters that with his most recent purchases, his company now had more than $2 billion in cash reserves he intended to use for continued expansion and long-term growth in the beer industry. He declined to comment when questioned about recent rumors that he was considering the purchase of Stroh Brewing.

The very next day industry analysts reacted to Bond's rosy outlook. They reported that Heileman sales and profits were decreasing and overall sales for the brewing industry were flat. Heileman faced an increasingly difficult battle against Anheuser-Busch and Miller, not to mention Stroh and Coors, and while Heileman might want to purchase Stroh, the opposite was just as possible. Stroh had declared its desire to remain independent and was looking into acquisitions or mergers.

Third-quarter numbers supported what the analysts had said. Heileman sales were down 11 percent according to beer industry analysts, but company officials disputed the numbers, putting sales down only 6.6 percent. No matter which numbers were correct, all of Heileman's competitors, including Anheuser-Busch, Miller, Coors, and even Pabst, had increased sales. The only other company to lose business was the struggling Stroh. Anheuser-Busch had widened its lead to more than 40 percent of total beer sales in the United States.

Bond turned his attention to exporting beers outside the United States. Lone Star was sold in the United Kingdom and Special Export, Lone Star, and Lone Star Light in Japan. Rainier Special Dry and Henry Weinhard's Special Reserve were exported to France, Spain, and Italy, and long-term plans were to ship several more brands all over Europe. The Canadian export battle continued into July 1989, when the Ontario Liquor Control Board raised the retail price of a six-pack of American beer by 70 cents. As a result, Canadian dealers canceled orders for thousands of cases of Heileman beer, resulting in a 40 percent drop in Canadian sales at an estimated $1 million per month loss.

So, by the end of 1988, Heileman had closed several breweries and sold off most of the non-brewing assets. Total beer production was down slightly from 1987 and, worse yet, over the past few years Heileman had slipped badly from the No. 1 position in its stronghold of Wisconsin. Miller Brewing had easily passed Heileman and now owned about 39 percent of the market, compared with Heileman's 22 percent.

On January 16, 1989, Cleary and Bond announced jointly that Cleary was retiring from Heileman at age 55. Cleary had been with Heileman since 1960 and was president for 18 years. Cleary and his father-in-law, Roy Kumm, had taken the company from a struggling regional brewery, 39th largest in the United States, to the fourth-largest brewery with annual sales exceeding $1 billion.

Replacing Cleary was Murray S. Cutbush, a 43-year-old Australian with more than 20 years of experience in the brewing industry who came from Bond's North American headquarters in Chicago. The senior management team now consisted of three Heileman managers and three managers from Bond's corporation.

The immediate reaction in La Crosse was fear and concern. La Crosse Mayor Patrick Zielke was especially uncertain about not having Cleary on board to look out for the city. Bond and Cutbush assured La Crosse that the existing management team would remain in place, and Cleary would continue to provide management consulting to Heileman. They also announced they would pump massive dollar amounts into Heileman advertising and marketing. If there was one thing Bond could do well, it was spend money.

With Cleary retired, Bond and his management team were now firmly in control of Heileman. It didn't take long for things to turn from bad to worse.

At the end of April 1989, Heileman announced 267 workers would lose their jobs when it closed the brewery in Perry. Heileman officials placed much of the blame for the closing on Pabst, but industry analysts pointed at the Bond corporation's debt load after the Heileman purchase.

On the same day, it was announced Heileman officials had met with Stroh executives in Detroit to begin discussions about a possible merger between the two companies. Stroh officials were less enthusiastic about the potential merger. They were more interested in finding a foreign investor with deep pockets, someone willing to spend money on marketing and to buy a minority interest in the company.

Analysts questioned the entire merger. Stroh had recently announced plans to close its breweries for the first week of July because of lack of demand. No other brewery had ever been forced to do this during the peak summer months. They could see no good that could come from merging two companies with declining sales.

In an attempt to reverse falling sales, Crichton said Bond had decided to focus on only 11 core brands and market those brands only in geographic areas where they already had an established market share. Heileman reorganized into four divisions to support this new strategy.

By late June, the Bond empire had begun to stagger under its huge debt load. The Australian Stock Exchange suspended trading on Bond stock after he announced a complicated plan to restructure. The plan involved selling some of his assets to another of his own subsidiaries, Bell Resources. In addition, Bond was facing potential legal problems over an out-of-court settlement of a libel suit and concerns that his television stations had gathered negative information on a business competitor.

The Australian press reported rumors that Bond would sell off his beer interests. Cutbush denied those rumors. Days later, new reports named Heileman as part of the assets Bond wanted to transfer to Bell Resources. Company officials said they wanted to consolidate all brewing assets in a single company.

Shortly after this news, the *Wall Street Journal* reported Bond was selling the St. Moritz Hotel in New York City, which he had purchased six months earlier from Donald Trump for $180 million, in an effort to raise cash. It was also reported that Bond had raised another $80 million in cash by selling off half of his interest in some prime London real estate.

The *Financial Times* of London reported Heileman was now losing money. Initial statements from Bond confirmed that, but said the situation was temporary and would last only 12 to 18 months. Later reports from Bond claimed Heileman had operated at a break-even level since the acquisition.

In August, Heileman announced it was closing Val Blatz in Milwaukee, a highly automated brewery open only since September 1986. All 12 employees were laid off. A September *Wall Street Journal* article reported Bond and Bond Corporation Holdings Limited were the subject of a formal investigation by the Australian National Companies and Securities Commission.

News of the investigation caused the price of Bond stock to dive to 43 Australian cents, down from $1.80 at the start of the year. Analysts estimated Bond's debt at this point had grown to around $6 billion.

Fresh rumors surfaced that Elders IXL Limited had proposed a "rescue" of Bond's corporation, but Bond officials denied Heileman was part of the assets that were being considered for sale to Elders. Business experts speculated Bond had paid too much for Heileman originally and now faced enormous interest payments on the borrowed money. Worse yet, the investments weren't producing enough income to cover the debt payments. They predicted that essentially everything owned by Bond would have to be put up for sale.

Bond went from national hero in Australia to the subject of jokes and suspicion. There were increasing questions about his business dealings and pattern of buying assets, revaluing them, and then borrowing against the assets to purchase additional assets. There also were more charges and findings of political and business problems.

Bond's debt now represented almost 10 percent of the total debt of Australia, whose entire economy was threatened by outstanding loans to Bond, not to mention the international banks that had made them. Owners of Bond stock were close to holding totally worthless paper.

In late September, the chief executive officer of Minneapolis-based First Bank System resigned after it was announced the company faced an $83 million loss from loans, part of which was rumored to be from the leveraged buyout of Heileman. Company officials were quick to deny the rumors and stated it was current on all its loan payments.

With the Bond corporation struggling, beer industry analysts speculated on what the future might hold for Heileman. They predicted that somehow Heileman, Stroh, Pabst, and Coors would need to be consolidated.

Recent talk of a potential merger between Heileman and Stroh had ceased with all the Bond problems. There also had been a failed leveraged buyout of Stroh by company management and an unsuccessful offer from Pabst to buy it. Stroh had recently reorganized, and had laid off 300 workers, down to 1,200 from a high of 2,100.

Heileman now faced an $850 million debt and market share had slipped from 9 percent to 7 percent, although that erosion had started prior to the Bond acquisition. But Cleary had still managed to keep the company profitable. After he left, management became increasingly complex and difficult to deal with. Distributors reported that Heileman had cut marketing field personnel, and when there was a problem they had to work through multiple levels of bureaucracy to get a resolution.

Under Cleary, stockholders and customers had been extremely loyal to Heileman products, but under Bond they no longer considered it to be a local company and in many cases had turned to other brands. Finally, Bond's plans to bring Australian brands into the United States and take Heileman brands to international markets had backfired.

Late in September, the Bond corporation stated it was selling half of its Australian brewing assets to

New Zealand's Lion Nathan Limited. However, Heileman was not for sale—for at least a year.

Cutbush disputed analyst estimates that Heileman was losing up to $100 million a year, and suggested part of the reason Heileman wasn't for sale was it was still negotiating with Stroh for a purchase or merger between the two companies.

But, a few days later, Coors announced a $425 million offer to buy Stroh, and Bond filed papers with the Australian Stock Exchange indicating Heileman might be sold to Bond subsidiary Bell Resources Limited. Cutbush assured worried employees and residents that the sale was just a transfer of assets between Bond's subsidiaries and there would be no impact on the plant in La Crosse.

The Coors offer did not include purchase of the Stroh breweries in California or Tennessee. Heileman officials quickly announced they were against the deal and would fight it in court. Ironically, if the merger were allowed, Heileman would once again move up to fourth-largest brewery in America.

In early October 1989, Cutbush issued a memo to employees that outlined three major business goals for Heileman. First, it established sales and profit targets to put Heileman in a leadership role in its targeted regional markets. Second, it reaffirmed that the company did not intend to pursue sales for the sake of volume. It was more interested in profitable sales. Third, it committed to major investments in equipment, facilities, advertising, and promotional programs. The memo went on to assure employees that sales for the international division were up 50 percent for the last three months, and Heileman now controlled almost 40 percent of beer exports to Canada.

In November 1989, the *Wall Street Journal* reported that Heileman audit results showed the company probably didn't have sufficient cash flow to cover its

Bond's Fiscal Results for 1989

When Bond Corporation Holdings Limited announced its fiscal results for 1989, the figures were staggering. The company had lost $726.4 million, the largest loss in Australian corporate history.

Earnings for its brewing assets in both Australia and America were down 50 percent from a year earlier. While revenue was up 69 percent, the telling number was that interest payments were up 85 percent.

Bond remained confident and issued a statement that the company had taken it on the chin, but he intended to remain in business and recover. He predicted by June 30, 1990, he would have debt reduced by another $3 billion. Furthermore, he expected to have a stable balance sheet and be focused on a reduced set of good quality assets.

On the Australian stock market, Bond corporation's stock price went even lower, and there was speculation the conglomerate might be forced into liquidation.

debt payments. The paper also raised doubts about the long-term ability of Heileman to continue.

Cutbush disputed the audit findings, and Heileman announced it had negotiated loan waivers from several creditor banks in Canada and the United States until June 1990. Industry analysts estimated Heileman still had outstanding loans of $850 million from the original $1.3 billion purchase price by Bond.

As 1989 came to a close, it appeared the entire Bond corporation was on the verge of collapse. An Australian court placed Bond Corporation Holdings Limited of Australia in receivership and appointed managers to run Bond's Australian brewing interests. With January 1 just days away, the *Wall Street Journal* reported Bond's corporation would have $52 million in interest payments due to various American banks, and speculated that if they were not made, creditors would take legal action. In Australia, trading was suspended on Bond stock.

Some analysts felt that since Heileman's debt was separate from Bond's there was still hope, but others feared that if Bond were forced to liquidate, Heileman would be torn apart and sold in piecemeal fashion. It was a buyer's market and any sales would be a financial bloodbath for the company.

Alan Bond in Prison

Alan Bond's legal and financial troubles in Australia did not go away.

In 1992 Bond was charged with criminal dishonesty in his business dealings and was sent to jail for 30 months. A retrial, however, resulted in his early release.

In 1995, Bond paid creditors less than 1 cent on the dollar in a personal bankruptcy settlement.

In August 1996, he was sentenced to prison for fraud after a West Australian District Court jury convicted him on four charges of defrauding his corporation over the purchase and resale of a French impressionist painting.

In 1997, Bond pleaded guilty to defrauding Bell Resources out of $1.2 billion and served almost four years in jail. He was released from prison in March 2000 and currently resides in London.

Bond was ranked as one of the richest Australians until his financial, brewing and real estate empire collapsed under the weight of huge debt in the late 1980s.

Chapter 15

Bankruptcy Looms

HEILEMAN DECLARES BANKRUPTCY FOR THE FIRST TIME 1990–1993

Alan Bond resigned as chairman of Bond corporation in September 1990, just ahead of the corporation's announcement of its yearly results, which showed a loss of $1.86 billion, again the largest loss in Australia's history.

Murray Cutbush was managing Heileman for the Bond corporation as he entered 1990, but he still felt like he was living in the shadow of Russ Cleary. Cutbush said he loved La Crosse, but he was a bit homesick, and had not been back to Australia where his family lived since July.

Heileman had recently benefited from lower malt and barley expenses, and sales of La Croix water, Special Export, Special Export Light, Henry Weinhard, and Kingsbury were all doing well. Unfortunately, sales for Old Style were down, which he blamed on a lack of advertising and not reaching younger drinkers. Heileman was rapidly losing market share in Wisconsin to Miller and Anheuser-Busch.

Cutbush hoped that Heileman could restructure its debt and isolate itself from Bond's troubles. The company had too many brands, he thought, and he put plans in place to reduce the 70 brands to 15 during the next 18 months. Brands he intended to keep included Old Style, Special Export, Rainier, Lone Star, Iron City, and Henry Weinhard. Blatz, La Croix, Schmidt, and Kingsbury nonalcoholic ranked in the second tier. He hoped to sell the remaining 55 brands rather than discontinue them.

Cutbush speculated that a three-way merger with Stroh and Coors still made sense and might be pursued. Coors had been negotiating for the purchase of Heileman, and Cutbush had been negotiating with Stroh, but those talks had been called off for now.

By mid-January, Heileman employees were starting to feel nervous about the future. The company laid off 70 union employees, which was attributed to normal seasonal slowdowns. But industry analysts were quick to point out Miller hadn't needed layoffs at any of its six plants.

By the end of January 1990, corporate reports to the Securities and Exchange Commission showed Heileman had lost $126.7 million on sales of $796.4

million. Worse yet, it owed more than $1 billion in long-term debt and another $221 million in current liabilities. The future of Heileman was totally in the hands of the banks, which could sell off the assets or take ownership to get their money back through future profits.

Meanwhile, the Supreme Court for the Australian state of Victoria was considering a request to reverse the decision that had forced Alan Bond's Australian breweries into receivership. Bond won an initial victory when the courts dismissed a government agency request to have Bond Corporation Holdings Limited liquidated. However, the victory was short-lived and the decision overturned.

The battle didn't end there, and just weeks later the decision was reversed again in Bond's favor. It still wasn't clear what would happen to American holders of Bond debt if his company were liquidated. In most cases they ranked behind the Australian creditors.

With the Bond corporation's future in doubt, a 28-year-old American investor named Jeff Reynolds suddenly and unexpectedly made an offer of $250 million to buy out Bond, and as part of the offer he indicated he intended to keep Heileman. Reynolds, from a long line of Texas oilmen, described himself as an intensely private businessman.

However, a check into Reynolds' claims and his past proved baffling. The Bond corporation said it was embarrassed by the offer and doubted Reynolds really had the resources to take over Bond corporation and the estimated $6 billion in debt. Analysts also doubted the offer was legitimate. A few days later, Reynolds gave up the takeover, saying there were too many legal problems.

Bond corporation sold off its Australian coal-mining operations to an insurance company, and Labatt Brewing made an offer to buy Bond's troubled Australian breweries. Those breweries had been denied an extension on a deadline for a $32 million debt payment to several American banks, and that decision would probably force liquidation of Bond's assets to pay off the outstanding loans.

In March 1990, Bond was still trying to get his personal and corporate finances in order. He sold his Vincent Van Gogh painting, *Irises,* to the J. Paul Getty Museum in Los Angeles, and was finally able to pay off his debt to Sotheby's Holding Incorporated, the New York auction company that had sold him the painting in 1987.

Finally, at the end of May, Bond corporation announced it had reached an accord with a group of international banks to avoid legal proceedings against its Australian brewing holdings. As part of the same announcement, Bond announced plans to restructure some of the other debts against his company. By early June 1990, however, his holdings were unraveling quickly and plans were announced to sell off some of the television and radio empire to another Australian company.

Late in September, Bond resigned as chairman of Bond Corporation Holdings Limited. Two days later the Bond corporation announced its yearly results, and the numbers were again staggering—a loss of $1.86 billion, the largest loss in the history of Australia.

A special Australian commission was ordered to investigate allegations of corruption and improper business dealing by the corporation. In early December, Bond was arrested and charged with concealing information from investors in some of his business dealings. He maintained his innocence, paid a $100,000 bond, and was ordered to appear before the court in Perth, Australia.

The Schmidt brewery in Saint Paul, and the Grain Belt, Hauenstein, and Stag brands, were put up for sale. The estimated value of the brewery was only $4 million, although Heileman had spent more than $45 million modernizing it since 1972. By the end of April, none of the offers on the brewery had come to fruition, and Heileman announced it would close the plant on June 23 unless a buyer could be found.

News of the closing elicited a prompt response from Saint Paul Mayor Jim Scheibel, who organized support from Minnesota Governor Rudy Perpich and arranged to meet with Cutbush. He also applied for funds for retraining programs for employees and offered state-funded grants for other potential buyers.

Employees and distributors of Heileman products pointed out that closing the brewery would cause ill will toward Heileman throughout Minnesota, and boycotts of Heileman products were threatened. But time was running out for Heileman, which needed immediate cash just to survive short-term.

Sohan S. Sahota, owner of North Country Beer Wholesalers of Oakdale, Minnesota, announced he was looking for financing to pay the reported $15 million being asked for the brewery, brands, and current inventory, and for a while it looked like a deal would be made. But it fell through when it was discovered that Sahota was not only $5 million short, but wanted the union workers in Saint Paul to take a 14 percent pay cut and to give up rules allowing them to select jobs based on seniority. Union officials angrily rejected the offer.

The May 31 deadline for financing passed and Sahota withdrew his bid. Then rumors cropped up that Kevin McHale, a Minnesotan and professional basketball player, had expressed interest in buying the company. Dave Thane, a Saint Paul city council member, also offered a plan for the city of Saint Paul to acquire the brewery through eminent domain and keep it operating.

When McHale discovered that Heileman officials were transferring some of the equipment to the brewery in La Crosse, he was no longer interested. Without it, he felt the brewery had no chance to survive. Heileman officials defended the decision to move the equipment, but Saint Paul city officials started to research the legalities of the situation.

As promised, Heileman closed the brewery in July, and a few days later a group named Red Oak Investments announced it would join forces with investors from Old Home Foods, a Saint Paul-based dairy products company, to purchase the brewery. The plan called for the new company to brew Grain Belt and for Old Home to use the plant to produce non-alcoholic products such as bottled water.

It initially planned to rehire about 40 of the 150 workers who lost their jobs when the brewery closed. Saint Paul officials were thrilled by the announcement and promised additional funding from both the city and state in support of the plan. But by early December 1990, Red Oak still had been unable to obtain all of the necessary financing. In January 1991, Heileman completely shut down the plant.

In April 1992 Bruce Hendry, a liquidation specialist who had made a previous unsuccessful attempt to buy Schmidt, offered $4.2 million for the brewery and Grain Belt brand. He made it clear that the deal depended on full support from the laid-off union workers and low-interest loans from the state of Minnesota and the city of Saint Paul.

At the end of August 1992, Heileman sold the plant to Hendry and his group of investors for about $3.2 million, a far cry from the $15 million they had hoped to get. As part of the agreement Heileman allowed them to keep the historic Schmidt sign on the plant, even though the Schmidt brand was not part of the deal. The brewery reopened in October 1992 as Minnesota Brewing, making Grain Belt and a new brand, Pig's Eye, as well as contract brewing for Pete's Wicked Ale of California.

The sale of the Schmidt Brewery in Saint Paul was only one of the events that consumed the Heileman management team during the early 1990s, and there were even bigger storm clouds on the horizon.

Sales for the last quarter of 1990 were the best since 1987, but unfortunately much of the demand was due to distributors stocking up prior to the excise tax increases on beer taking effect on January 1, 1991. Total 1990 sales were down more than 6 percent from 1989, in a year when the three largest competitors in the beer industry had increased volume by 20 percent.

Cutbush resigned days after the 1990 results were announced. The new chief executive officer was Thomas J. Rattigan, a principal partner in Riverside Partners, an investment firm from Cambridge, Massachusetts. He had been hired at a salary of $750,000. Rattigan brought on a new chief financial officer, Michael B. Evans, who was known for turning companies around.

Rattigan inherited a company which was $780 million in debt and had a declining market share. He had no experience in the brewing industry, but had a history of bailing companies out of trouble. Heileman was down to just five breweries: La Crosse, Seattle, Portland, San Antonio, and Baltimore. Total employment for the company had been reduced to about 2,500, about 1,050 of them in La Crosse. Rattigan's first task was to officially declare Chapter 11 bankruptcy for Heileman, which gave the company 120 days to finalize debt restructuring with its major secured creditors. He hoped to reduce its total debt to around $300 million to $400 million.

The corporate message was optimistic. Rattigan vowed Heileman would fight its way through bankruptcy and emerge stronger. Heileman executive Randy Smith predicted that once the debt was settled, Heileman could just as easily emerge as an acquirer rather than a company to be acquired. He called Cutbush's exit part of a plan to "de-Bond" the company.

Those who owned $200 million in unsecured junk bonds would be the big losers in the settlement, while holders of secured debt were offered an ownership stake in the company. Heileman assets were estimated to be worth $1.2 billion, but debts were $1.4 billion. Some analysts disagreed with these estimates and said the entire company was worth no more than $350 million.

With the bankruptcy under way, the company looked for new ways to get back to the business of selling beer. In a period of six months it offered 15 new brands. A $3 million line to produce packaged draft beer was put into La Crosse to make Old Style Classic Draft and Old Style Classic Draft Light. The brands were introduced in restaurants in Chicago and later expanded to other markets.

Heileman test-marketed a dark bock malt beer brewed in its San Antonio brewery, introduced Rainier Draft and Rainier Draft Light, and repackaged Old Style and Special Export. Analysts questioned how successful these moves would be without an advertising budget to support them, and predicted it would take more than packaging changes to turn the company around. They suggested Heileman consider selling off Colt 45 malt liquor and perhaps merging with Stroh.

Heileman also introduced a new malt liquor named Powermaster during the summer of 1991 and immediately found itself in a fight with a variety of groups opposed to Powermaster's high 5.9 percent alcohol content. They also claimed that the advertising was targeted at inner city blacks. After several months of controversy, Heileman was forced to withdraw the product.

By late April, rumor had it that Stroh was interested in Heileman. Stroh had recently sold its brewery in Spain for $300 million and had also obtained another $100 million from the sale of its Sundance soft drink subsidiary. Rattigan said he'd consider any offer that would move the company in a positive direction.

First quarter results for 1991 showed sales down another 13.5 percent, still attributed to distributors stocking up prior to the excise tax increase. The only brewer able to increase sales in the first quarter was Anheuser-Busch. As internal chaos continued, so did Heileman's slide in sales. In the second quarter Heileman was showing large losses in Wisconsin market share.

As the summer progressed, however, things picked up and in early July the brewery in La Crosse was operating at maximum capacity around the clock and on weekends. The result was a record for the most beer produced in a single month.

Details of the Heileman bankruptcy were made public in August. The plan called for secured creditors to receive $325 million in new debt along with a 70.5 percent share in the newly restructured company. In exchange, Heileman was forgiven $663 million in debt. The holders of junk bonds had to settle for splitting up 18 percent of the new common stock. The Heileman management team received 8.5 percent of the stock. Other trade creditors were paid 70 percent of their claims and the rest of the creditors proportionately split $11 million. Under bankruptcy law Heileman was required to pay all of the creditor legal fees, which, before it was all over, added up to more than $3.5 million.

The Bond corporation, which was finally close to a return to the Australian stock market after its own reorganization, retained 3 percent of the stock. Meanwhile, Alan Bond told the courts in Australia he had run out of money. He declared less than $40,000 in his accounts other than a $2 million retirement fund. There were rumors he might be sent to jail.

The plan also had a relatively conservative estimate of future revenue for Heileman, predicting a decline in 1992 and 1993 before stabilizing at about

$500 million per year. The plan put the total worth of the new company at $495 million following the restructuring, not a figure believable to all.

Industry analysts were somewhat surprised by the plan. They thought the secured creditors made out well, but that the unsecured creditors stood to lose a lot of money. They also questioned the 8.5 percent stock for the Heileman management team, along with $8 million in golden parachutes for the company's top 35 executives. If the restructured company hit its targets, the executives stood to collect large bonuses on top of their salaries.

The documents also disclosed that Rattigan and his wife were entitled to monthly trips, at company expense, to their homes in Connecticut and on Cape Cod. Some creditors were angered that they were paid only partially while company executives received large salaries and special perks.

Heileman put La Croix Sparkling Water and Champale up for sale, hoping a buyer could be found who would continue to contract with the brewery for the bottling. But Heileman executives had no plans to sell any other assets except the four idle plants in Perry, Georgia, Frankenmuth, Michigan, Saint Paul, and Milwaukee.

Finally, in October, the restructuring deal was close to being finalized. The major creditors and banks had agreed to it, although other creditors were still upset, saying it would be very difficult to sell off the breweries and brands to raise $100 million in cash, which was part of the deal. Despite the concerns, a judge ruled Heileman could submit it for final approval, and by late November the bankruptcy plan was in the hands of the banks and creditors. An entirely new board of directors was elected that was heavy on business experience, but not in the brewing industry.

The company reported sales for the fourth quarter were up.

Canadian Problems

Heileman executives faced several business and legal problems, besides bankruptcy issues, in the early 1990s. One of the biggest problems facing the company was the continuing border battle with Canada over beer imports.

In March 1991, U.S. Senator Bob Kasten of Wisconsin announced he had sided with Heileman in its fight against beer import regulations in Canada. He vowed to help Heileman fight the regulations and make it easier to export beer into Canada. Meanwhile, the Brewers Association of Canada brought charges that Heileman, Stroh, and Pabst were "dumping" beer into Canada by selling beer below cost in British Columbia in an effort to gain market share.

The dispute with Canada dragged on until later in 1991, when United States trade representatives sided with Heileman. They agreed to levy a duty against Canadian beer entering the United States unless Canada dropped or lowered the duties on American beer entering Canada. Kasten was thrilled by the ruling and noted it would help both the United States and beer drinkers in Canada.

The battle between the two countries raged on into 1992, when Canada asked 108 nations that participated in the General Agreement on Tariffs and Trade (GATT) to declare the new tax breaks for American brewers to be discriminatory. Heileman officials responded by stating Canada had always been known for being exclusionary in its dealings with other countries over alcohol.

Finally, Canada tried to negotiate a settlement by agreeing to open up its provinces to sales of American beers within three years. Heileman officials were incensed by the announcement and called the timetable totally unacceptable. It also rejected clauses that would allow Canada to establish minimum prices in three provinces after the three-year period.

In July 1992, Canada fired another shot in the battle by placing an environmental tax on beer cans. The tax increased the cost of a case of American beer by more than $3. Heileman officials argued the tax was intended only for American beers because they were required to import only cans while most Canadian beer was sold in bottles. Heileman asked the U.S. government to help resolve the issue.

The United States responded by levying a $3-per-case excise tax on Canadian beer imported from Ontario. Within hours Canada responded by slapping a 65-cent tax on each six-pack of Lone Star and other American brands sold in Ontario. When Heileman first introduced Lone Star into Canada it sold for about $3 a six-pack and sales increased rapidly. With the new tax the price of Lone Star had risen to about $7 a six-pack, and sales dropped along with the price increases.

By January 1993, it was clear Canada had found a way to deal with the new excise tax. It simply shipped its beer from Ontario to another province and then sent it into the United States. As a result, sales of Canadian beer were up slightly, while exports of American beer to Canada had fallen by 45 percent. To help fight the battle, Heileman officials asked the U.S. government to expand the tax to apply to all Canadian beer.

Walk, Don't Run, to the Beer Cooler

"Medical evidence continues to build, supporting the fact that moderate consumption of beer has a positive health impact," according to an item in the 1982 annual report published by G. Heileman Brewing Company.

The article stated that "a number of medical reports in recent years have concluded that the moderate daily consumption of beer reduces the threat of heart attacks and promotes healthy social attitudes in geriatric patients."

Furthermore, the article continued, "numerous medical studies have indicated that drinking three beers a day can offer the same level of protection against heart disease as jogging."

The article specifically identified a study done by the Baylor College of Medicine which concluded that people who don't exercise can maintain levels of high-density lipoprotein cholesterol "similar to those individuals who jog regularly by ingesting three beers a day." The data was reported in the February 13, 1983, issue of the *Journal of the American Medical Association.*

Chapter 16

Banking on Beer

OWNERSHIP BY BANKS, AND RUSS CLEARY RETURNS 1992–1994

In November of 1993 Heileman was sold to a Dallas investment firm.

Heileman emerged from bankruptcy a different company, one now firmly in the control of its banks and its creditors.

Thomas Rattigan, Heileman's president, announced in late January 1992 that he and 10 other senior managers would relocate to Rosemont, Illinois, in an effort to consolidate sales and marketing with the 50 Heileman staff already located in Chicago.

Restructuring had essentially wiped away almost $1 billion in debt from the company. The old Gund brewery structures Heileman had owned for years, near Lutheran Hospital in La Crosse, had been torn down to make the property more attractive to a buyer. Other properties in La Crosse, along the Mississippi River near the Main Channel Bridge, were for sale. La Croix water and Champale were still for sale, but no credible offers had been received.

In the first quarter, sales were up just more than 2 percent, attributable to new marketing and packaging such as a 30-can pack for Old Style. Still, with the declines over the past years, Heileman had slipped from its lofty positions of the 1970s and 1980s to a ranking of 23rd among all beverage companies in the United States.

La Croix was eventually sold to WinterBrook Beverage Group of Seattle, Washington, but the Champale brand was no longer for sale because of a lack of interest from buyers. Heileman executive Randy Smith announced that the company had decided to keep the brand because it was a good product and highly profitable. In December 1992, Heileman announced it was considering a menthol-flavored malt liquor named Cool Colt. The product, packaged in a 22-ounce bottle called the "Double Deuce," was initially produced at the brewery in Baltimore, but plans were to move production to La Crosse. Industry analysts were unimpressed and correctly predicted a poor reception for the product. As 1992 came to a close, Heileman sales for the year were down another 2 percent.

Early in 1993 Foothill Capital Group, a California corporate investments firm, had increased its ownership in Heileman. It was a significant shareholder, but not the largest, that being the syndicate of banks that held most of the Heileman debt prior to the bankruptcy.

In an effort to capitalize on the growing trend toward microbreweries, Heileman introduced several specialty beers, including Emerald City Ale in Seattle and Windy City Ale in Chicago. Heileman also introduced Old Style Royal Amber, a new nonalcoholic brand that was designed to recapture some of the market that had been lost by declining sales of the Kingsbury near beers. The Royal Amber brand was originally a premium beer owned by Wiedemann.

Heileman continued introducing new brands in an effort to find a product that would increase sales. In May 1993, production of the new Colt 45 Premium and Colt 45 Premium Light were moved to La Crosse. By September, Heileman had expanded sales of Special Export and Special Export Light into the Pacific Northwest market, packaging them under the Henry Weinhard name instead of Heileman because they were brewed at the Blitz-Weinhard brewery in Portland.

When results for the first half of 1993 were released, Heileman sales were up slightly, running ahead of projections made during the bankruptcy settlement. In Chicago, Heileman's market share fell to about 24 percent, well behind Miller's 45 percent.

In the fall of 1993, Rattigan sent a letter to employees saying the banks that currently owned Heileman were eager to get out of the brewing business and sell the company. Merger rumors were rampant.

Then, early in November, Heileman was sold to a Dallas investment firm, Hicks, Muse, Tate & Furst Incorporated, for $390 million. The deal affected Heileman's 2,200 employees in La Crosse, Baltimore, San Antonio, Portland, and Seattle.

Similar to the Bond takeover, the purchase was a leveraged buyout; the buyer put down only $78 million of the price and financed the rest against the assets. A spokesman for the investment firm assured the public that it had not overpaid for the company and that cash flow was adequate to finance the debt and interest payments. Employees were notified by press releases posted on company bulletin boards.

The firm specialized in leveraged buyouts and was best known for the successful takeovers of Dr. Pepper and 7-Up, which it merged into a single company. While not all of the purchases by Hicks, Muse, Tate & Furst Incorporated were successful, it had an impressive track record, averaging a 191.6 percent return on investments in the latest nine companies it had bought.

William J. Turner was named temporary chief executive officer of Heileman to replace Rattigan, and an entirely new board of directors was put in place. Turner announced a five-part plan for the future of Heileman:

1. Broaden the market area for core products such as Old Style, Special Export, Henry Weinhard, Rainier, Lone Star, and others.
2. Add extensions such as light, dry, and draft to existing product lines.
3. Use new and creative packaging.

4. Use major in-store merchandising displays.
5. Advertise core products tailored to individual markets.

Turner assured employees there were no plans to move any jobs out of La Crosse or close any of the Heileman breweries.

Rattigan and Michael Evans, his executive vice president, received generous severance packages.

The final purchase price was $427.7 million, about $250 million of which went to Bank of Boston, Bank of Nova Scotia, and Foothill Capital Corporation of Los Angeles. Another $140 million went to stockholders, including nearly $12 million that was paid to other senior managers. Hicks, Muse, Tate & Furst Incorporated was selling $160 million in debt—senior subordinated notes—to finance the deal.

The new owners were greeted with the news that sales for the third quarter were down another 2 percent and were flat for the previous 12 months. Only 8.93 million barrels had been produced, or about half of the 17.5 barrels during the peak year of 1983. Market share in America had fallen from 10 percent to 4.5 percent.

Richard F. Gaccione was named the new chief executive officer. Formerly president of Bristol-Myers Squibb Company, he had a background of launching new products and was best known for his successful introduction of Sunlight dish detergent and Snuggle fabric softener and increasing health and beauty products sales by 30 percent.

The new head man's lack of experience in the brewing industry led Hicks, Muse, Tate & Furst to ask Russ Cleary to come back as an adviser. The former Heileman president accepted, which reestablished some of the company's credibility in the industry. He would spend half his time rebuilding relationships with Heileman wholesalers and half on possible acquisitions.

Union officials and Heileman distributors were glad to see Cleary back. However, they were realistic enough to know that he was no longer calling the shots. The company still faced a long uphill battle, and the beer industry was very different than it was in the 1980s.

Explaining the Bond takeover, Cleary said he had tried to negotiate the best possible deal for employees, stockholders, and La Crosse.

Those who knew Cleary knew how painful it had been for him to watch the company being dismantled during the Bond era. He said he could look anyone in the eye and tell him he had never met Bond or had any communication with him prior to the phone call on that fateful evening in September 1987.

In late January 1994, Gaccione and members of the board met with the press to outline their vision for the company. They promised they would look to the past to guide them in the future. He repeated the old Heileman advertising theme, "We don't aim to make the most beer, only the best," and vowed to expand the company's stable of regional brands.

They wanted to promote Old Style, Colt 45, Mickey's, and Champale, and take Special Export and Henry Weinhard into new market areas. Lone Star could be a dark horse for the company, they said, capitalizing on a current country-western craze. And while they admitted they knew little about microbrews, they saw them as the next big growth area in the beer industry.

The Perry, Georgia, brewery remained idle, and the company had been approached to sell the Val Blatz Brewery in Milwaukee. But with an increasing demand for contract brewing for microbrewers, that didn't look likely. Contract brewing had been up 50 percent in the previous year, and the company had a solid reputation as a low-cost producer.

In the Chicago market, Heileman reduced the cost to wholesalers for a case of Old Style from $7.89 to $6.71 in order to be at least $1 below competition. It lowered prices for Special Export and discontinued many of the odd-sized packages.

Thomas A. Koehler replaced Ian Crichton, who had led Heileman sales since 1988 and was one of the last remaining members of the management team brought in by Bond. Koehler had a 22-year history with Miller and vowed his first task would be to meet face-to-face with the 1,500 Heileman distributors.

Sales continued to dive, with another 11 percent decline in the first quarter. Company officials blamed the poor showing on an unusually harsh winter and intense price competition from Anheuser-Busch and Miller.

But the Heileman decline was the worst among the six largest brewers in the United States. In June 1994, Gaccione shocked everyone by resigning, less than six months after he was hired. He blamed personal reasons, among them job travel requirements that were too hard on his family, although reportedly he was in the process of moving them to Chicago from New York.

Cleary was willing to return to the company as joint chief executive officer along with William Turner from Hicks, Muse, Tate & Furst. Turner would concentrate on finances and Cleary on marketing, working with the top 300 Heileman wholesalers. Later he said that this was a mistake that took an immense toll on him and his family, and he resigned in less than a year after major disagreements. He felt he could help but said that others in management did not want to listen.

The new joint chiefs reopened the Val Blatz Brewery in Milwaukee and announced a new Henry Weinhard Boar's Head Red brand to compete with Killian's Red and Leinenkugel's Red. A few weeks later, Turner reported the company would introduce as many as 150 new products and line extensions within six months, and that 30 of those products would be produced in La Crosse.

One of the first introduced was an ice version of Special Export. Heileman also turned to the world market in an effort to increase sales. In November 1994, the company announced a joint venture with Hong Kong Investments Limited to export Lone Star and Henry Weinhard to China and produce Lone Star at 23 breweries in China. Heileman also finally discovered a new use for the idle brewery in Perry, and made plans to retool the facility to brew and package Arizona Iced Tea, the No. 3-ranked tea in the United States.

In a major reorganization of marketing and sales, Joseph Martino, formerly with Anheuser-Busch and Miller, came to Heileman. Martino had recently served 10 months in federal prison for violating Internal Revenue Service rules governing the reporting of gifts he received while working for Anheuser-Busch, but he still had a reputation in the brewing industry for his marketing skill.

The Henry Weinhard brand was expanded from the Pacific Northwest to become a national brand,

and the Val Blatz Brewery began to produce stout, wheat, dark bock, and a variety of specialty beers and flavors. The brewery had only the capability of producing half-barrel kegs, which had to be shipped to La Crosse via rail cars and bottled or canned there.

Heileman ended the year with sales off by almost 6 percent. Meanwhile, Anheuser-Busch and Miller continued to gain share at the expense of Coors, Stroh, Heileman, and Pabst.

M.L. "Lou" Lowenkron was named chief executive officer early in 1995, replacing Cleary and Turner.

During the fourth quarter of 1994, the company had suffered a negative cash flow, attributed to spending too much to promote its new products. The investment firm notified the federal government it intended to borrow up to $25 million.

But Heileman lost $24.4 million in the first six months of the year and did not expect cash flow to meet debts in the coming years. Banker's Trust, Heileman's largest creditor, was losing patience. Heileman executive Randy Smith blamed the poor results on increased costs of aluminum and continued decreasing sales, which in Heileman's Midwest stronghold had fallen dramatically. Sales were down in Indiana, Michigan, and Ohio, but the biggest drop of all was in the brewer's home state of Wisconsin.

The contract brewing business had been especially hard hit. Heileman had reopened the Perry plant specifically to bottle iced tea, but shortly afterward Coca Cola entered the tea market with a line of specialty teas and fruit drinks which devastated Arizona Iced Tea sales. Standard and Poor's reduced Heileman's credit rating twice during the first six months, to a CCC+ rating, and indicated it could be reduced again if finances didn't improve. Sales of assets or a merger seemed likely.

As Heileman struggled, a new opportunity appeared. Pabst asked its union employees to take a $9.60-per-hour cut in wages and benefits in an attempt to save about 280 out of 400 jobs. The average Pabst union employee was making $16 an hour, but benefits brought the total to $40. When Pabst employees rejected the pay cuts, Pabst contacted Heileman about brewing its beer on contract, and two-thirds of Pabst production moved to Heileman's breweries in La Crosse and Baltimore. Nearly 280 Pabst employees with up to 29 years of seniority lost their jobs in Milwaukee, leaving only 12 employees at the Milwaukee brewery. The 1.4-million-barrel deal increased Heileman production by 18 percent.

Heileman retained the Blackstone Group to restructure the company, but Lowenkron was still hopeful Heileman could avoid bankruptcy. Standard and Poor's lowered the Heileman credit rating to low triple C, saying the company had extremely limited financial flexibility.

In mid September 1995, Heileman sold the Val Blatz microbrewery in Milwaukee to Jacob Leinenkugel Brewing. The deal was financed by Miller, parent company of Leinenkugel.

In another effort to save cash as the September 30 deadline approached, Heileman shut down its entire brewing operation for a week in La Crosse. In the past the brewery had had partial shutdowns, but all 460 production workers and 30 supervisors were affected and eligible for unemployment pay.

When the third quarter came to a close, the situation looked even bleaker than at the start of the year. Heileman had lost another $22 million, more than half of it interest on loans taken out by the Dallas-based investment firm when it purchased the company. Sales were down by 17 percent. Heileman's own products had fallen by about 11 percent, but the worst decline came in contract brewing, which was down by 32 percent.

By this time, Heileman had quit filing reports with the U.S. Securities and Exchange Commission. A *La Crosse Tribune* article on December 21, 1995, reported, "Following several quarters of losses, the company has stopped filing reports with the U.S. Securities and Exchange Commission. Recently (Randy) Smith said Heileman had changed its method of distributing financial information because of negative publicity. Instead, the privately held company gives reports directly to investors and creditors, as allowed by the SEC rules."

At the end of January 1996, Heileman failed to make its required interest payments and its Standard & Poor's rating fell to a D, the lowest yet. Industry analysts predicted a second bankruptcy.

The Heileman Corporate Headquarters II office building at Second and State streets in La Crosse, empty for almost 18 months, went up for sale for $375,000. Ever since the 1992 move of executives and sales staff to Chicago, there had been an excess of office space in La Crosse.

Heileman was actively trying to sell the Colt 45 brand for $150 million. Both Anheuser-Busch and Miller were interested, but neither offered more than $100 million. Henry Weinhard sales in the Midwest and Eastern markets proved disappointing, and the brand was withdrawn there. Smith announced the company still intended to introduce Henry Weinhard in all 50 states, but the goal was moved out another four years.

As it closed in on the end of the 30-day grace period after the missed debt payments, it appeared the only remaining options were to sell the company outright or attempt another bankruptcy and restructuring. Even after the previous bankruptcy, Heileman was $300 million in debt, including about $160 million from bonds sold in January 1994 by Hicks, Muse, Tate & Furst Incorporated when it purchased the company.

On March 1, 1996, a headline in the *La Crosse Tribune* confirmed Stroh had purchased G. Heileman Brewing Company and the end of the line had come. William Henry, president of Stroh, and Lowenkron made a joint announcement. They stressed that together the two companies had an excellent portfolio of brands and strategically located breweries around the United States. Heileman breweries included in the sale were those in La Crosse, Baltimore, San Antonio, Portland, and Seattle; brands were Old Style, Special Export, Rainier, Henry Weinhard, Schmidt's, Lone Star, Champale, Colt 45, and Mickey's. At the time of the purchase, Heileman had 2,200 employees, including 831 in La Crosse.

Stroh had about 2,300 employees and operated breweries in: Saint Paul, Minnesota; Longview, Texas; Lehigh Valley, Pennsylvania; Winston-Salem, North Carolina; and Tampa, Florida. Its primary brands were Stroh, Schlitz, Old Milwaukee, Schaefer, and Schlitz Malt Liquor. The deal was expected to be completed by July 1. Heileman would file for bankruptcy, after which Stroh would pick up the remainder of the estimated $317 million in Heileman debt.

Closing Saddens La Crosse

Residents of La Crosse were shocked, saddened, and fearful when the closing of G. Heileman Brewing Company was announced. Patrick Zielke, La Crosse's mayor, noted it was the end of a long era in La Crosse. He hoped Stroh realized just how special Heileman was to La Crosse and would support not only the brewery, but also the city.

Russ Cleary blamed Heileman's eventual demise on the 1981 decision by the U.S. Justice Department, which blocked a proposed Heileman-Schlitz merger. He also predicted there would be three keys to its success under Stroh ownership: consolidation of the company's 10 breweries, increased contract brewing, and the intelligent incorporation of Heileman brands into the Stroh mix. He described the Stroh team as good people and beer people.

Shortly after the announcement, more than 100 former and soon-to-be former Heileman employees gathered at Sloopy's Alma Mater tavern near the La Crosse brewery for a farewell party. Dave Berger, owner of Sloopy's, provided the food and drink to thank the employees and Heileman for years of support. Employee emotions ranged from sadness to anger.

Still, most felt they had been treated fairly by Stroh, which offered severance packages, resume and interview training, job search support, and classes in stress management.

In the meantime, the company would be run by an oversight committee composed of representatives of investment firms, along with Lowenkron, Smith and Daniel J. Schmid Jr. from the brewery. In early May 1996, Lowenkron was terminated with a severance package. Smith, long-time Heileman vice president and corporate counsel, and Schmid, the chief financial officer, also were terminated and received severance packages.

Stroh announced that headquarters for the merged company would be in Detroit, Michigan, but that production would continue in La Crosse. Heileman facilities in Rosemont, Illinois, would be closed, and most of the headquarters operations in La Crosse would move to Detroit.

Heileman breweries in Portland and Seattle were especially valuable to Stroh, which was selling beer in 80 foreign markets, especially in Japan and Hong Kong. Prior to the merger, Stroh's closest brewery to the Pacific Northwest and overseas markets was its aging plant in Saint Paul.

In early April 1996, Heileman officially declared bankruptcy for the second time, $753.6 million in debt. The largest creditor was U.S. Trust Company of New York, which held almost $169 million in bonds. The list included many other creditors, all the way down to the Wisconsin Department of Revenue, which was owed $25. Stroh agreed to issue $70 million in bonds to assume Heileman's debt as fiduciary for beneficial owners.

The Cleary Alumni &Friends Center, completed in June 1995 at 615 East Avenue North, houses the offices of the University of Wisconsin-La Crosse Foundation, which had the building constructed with the assistance of the Cleary family. Both Russ and Gail Cleary graduated from UW-L.

PHOTO COURTESY OF UW-L FOUNDATION

Chapter 17

Fire Brewed Owners

THE STROH YEARS

1996–1999

Union members were upset that the existing balance of $800,000 in their treasury didn't belong to them.

The G. Heileman Brewing Company officially ceased to exist on July 1, 1996.

William Henry, Stroh's chief executive officer, assured employees and La Crosse residents the Heileman brands would live on. He also vowed that the giant Heileman six-pack would not be painted over, and said he had no intention of placing a big Stroh sign on the brewery.

Some corporate employees were offered full-time work with Stroh in Detroit and some were offered up to six months of transitional employment. About 60 employees at Heileman's headquarters and sales office in Chicago also lost their jobs.

The combined company had more than 1,400 distributors, and about 500 already carried products from both breweries. Henry wanted to reduce the number of distributors.

He made it clear he wasn't satisfied with a fourth-place standing in the brewing industry, but the beer business was highly competitive and profit margins in the United States were the lowest in the world. For example, in the United States beer sold for as little as $6 to $7 a case, while in Canada it sold for almost $30 and in Japan for $48.

Stroh, which advertised its beer as being "fire brewed," began to consolidate the two brewers' assets less than a month after the merger was completed. The Heileman Lone Star Brewery in San Antonio closed and production of Lone Star was transferred to the Stroh Brewery in Longview, Texas. A seven-person field sales office was kept open.

The Perry, Georgia, plant was also closed, on September 27, and between 100 and 150 more workers lost their jobs. The closing was blamed on the non-renewal of the contract to brew Arizona Iced Tea.

Next, the Carling Brewery in Baltimore closed on December 20. Stroh facilities in Lehigh Valley, Pennsylvania, and Winston-Salem, North Carolina, were more modern and would assume the bulk of the production from Baltimore.

Shortly after the announcement of the Baltimore closing, Henry and eight of the nine members of the Stroh board of directors visited La Crosse. Although they had no plans to close additional breweries, they said they would be shifting production to breweries as geography dictated.

Employees at the La Crosse brewery were upbeat after the visit. Baltimore production would move to La Crosse, they were told, as well as some production of Old Milwaukee. Stroh wanted to have the facility running as close to its 4.4-million-barrel capacity as possible.

But Stroh's third quarter sales dropped by a half million barrels, down 1.15 million barrels for the first nine months. Sales were down for every major brewer except Anheuser-Busch.

In December 1996, Russ Cleary, former Heileman president, announced he was going to purchase the Heileman Corporate Headquarters building in La Crosse for about $4 million from Stroh and would lease the building to the Postalsoft software company. Things were looking good in La Crosse, with sales for April 1997 up more than 16 percent over 1996. The brewery was running near capacity and shipping products to a larger geographic area than ever before. It was working 9.5-hour shifts, six or seven days a week. Not only had all of the laid-off workers been recalled, but also an additional four production workers had been hired. The plant was producing Old Style, Special Export, EX-Light, Old Milwaukee, Schlitz, and Schlitz Malt Liquor.

But in late May 1997, Stroh announced that sales for the entire company had declined 6.5 percent for the first quarter. By August, the news was even worse. Sales were down 12 percent for the second quarter and Stroh announced its Saint Paul plant would close in November. Good news for La Crosse was Stroh's announcement of plans for $9 million in improvements to the brewery there in 1997 and 1998 to handle the additional production of Schmidt's City Club and Augsburger brands from Saint Paul.

Sales of specialty beers had slowed dramatically throughout the industry, and Anheuser-Busch and Miller initiated a brutal price-cutting war. Stroh officials said they wouldn't be leaders in the price war, but had no alternative but to react in markets where it was attacked. Analysts doubted Stroh could survive for long under these conditions.

Year-end results for 1997 showed Stroh's market share had dropped from 8.9 percent to 7.9 percent, and it had shipped only 15.87 million barrels. At their peak in 1983, Heileman and Stroh together had shipped more than 41 million barrels. Anheuser-Busch's market share was up to 45.8 percent, Miller remained in second place with a steady 21.8 percent, and Coors was in third place with a slight increase to 10.2 percent.

Sales for the first quarter of 1998 were down another 17 percent, and for the first time there were rumors that the entire Stroh company, or the brewery in La Crosse, might be put up for sale. By May, Stroh had been severely hurt in the price wars between Anheuser-Busch and Miller. In late June, Pabst announced it had reached an agreement with Miller to be the brewer for all of the Pabst brands. Stroh had been producing 2.35 million barrels for Pabst, about a third of the production in La Crosse, and word of the new agreement sent yet another shock wave through the city, as the lost contract meant production there would drop by 20 percent effective September 1. It was the first time in history one of the three major beer companies had entered into a contract brewing arrangement. Analysts agreed on one thing—the news was not good for Stroh, and they didn't know how the company could survive the blow.

By mid-August, Stroh had laid off about 100 seasonal temporary employees, and in the next two weeks another 100 regular full-time employees were laid off, some with as much as 18 years of seniority at the brewery. Stroh said staffing would be analyzed on a month-by-month basis, but future layoffs were expected. Stroh also laid off workers in Winston-Salem, Lehigh, and Tampa.

When Stroh announced third-quarter results, profits were up more than 20 percent. But the bulk of the increase came from the sale of $11 million in assets during the first half of the year, including several breweries and specialty products.

By the end of October, a story in the *Milwaukee Journal Sentinel* reported that Pabst and Miller were going to buy Stroh.

In December, Stroh suddenly announced it would close its Tampa brewery in January 1999, and most industry analysts predicted Stroh could not survive the year. Shipments for 1998 had declined another 15 percent and market share fell from 7.9 to 6.7 percent. Because of sales of assets, Stroh was financially strong and reducing debt ahead of schedule, but analysts still saw no alternative for Stroh other than to sell the company.

Entering 1999, Anheuser-Busch gained another 1.1 percent to hold a commanding 46.7 market share. Miller was second after a slight decline to 21.2 percent and Coors had gained slightly to 10.5 percent. Stroh was fourth with 6.7 percent and Pabst was fifth, declining from 2.4 to 2 percent.

In early February 1999, Stroh sold most of its assets to Pabst for $400 million. John Stroh III, chief executive officer of the parent Stroh Corporation, said the company had struggled with the emotional decision, but in the end saw no alternative, and concluded it was time to exit the brutal world of brewing and concentrate on other ventures. He vowed to do everything possible to limit the impact on loyal employees.

The deal included Stroh's brewery in Lehigh, Pennsylvania, and most of the Heileman brands. But Pabst wasn't interested in buying the other five Stroh breweries, which included the one in La Crosse. Miller bought the Henry Weinhard, Mickey's Malt Liquor, Hamm's, and Old English 800 brands, boosting its presence in that market.

A mixture of fear, panic, disappointment, anger and, finally, guarded optimism hit La Crosse. The 495 hourly production workers and 80 salaried employees received a letter urging them to continue to work hard and produce a quality product. The letter reminded them the deal had not been completed and if it were to fall through, their future relied on the company's reputation.

Unemployment was very low in La Crosse at the time, and it was thought most management employees would be able to find other work. Production workers faced a more difficult task—finding work that paid as well. The average production worker was earning about $35,000 a year at the brewery. Local suppliers such as Niedfeldt Trucking and American Warehousing worried about the effect on their businesses, and La Crosse retailers and the city itself feared the worst. The brewery was a major contributor to the tax base and utilities in the city.

Heileman and its employees also played a major role in funding La Crosse community festivals such as Oktoberfest and Riverfest, and numerous charitable organizations. Events such as wedding receptions and parties held in Heileman Hall would have to be rescheduled elsewhere after September 1.

La Crosse Mayor John Medinger was doubtful a buyer could be found for the brewery. He set up a task force of 40 members representing the company, city, county, state, and other groups to brainstorm some sort of reuse for the eight square blocks that had been Heileman, as well as find new jobs for the brewery's displaced workers.

During the transition period production continued at the brewery until it could be moved to one of the Pabst or Miller breweries. Federal law required at least 60 days formal notice before the facility could be closed.

Ron Buschman, secretary-treasurer of Brewery Workers Local 1081, encouraged workers to start planning for the worst. He tried to answer their numerous questions about severance, pensions, and medical benefits, and also encouraged them to take advantage of the other services and benefits available. The Western Wisconsin Private Industry Council received a grant of $60,000 to assist employees in résumé writing, searching for job openings, and classroom training.

Medinger contacted Stroh to discuss the future of the Heileman home at 925 South Third Street, calling it a historical treasure and inquiring about the possibility of turning it into a bed and breakfast or brewery museum. He was also interested in preserving the World's Largest Six-Pack across from the brewery. Stroh officials understood that certain assets had a special meaning to the city and said they would do their best to work with them.

In early March, John W. Stroh III, a seventh-generation member of the Stroh brewing family, came to La Crosse to try to address local concerns. He said Stroh wouldn't sell the brewery until the deal was completed and said that no purchase price had been set. He cautioned it was unlikely a buyer could be found for it.

The union contract was set to expire on March 1. Several weeks earlier, the union voted to authorize a strike if a new agreement wasn't reached. At the same meeting, union members agreed to limit the negotiations to issues of pension and severance pay and thanked La Crosse residents and officials for their support.

A one-year contract agreement had been reached, with no wage increases, but guaranteeing existing pension benefits for retirees and active employees. Buschman noted the employees were realists and knew if they went on strike the brewery would be closed and employees would be left with nothing. But union members were upset that the existing balance of $800,000 in their treasury didn't belong to them. The constitution of the Teamsters Union contained a clause that such funds would go to the union's international treasury should a local union be dissolved.

Every possible avenue was pursued to prevent the brewery from closing, and state and federal lawyers were contacted to see if there was any hope that Wisconsin or federal anti-trust law could be used to block the deal. But state officials and the U.S. Department of Justice said they would not block the deal, and Stroh was free to sell or dismantle the brewery in any way it saw fit.

City officials sought interest from the investors from Saint Paul who had purchased the Schmidt brewery from Heileman back in 1991, but that company was losing money and didn't offer much hope. The Mayor's Task Force turned its attention to raising funds to hire consultants and finance trips to La Crosse for potential buyers. The group hoped for a budget of $262,000, and requested a $35,000 donation from Stroh, which contributed $10,000.

The commission asked the city of La Crosse and La Crosse County for donations. La Crosse County approved a $25,000 contribution. The request to the city met controversy, with some members of the Common Council arguing a donation would set a bad precedent, but the city eventually approved a $25,000 donation. The commission approached the brewery union for a donation, but Teamsters bylaws prevented it from making local donations. Wisconsin Governor Tommy Thompson announced that Forward Wisconsin, an agency to promote Wisconsin businesses, would donate $5,000.

As hopes for a domestic buyer for the brewery waned, officials started to investigate the idea of foreign investors. Medinger met with the Wisconsin Department of Commerce about the possibility of a foreign brewer taking over the facility, and U.S. Representative Ron Kind of La Crosse contacted Miller, Coors, and several Canadian brewers to see if they were interested in it. State Senator Brian Rude, who lived just south of La Crosse, offered to work with the state's foreign trade office to determine if there was anything it could do to help.

Then in mid-April, Stroh announced it had found a buyer for its brewery in Tampa, Florida—D.G. Yuengling & Sons, a small regional brewer from Pottsville, Pennsylvania. News of the purchase raised hopes in La Crosse that a similar buyer might still be found. Stroh announced it planned to close the La Crosse brewery in July, much earlier than expected. The announcement gave a new urgency to the search for a buyer and plans for the laid-off workers.

Shortly after the announcement of the July closing was made, a new proposal raised hopes of the employees. Ted Solie, a La Crosse resident, offered to sell rights to the Peerless label originally owned by John Gund's brewery and later La Crosse Breweries Inc. of La Crosse. The city buzzed with excitement about the possibility of brewing the local brand again. The proposal also called for a group of local investors to purchase the brewery and equipment from Stroh for $3 million to $4 million in order to produce the Peerless brand. The idea was a long shot, since the brewery and equipment had an assessed value of more than $28 million.

On April 30, 1999, the deal with Miller and Pabst was finalized, and Stroh Brewing Company ceased to exist. Miller Brewing contracted with Pabst to produce Old Style, Old Style Light, Special Export, and Special Export Light in Milwaukee and Trenton, Ohio. Miller officials promised beer drinkers there would be no noticeable difference in taste. As the closing date approached, sale of Heileman products began to drop in the La Crosse area, where it had accounted for 60 percent of the market.

More than 90 percent of the brewery's employees were male and almost 60 percent of them were 45 or older. Less than 5 percent of the workers indicated they would retire. Of the rest, almost 60 percent indicated they intended to obtain some type of retraining before looking for a new job, and more than 63 percent of the employees indicated they preferred to stay in the La Crosse area rather than relocate.

John Satory, a member of both the La Crosse Common Council and the La Crosse Historic Preservation Commission, nominated the Heileman home, 925 South Third Street, and the old Heileman brewhouse, 1000 South Third Street, for the city's historic preservation list. The original "City Brewery" name was still on the brewhouse. Once approved, the buildings could not be torn down without the permission of the commission.

Members of the La Crosse County Historical Society contacted Stroh and requested that anything of historical significance to Heileman be given to the society, saying it was willing to accept and preserve any such materials. Stroh responded it had very little other than a few barrels and one crate of advertising materials and bottles. They said the brewery had changed owners so many times that a lot had been lost.

Mayor Medinger sent a request to John Stroh III to keep all equipment in place in the brewery to make it easier to find a buyer. He also requested that Stroh make all financial records available to a brewery consultant involved in trying to find a buyer.

But Medinger's request appeared to be too late, as some of the bottling and packaging equipment from the brewery had been sold to Miller and Pabst as part of the deal. Stroh officials told Medinger that if a buyer were found for the brewery, similar equipment could readily be obtained from some of the other breweries it had closed.

The La Crosse Area Development Corporation produced a brochure with a photo of the King Gambrinus statue on the cover and an aerial photo of the brewery and statistics about it inside, which was mailed to hundreds of manufacturing companies around the country.

On May 29, Stroh gave employees of both the La Crosse and Winston-Salem breweries the required 60-day notice that the breweries would be closed on July 30, and their employment would terminate during the 14-day period from July 30 to August 13. The severance package offered included one week's pay for each three years of service and up to six months of continued medical coverage.

In the middle of the month, a German company contacted Medinger and inquired about the brewery. Later in June, James Ehrsam, the La Crosse County board chairman, organized a visit to the brewery by a group of Polish and German brewers. The Onalaska City Council donated $2,000 toward the cost of hosting the delegation.

The German delegation represented 15 regional brewers from the Bavaria region of Germany, while the Polish one included four high-level members of the Polish parliament. Both groups were interested in having their products available in the United States. They told officials they could not afford to purchase the brewery, but would be interested in having their products made there.

In the middle of July, Brewery Workers Local 1081 held a picnic for all current and retired employees of the brewery at the South Side Oktoberfest Grounds. People continued to hold out hope that foreign brewers or other investors would still be found, and there were new rumors that New York investors, led by a former La Crosse resident, had spent several days touring the brewery and were serious about buying it. Buschman, however, continued to encourage employees to plan for the worst and continue with their retraining and education plans.

Chapter 18

A Brand New Start

REBIRTH OF THE CITY BREWERY 1999–2003

I may be the first brewmaster at City Brewery, but I won't be the last. We're going to be here for a long time.

—RANDY HUGHES, BREWMASTER AT CITY BREWERY

With less than two weeks to go before La Crosse's brewery was to be closed, headlines proclaimed that a buyer had been found. James J. Strupp, a 55-year-old La Crosse native, and his business partner, John D. Mazzuto, purchased the brewery as Platinum Holding Investment Company.

Strupp, a 1961 graduate of La Crosse Aquinas High School and then Marquette University, grew up in La Crescent, Minnesota. Described as very outgoing and personable, Strupp had a reputation for being a workaholic and was known to put in 18-hour days. He had worked in the energy, textile, steel, and insurance industries, but had essentially no experience in the brewing industry. He had recently retired as human resources director for the specialty chemical division of GAF Corporation and had a reputation for being a top-flight union negotiator, respected by both union officials and company management. Above all else, he was known as a man with high values and exceptional integrity.

Strupp's business partner, Mazzuto, also had no experience in brewing. Mazzuto had recently retired to spend more time with his family. The two of them had known each other for 25 years and had started Platinum Holdings in 1997, acquiring nine small and medium-sized human resource companies. They also were actively pursuing the purchase of a savings and loan bank and a small insurance company, both located in New Jersey.

Brewery employees and residents of La Crosse were thrilled by the announcement. Strupp said they intended to either purchase or establish a brand of beer for regional distribution, and wanted to become involved in producing bottled water or juice. He attempted to purchase former Heileman brands but they had been sold to Pabst, which was not interested in giving them up. Strupp estimated the brewery could reopen as early as September, might employ 50 to 75 initially, and eventually could employ up to 250. As part of the announcement, Strupp also agreed to recognize the local union and call workers back based on seniority.

Randy Smith, former Heileman vice president, agreed to run the brewery, and he and his family returned to La Crosse from the Chicago area. It was hoped his return would give the brewery the expertise it needed. Smith and the rest of the management team contacted Pabst and inquired about contract brewing. They also studied the possibility of producing ready-to-drink tea and even ethanol at the plant.

Strupp and Mazzuto negotiated tax incentives and financing over a six-week period with: the city of La Crosse, La Crosse County, and the Wisconsin Department of Commerce. The plans called for Platinum Holdings to develop a final purchase agreement and business plan and acquire the company within the following 30 to 60 days.

Strupp set to work on obtaining local, state, and federal funding, and estimated he needed $50 million to purchase and restart the brewery. He set out to obtain $16.7 million of it from all three levels of government, along with funding from Northern States Power Company. He asked the city of La Crosse for $200,000 from its commercial revitalization program and asked the city and county together to provide $5 million. From Wisconsin, he sought $5 million in working capital, $500,000 for worker training, and $3 million in income tax credits. From the federal government he wanted $2 million in economic aid, and finally, $1 million from Northern States Power Company (now Xcel Energy) to help with marketing programs and strategic planning. Platinum Holdings would contribute the other $34 million. Strupp justified the amounts by noting he didn't want the company to start under an enormous debt load, as it had when Alan Bond had taken over Heileman.

The $8.5 million sought from the state was the largest request ever received by the Wisconsin Department of Commerce. The state asked Strupp to provide it with a copy of his business plan and monthly cash flow projections, and eventually agreed to offer $3 million in low-interest loans and funds for training.

Mayor Medinger and James Ehrsam, chairman of the La Crosse County Board, reacted to the request with concern and skepticism. Both the city and county board held special sessions that lasted all evening and were closed to the public. Ehrsam called it a "no-win" situation. If the county didn't approve the money it would be blamed for the lost jobs, but if it approved the loans and the brewery failed, they'd all look like suckers.

Strupp pressed the city and the county for a decision, saying he was spending $20,000 a day on expenses and needed action. Stroh threatened to begin removing and selling equipment from the brewery if the situation was not resolved soon.

After much debate, the city and county voted by a wide margin to approve $3 million in loans to Platinum Holdings. As part of the decision, they wanted viable collateral, a signed contract for specified production, and a letter of commitment from Platinum Holdings. In the event the brewery was sold within five years the loans would have to be repaid with interest. Strupp was pleased, but Ehrsam felt the city and county had been stampeded into a decision they might regret down the road.

Strupp and Mazzuto made it clear they intended to run the company very differently. They vowed to find ways to get employees more involved, give them a financial stake in the future of the company, and work closely with the labor union. But they also made it clear that concessions would be required to keep costs low.

Union leader Ron Buschman began labor negotiations with Strupp for a new contract with the union workers and, being realistic, knew they probably couldn't get the $17 an hour they had been earning. After several days of talks, the union overwhelmingly approved a new 4.5-year contract with Platinum Holdings for $15 an hour, with cost-of-living increases in the third and fourth years. Under previous Stroh contracts some overtime was paid double, but this contract was only for time and a half. However, seven percent of the operating profits would be distributed to the employees under a profit-sharing program. Buschman was pleased with the settlement and called it a fair deal.

As the deadline for Stroh's closure of the brewery approached, there was still no formal agreement. Stroh extended the deadline by several days to allow Strupp time to complete his financing. He traveled to Milwaukee to meet with Miller to discuss contract brewing and again expressed interest in obtaining either brands or contract brewing from Pabst. He was especially interested in brewing Old Style and Special Export, which Miller was making under contract for Pabst at this point.

As the new company searched for a name, it considered Golden Leaf, used by Heileman prior to the 1902 introduction of Old Style. Industry analysts warned that introducing new brands was very difficult, and that the key to success would be contract brewing or possibly the production of bottled water. However, contract brewing and the number of specialty beers had declined from 150 in 1995 to 91 in 1998. Strupp also announced Stroh had agreed to sell the brewery to him with all of the equipment included. Previously Stroh had said some of the equipment had been sold to Pabst as part of the earlier deal.

Platinum Holdings purchased the brewery for $10.5 million on August 7, the day after it closed. The new company would be named City Brewery, reverting to its original name from the 19th century, and would reopen in the fourth quarter with 50 workers. Long-term plans were to have 300 employees within three years. Strupp was thrilled by the purchase. He pointed out that the replacement cost for the brewery alone was probably close to $400 million.

Between 10 and 15 employees continued to work at the brewery to maintain the equipment and keep it operational during the transition. About 25 more stayed on doing final cleanup.

Smith announced that other former Heileman executives were considering joining the management team and that he would contact former Heileman distributors about carrying the new local brand of beer. He was optimistic that personal contacts from the past would prove beneficial to the new company.

Other local businesses also looked forward to the success of the new brewery. C&C Machine Incorporated had done contract machining and fabrication for the brewery for more than 20 years. In 1972, Heileman business accounted for 58 percent of its total business. Crown Cork & Seal had supplied aluminum cans to the brewery, but lost the contract when Stroh took over. The city of La Crosse hoped the brewery would once again attract tourism. Local tavern keepers and owners of liquor stores also welcomed the new brewery, noting a recent backlash against Heileman products and a corresponding decrease in overall sales.

But the purchase by Platinum Holdings dragged out into early October 1999, threatening Smith's plans to begin production of beer in October and have it available between Thanksgiving and Christmas. The new brands were to be named City Lager and City Lager Light.

Pabst officially announced it had no plans to sell the Old Style or Special Export brands to City Brewery, as the brands were two of its more popular and successful in Chicago, Milwaukee, and Madison. A 10-year contract with Miller would not allow Pabst to contract with City Brewery, but officials were still hopeful a contract could be obtained from Miller.

Things appeared to be going well for the new brewery initially. City Lager won a silver medal in June at the World Beer Cup awards, and City Brewery received high marks from the companies that had hired it for contract brewing. Brewmaster Randy Hughes was immensely proud of the silver medal—winning an award in the first year of operation was almost unheard of in the brewing industry.

But financial difficulties began to crop up in March 2000, and by May and June the company had begun to run out of money. With suppliers filing lawsuits against it for unpaid bills, City Brewery ran out of cans and bottles in August 2000 and had to lay off most of its 62 workers. Strupp admitted he had underestimated the capital required to get the brewery going again.

However, not everyone was ready to throw in the towel. A core team of employees continued to work without being paid. With Oktoberfest approaching, Hughes decided to develop a new beer specifically for Oktoberfest. With no money to buy new supplies, he used only ingredients he still had available in the brewery. The result was City Fest Bier, "The official beer of Oktoberfest USA."

Another buyout was proposed, this time by employees and an investor group. Smith felt the brewery was one of the best in the country and still a viable place to make beer. He also said the workers there deserved medals for going above and beyond the call of duty to keep it open.

On November 3, 2000, a dozen investors formed CBC Acquisitions to purchase City Brewing Corporation. Six former Heileman officials were in the group.

In addition to the 12 primary investors, employees put in their own money to buy the last 12 percent of the company. As of 2002, the brewery was the largest locally owned and employee-owned brewery in the United States. The CBC Acquisitions management team immediately moved to pay off some of the debt.

By September 2003, City Brewery employed about 330 people, and produced its own line of beers, including City Lager, City Lager Light, La Crosse Lager, La Crosse Light, City Cream Ale,

Work without Pay

Many Heileman workers continued to work without pay after the brewery was shut down in La Crosse. They had no other job to go to and their pride and loyalty left them feeling that somehow the brewery would survive.

One of those employees was brewmaster Randy Hughes. In the early 1980s, Hughes remembered working the night shift and watching the new brewhouse being built. Back in 1981, he gazed at the 40-foot-deep holes where the new giant brew kettles would be installed. He dreamed about the opportunities and possibilities those kettles would bring to Heileman. Now he found himself staring at those same brew kettles and wondering what the future would bring.

The actual closing of the brewery had an impact on La Crosse, as was expected. Unemployment in La Crosse jumped from 2.8 to 3.3 percent and the average manufacturing hourly wage decreased from $12.63 in July to $12.12 in August. Fortunately, many local employers were still hiring.

In November 1999, the U.S. Department of Labor announced $1.29 million in retraining money for workers in the La Crosse area who had lost their jobs at Heileman. The money included funding for job counseling, job search, vocational training, and other job and educational services. Workers formed a weekly club that met from 8:30 to 10 A.M. every Tuesday morning in the Wisconsin Job Center in La Crosse. They discussed job tips, job openings, and interviewing, and provided support for each other.

The laid-off workers indicated they didn't miss the work as much as they missed their coworkers. As of June 30, 2000, Workforce Connections had helped 441 former Heileman workers. Of those, 194 had found other jobs, but their average hourly wage was $14.71 versus $17.53 at the brewery. More than 250 former workers received training at Western Wisconsin Technical College. The average wage in La Crosse continued to drop to $12.58 from $13.01 a year earlier.

City Pale Ale, City Fest Bier, City Winter Porter, Kül, and Kül Light. The company also relied heavily on contract brewing for Stroh brands for Sleeman Breweries Limited of Canada and a variety of malt beverages including Smirnoff Ice, and Mike's Hard Lemonade. It also had contracted to brew and bottle Arizona Teas.

In 1999, when Stroh closed the brewery, the famous Old Style Six-Pack had been painted white. Four years later, on September 26, 2003, City Brewery held a ceremony to unveil the new La Crosse Lager Six-Pack with the new logo. Hundreds of employees, former employees, and loyal beer drinkers gathered in the rain across from the brewery to watch the ceremony. Jon Reynolds, City Brewery director of marketing and sales, introduced Smith and La Crosse Mayor John Medinger, and each spoke briefly about the importance of the brewery to La Crosse.

Helping with the unveiling ceremonies for the City Brewery's Six-Pack were, from left: John Medinger, mayor of La Crosse; Randy Smith, City Brewery's chief executive officer; and Paul Ricker, investor in City Brewery.
PHOTO COURTESY OF PAUL D. KOELLER

Following the speeches, investor Paul Ricker counted down as groups of employees, dressed in matching T-shirts and red baseball caps, lowered the blue tarps. They unveiled the new six-pack, once again standing proud and tall as a tribute to the thousands of employees, distributors, and customers who had been part of the long brewing history in La Crosse.

After the ceremony the crowd headed to a beer tent set up behind the visitor center to continue the celebration. At 4 P.M., Hughes tapped a wooden keg of City Fest Bier and declared the 2003 City Fest officially open. "I may be the first brewmaster at City Brewery, but I won't be the last. We're going to be here for a long time," he said.

Chapter 19

Heileman Highlights

1824–2003

1872—Gottlieb Heileman wins a coin toss and takes sole control of City Brewery.

1824	Johann Gottlieb Heilemann is born on January 6 in the southern German province of Wurttemberg in the village of Kirchheim unter Teck.
1830	John Gund is born on October 3 in Baden, Germany.
1848	John Gund immigrates to the United States and settles in Galena, Illinois.
1852	Gottlieb Heilemann immigrates to the United States and settles in Philadelphia. John Gund moves to Dubuque, Iowa, and works in a brewery owned by Anton Heeb.
1853	Gottlieb Heileman moves to Milwaukee and opens a bakery with Gottlieb Maier.
1854	John Gund moves to La Crosse, and opens a small brewery in a log cabin on the southeast corner of Front and Division streets.
1857	Gottlieb Heileman sells his interest in the bakery in Milwaukee and moves to La Crosse.
1858	Gottlieb Heileman marries Johanna Bandle in Milwaukee. Gottlieb Heileman and John Gund enter into a partnership and open City Brewery in La Crosse.
1870	Gottlieb Heileman completes a new large brick home at 925 South Third Street in La Crosse.

1872	Gottlieb Heileman and John Gund decide to part ways. Heileman wins a coin toss and takes sole control of City Brewery. Gund gets control of other property and opens his own Empire Brewery on South Avenue, near the present site of Lutheran Hospital.
1878	Gottlieb Heileman dies on February 19. His wife, Johanna, takes control of the brewery.
1881	Emil T. Mueller marries Louisa Heileman on May 17 and begins employment at City Brewery.
1884	Emil T. Mueller is named general manager of City Brewery and leads the company to a period of unprecedented growth over the next several decades.
1885	The brewery opens its first agency (later called branches) in Glencoe, Minnesota. Additional branches are quickly established in other cities in Wisconsin, Minnesota, Iowa, Illinois, and South Dakota.
1890	The company is incorporated on May 5 as G. Heileman Brewing Company. Johanna Heileman is elected president. She is the first female chief executive officer of a brewery in United States history.
1900	Heileman introduces the Old Times Lager brand in addition to its existing Golden Leaf brand.
1902	Heileman changes the Old Times Lager name to Old Style Lager and copyrights the Old Style Lager label.
1919	The 18th Amendment is ratified on January 16. Effective May 1, brewing beer is prohibited in the United States. Heileman survives Prohibition by selling near beer, malt syrups, and extracts.
1932	Roy E. Kumm joins Heileman as an accountant.
1933	The sale of 3.2 percent (alcohol by volume) beer becomes legal on April 7. Heileman immediately begins to ship beer, and is reincorporated as G. Heileman Brewing Company on July 19.
1934	Heileman introduces the Special Export brand.
1935	Heileman begins selling Old Style Lager in metal cone-top cans.
1957	Roy E. Kumm becomes president of Heileman. He decides the company must acquire other breweries in order to survive in the brewing industry.
1959	Heileman buys Kingsbury Brewing Company of Sheboygan, Wisconsin. In addition to the brewery Heileman gets the Kingsbury, Fox Head, Weber, and Old Waukesha brands. A massive fire destroys the original Heileman Bavarian-style bottle house and corporate offices.
1960	Roy Kumm hires Russell G. Cleary as a lawyer for Heileman.
1961	Heileman and the city of La Crosse jointly sponsor the first Oktoberfest in La Crosse.

1962	Heileman buys the assets of the Independent Milwaukee Brewery and gets the Braumeister brand.
1963	Heileman buys Duluth Brewing and Malting Company of Duluth, Minnesota.
1964	Heileman buys the assets of the Gluek Brewery in Minneapolis, and gets the Stite brand.
1967	Heileman buys the George Wiedemann Brewery of Newport, Kentucky, getting the Wiedemann brands and a brewery in Newport, Kentucky. Heileman buys the Oertel Brewing Company of Louisville, Kentucky, and get the Oertel brands. Heileman buys Machine Products Company of La Crosse. The company manufactures precision parts for the aerospace industry.
1969	Heileman buys Blatz Brewing Company assets from Pabst and gets the Blatz brand.
1970	Heileman buys Erickson Bakery in La Crosse and Federated Bakery in Winona, Minnesota.
1971	Roy E. Kumm dies and Russell G. Cleary is elected chief executive officer by the board of directors.
1972	Heileman buys Associated Brewing Company of Detroit, Michigan. The purchase includes the Jacob Schmidt brewery in Saint Paul, Minnesota, the Sterling brewery in Evansville, Indiana, and the Drewry's brewery in South Bend, Indiana, which it closes. Brands acquired include Schmidt, Drewrys, Sterling, and Pfeiffer.
1975	Anheuser-Busch suffers a lengthy strike and Schlitz makes a negative change to its brewing formula. These events allow Heileman to make significant inroads into the Chicago market.
1976	Heileman buys the Grain Belt brands. Heileman buys the Rainier brewery of Seattle, and gets the Rainier brands.
1978	Heileman buys the Falls City and Drummond Brothers brands.
1979	Heileman buys Carling National Breweries Incorporated of Baltimore, also obtaining breweries in Frankenmuth, Michigan, Belleville, Illinois, Phoenix, Arizona, and Tacoma, Washington (which it closes). Heileman gets the Carling, National, Stag, Heidelberg, Colt 45, Tuborg, and Carlsberg brands. Heileman buys Our Own Bakeries of Marquette, Michigan. Heileman named sole distributor in 21 states for Beck beer from Germany. Heileman moves into new corporate headquarters in Harborview in La Crosse.
1980	Heileman buys Duncan Brewing Company of Auburndale, Florida. Heileman buys Bake Rite Baking Company of Plover, Wisconsin. Heileman surpasses Trane Company in sales to become the largest company in La Crosse.

1981	Heileman buys Barrel O' Fun Snack Foods of Perham, Minnesota.
	Heileman announces a merger with Schlitz. The merger is blocked by the U.S. Justice Department.
1982	Heileman, Pabst, and Olympia announce a complicated three-way merger. Heileman gets the huge Pabst brewery in Perry, Georgia, the Lone Star brewery in San Antonio, Texas, and the Henry Weinhard brewery in Portland, Oregon. Heileman also gets the Henry Weinhard, Lone Star, and Red White and Blue brands, along with contracts to brew Pabst.
	Alan Bond decides to get into brewing and buys the Swan Brewery in Perth, Australia.
1983	Heileman buys Red Seal Quality Foods Incorporated of Denver.
	Annual sales at Heileman exceed $1 billion for the first time.
1984	Heileman buys Cold Spring Sparkling Mineral Water from Cold Spring Brewery of Minnesota.
	Heileman named sole importer of Presidente Pilsner from the Dominican Republic.
	Heileman buys Mrs. Howe's Food Products of Milwaukee, Wisconsin.
	Heileman attempts to buy Pabst Brewing, but the deal is blocked by the U.S. Justice Department.
1985	Heileman buys New Process Bakery of Chicago.
	Heileman buys Johnson Nut Company of Willmar, Minnesota.
	Alan Bond buys Castlemaine Toohey Brewery in Brisbane, Australia.
1986	Alan Bond buys Pittsburgh Brewing Company.
	Heileman named sole importer of Moravia Super Premium beers from Germany.
	Heileman opens new state-of-the-art Val Blatz microbrewery in Milwaukee.
	Heileman buys National Baking Company of Chicago.
	Heileman buys the Champale brands from Champale Incorporated of Trenton, New Jersey.
1987	Heileman buys Christian Schmidt Brewing Company of Philadelphia. It gets the Christian Schmidt, Erie, Coqui, Classic, Reading, Rheingold, Ortlieb's, Kohler, Valley Forge, Duquesne, and McSorley's brands.
	Heileman buys Taystee Division of bakeries from American Bakeries Company of New York.
	Alan Bond, and Australia-based Bond Corporation Holdings Limited, buys Heileman.
1988	Heileman brewery in Evansville, Indiana, closes.
	Heileman brewery in Belleville, Illinois, closes.
	Bond corporation sells Heileman Baking and Machine Products.

1989	Russ Cleary announces he is retiring and will run Cleary Management Consultants. Murray S. Cutbush replaces Russ Cleary as Heileman's chief executive officer. Heileman brewery in Perry, Georgia, closes, but is later reopened.
1990	Heileman brewery in Saint Paul closes. Heileman brewery in Frankenmuth, Michigan, closes. Stroh considers buying Heileman, but the deal isn't completed. Heileman declares bankruptcy and essentially is now owned by banks and creditors.
1991	Thomas Rattigan takes over as chief executive officer for Murray Cutbush. Heileman almost introduces Powermaster. The brand prompts controversy and criticism.
1992	Heileman finds more legal trouble over the Crazy Horse brand. Heileman gets into a legal border battle with Canada over beer prices. Thomas Rattigan moves the Heileman senior management team to Chicago.
1993	Heileman is sold to Hicks, Muse, Tate and Furst Incorporated, a Dallas investment firm. William Turner replaces Thomas Rattigan as chief executive officer. Turner is replaced by Richard F. Gaccione a few months later.
1994	Richard F. Gaccione resigns after only six months as chief executive officer. He is replaced by William Turner and Russ Cleary, who returns to Heileman to concentrate on marketing and distributors.
1995	M.L. "Lou" Lowenkron takes over as chief executive officer to replace Turner and Cleary.
1996	Heileman announces another corporate restructuring. Stroh buys Heileman, and G. Heileman Brewing Company ceases to exist. Former Heileman brewery in San Antonio, Texas, closes. Former Heileman brewery in Perry, Georgia, closes. Former Heileman brewery in Baltimore closes.
1999	Stroh decides to exit the brewing business and announces it will close the La Crosse brewery. Former Heileman brewery in La Crosse closes. Platinum Holdings, owned by James J. Strupp and John D. Mazzuto, buys the La Crosse brewery and reopens it as City Brewery. By the end of the year it is producing the first City Lager beer.

2000	City Brewery gets into financial problems and in November is sold to CBC Acquisitions, a company formed by 12 investors, including six former Heileman officials. Former Heileman executive Randy Smith is chief executive officer of City Brewery.
2003	City Brewery employs more than 200 people and is producing several of its own brands along with handling contract brewing for other companies. City Brewery unveils new La Crosse Lager Giant Six Pack at second annual City Fest.

Russ Cleary in front of control center for new brewhouse, 1982.

PHOTO COURTESY OF CLEARY-KUMM FOUNDATION

Above: Roy Kumm painting; right: Roy and Hope Kumm.
PHOTOS COURTESY OF CLEARY-KUMM FOUNDATION

Above: Russ Cleary at his desk mapping out Heileman strategy.
PHOTO COURTESY OF CLEARY-KUMM FOUNDATION

Emil Traugott Mueller, the marketing genius behind Heileman's Old Style Lager.
PHOTO COURTESY OF CLEARY-KUMM FOUNDATION

The Heileman Corporate Center, 100 Harborview Plaza, opened in September 1979 and featured views of the nearby Mississippi River.

PHOTO COURTESY OF CITY BREWERY

Egyptian scene—pre-Prohibition Old Style Lager advertising lithograph.
FROM THE COLLECTION OF GARY SCHULTZ

The Virgin's Dream—pre-Prohibition Old Style Lager advertising.
FROM THE COLLECTION OF GARY SCHULTZ

Russ Cleary with King Gambrinus statue along South Third Street in La Crosse.

PHOTO COURTESY OF CLEARY-KUMM FOUNDATION

Randy Hughes taps a keg on September 26, 2003, during City Fest.

PHOTO COURTESY OF PAUL D. KOELLER

FROM THE COLLECTION OF DAVID DELANO

FROM THE COLLECTION OF GARY SCHULTZ

FROM THE COLLECTION OF GARY SCHULTZ

Grenadiers: The painting at left above is from 1948; the advertising pieces are pre-Prohibition.

Old Style Lager advertising, 1940s.
FROM THE COLLECTION OF GARY SCHULTZ

Old Style Lager "Sign of a Friendly Host," 1940s.
FROM THE COLLECTION OF GARY SCHULTZ

The Legend of
The Old Style Label

Mere words, my friend, will ne'er be able
To tell what's on an "Old Style" label.

First thing you see are woods of pine;
Some oxen, too, are 'neath a sign.

And brewer's vats, and casks galore
Near where two men are kegging more.

You'll also find one big bull frog,
One billy goat, one shaggy dog.

And those three chaps around that table
Are hoisting steins, and that's no fable.

While on the Inn a shield appears
That proudly names the best of beers.

Old Style

Upon a horse there sits a gent
Who quaffs his brew with merriment.

From castle high upon a hill
One chap descends to fire a still.

To you, my friend, don't these suggest
A brew of sparkling, cooling zest?

There are civilized people and wild ones too,
Some lucky ones are sampling the brew.

In closing this rhyme we'd like to say
"You'll be glad tomorrow you drank 'Old
Style' today."

9801120 G. HEILEMAN BREWING CO., INC. LA CROSSE, WISCONSIN

The Legend of the Old Style Label.
FROM THE CLEARY-KUMM FOUNDATION

Heileman Brewery etched glass, pre-Prohibition.
FROM THE COLLECTION OF GARY SCHULTZ

Special Export S.S. United States bar sign, 1952.
FROM THE CLEARY-KUMM FOUNDATION

Old Style Lager advertising, 1940s.
FROM THE COLLECTION OF GARY SCHULTZ

Pre-Prohibition metal sign showing original Heileman bottle house that burned in 1959.
FROM THE COLLECTION OF GARY SCHULTZ

Creative license painting showing all brewery buildings in single setting. The malt house building on left was actually located near Lutheran Hospital. The old German-style bottle house actually faced Third Street. 1940s.
FROM THE CLEARY-KUMM FOUNDATION

Another tough day in the beer business.

Heileman executives enjoy a Mississippi River outing in the 1980s aboard Heileman's houseboat, the Hi Hope.

PHOTO COURTESY OF CLEARY-KUMM FOUNDATION

July 1984 Heileman sales team meeting in front of Heileman Corporate Headquarters. Note "top gunners" in front row.

PHOTO COURTESY OF CLEARY-KUMM FOUNDATION

Heileman product line 1984,

FROM 1984 HEILEMAN ANNUAL REPORT

The Mariners Return—this painting served as the model for design of the Heileman beer stube.
FROM THE CLEARY-KUMM FOUNDATION

Heileman introduced cone-top cans in 1935.
FROM THE COLLECTION OF GARY SCHULTZ

Label
FROM THE COLLECTION OF PAUL D. KOELLER

Roy Kumm and brewery workers Ken "Blackie" Minor, left, and Don "Doc" Olson, center, deliver the golden keg to open Oktoberfest.
PHOTO COURTESY OF CLEARY-KUMM FOUNDATION

These steins, from the House of Heileman employee series, were mainly given to employees and distributors. They were issued from 1979 through 1996 and have become popular items for collectors of memorabilia from the brewing industry. The initial stein in the series—the clear-glass one on the left in the second row above—is generally regarded as the hardest one to obtain because just 2,000 of them were made. Additional information about the steins can be found in chapter 32.

FROM THE COLLECTION OF PAUL D. KOELLER

These steins are from the Old Style series, which was produced for Heileman and sold to the public. The steins were made between 1981 and 1998.
FROM THE COLLECTION OF PAUL D. KOELLER

PART II

Places & Products

Sculptor Elmer Petersen (right) and his nephew, Kenneth Ness, position a statue of King Gambrinus during a trial installation near the west side entrance to the Heileman Corporate Center in La Crosse in 1980. PHOTO COURTESY OF MURPHY LIBRARY, UNIVERSITY OF WISCONSIN-LA CROSSE

". . . One who comes to La Crosse
definitely wants to see
the unique and outstanding brewery
where beers are made of hops and malt
with just a touch of kindness and poetry
and God's promise to preserve."

EXCERPT FROM ADVERTISING FOR OLD STYLE LAGER IN 1908

Chapter 20

The Breweries

HEILEMAN BREWERIES IN ORDER OF ACQUISITION

In 1968, Roy Kumm announced that his strategy for Heileman was to rely less on a single brand (Old Style), a single brewery (La Crosse), and a single product (beer). By 1983 Heileman was operating 13 breweries throughout the United States.

G. Heileman Brewing Company
La Crosse, Wisconsin
1858 - 2003

Kingsbury Brewery
Sheboygan, Wisconsin
1962 - 1974

Duluth Brewing and Malting Company
Duluth, Minnesota
1963 - 1966

George Wiedemann Brewery
Newport, Kentucky
1967 - 1983

Jacob Schmidt Brewery (Associated)
Saint Paul, Minnesota
1972 - 1990

Sterling Brewery (Associated)
Evansville, Indiana
1972 - 1988

Rainier Brewing Company
Seattle, Washington
1977 - 1999

Frankenmuth Brewery (Carling National)
Frankenmuth, Michigan
1979 - 1990

Stag Brewery (Carling National)
Belleville, Illinois
1979 - 1988

National Brewery (Carling National)
Baltimore, Maryland
1979 - 1980

Carling Brewery (Carling National)
Baltimore, Maryland
1979 - 1996

Arizona Brewery (Carling National)
Phoenix, Arizona
1979 - 1990

Duncan Brewery
Auburndale, Florida
1980 - 1984
Pabst Brewery

Pabst Brewery
Perry, Georgia
1983 - 1995

Blitz-Weinhard Brewery
Portland, Oregon
1983 - 1999

Lone Star Brewery
San Antonio, Texas
1983 - 1996

Val Blatz Microbrewery
Milwaukee, Wisconsin.
1986 - 1995

Heileman sound truck from the 1950s.

PHOTO COURTESY OF MURPHY LIBRARY, UNIVERSITY OF WISCONSIN-LA CROSSE

Chapter 21

Heileman Brands

APPROXIMATELY 400 LABELS ONCE DECORATED HEILEMAN BEVERAGES

The brewery owned, produced, or distributed brands from A (A-1) to Z (Zing Near Beer)

The following labels were all owned, produced or distributed by G. Heileman Brewing Company. The list also identifies the breweries that originated the brands. Some of the approximately 400 individual brands were sold several times before gaining a connection with Heileman. In those cases, the originating brewery is listed first.

A

A-1 (Arizona Brewing/National)
Ace Wisconsin Pilsner (Ace)
Apple Malt Duck (Carling)
American (Pittsburgh Brewing)
American Light (Pittsburgh Brewing)
Ansbach Light (Val Blatz brewery)
Atlas Prager Bohemian Light Lager (Sterling)
Altes (Carling)
Altes Light (Carling)
Altes Golden Lager (National/Carling)
Auer Brau Pilsner (Heileman 1960)

B

Bavarian (Christian Schmidt)
Bavarian Light (Christian Schmidt)
Beck's Light (imported from Germany)
Beck's Dark (imported from Germany)
Billy Beer (Falls City)
Blatz (Blatz)
Blatz Bavarian Style Dark Beer (Blatz)
Blatz Bock (Blatz)
Blatz Cream Ale (Blatz)
Blatz Draft (Blatz)
Blatz Draft Light (Blatz)
Blatz Ice (Heileman)
Blatz Light (Blatz)
Blatz Light Cream Ale (Heileman)
Blatz Low Alcohol (Blatz)
Blatz Malt Liquor (Blatz)
Blatz Old Heidelberg Private Stock (Val Blatz brewery)
Blatz Private Stock (Val Blatz brewery)
Blatz 1851 (Blatz)
Blatz 1851 Light (Blatz)
Blitz Weinhard (Blitz/Weinhard)

Blitz Weinhard Light (Blitz/Weinhard)
Blue Boar Red (Weinhard)
Boar's Head Red (Weinhard 1994)
Bock Beer (Heileman)
Bohemian (National/Carling)
Bohemian Light (National/Carling)
Boh Ice (Heileman)
Boh Ice Light (Heileman)
Brew 66 (Rainier)
Braumeister Special Pilsner (Independent Milwaukee Brewery)
Buckhorn (Lone Star)
Burgermeister (Blitz/Weinhard)
Burgermeister Light (Blitz/Weinhard)
Burgie Draft (Heileman)

C

Carling Black Label (Carling)
Carling Black Label Bock (Carling)
Carling Black Label Light (Carling)
Carling Black Label L.A. (Carling)
Carling Black Label nonalcoholic malt (Carling)
Carling Black Label 11-11 Extra Special Malt Liquor (Carling)
Carling Near Beer (Carling)
Carling Red Cap Ale (Carling)
Carling Red Cap Cream Ale (Carling)
Carling 71 (Carling)
Carlsberg (Danish import/Carling)
Cascade (Blitz/Weinhard)
Champagne Velvet (Terre Haute Brewing / Associated Brewing)
Champale (Champale)
Champale Apple-Fireside Wine Cooler (Champale)
Champale Citrus Malt Cooler (Champale)
Champale Golden (Champale)
Champale Pineapple-Coconut Malt Cooler (Champale)
Champale Pink (Champale)
Champale Spicy Plum Wine Cooler (Champale)
Champale Strawberry Citrus Malt Cooler (Champale)
Champale Extra Dry (Champale)
Classic (Christian Schmidt)
Crème de Luxe (Heileman—Prohibition)
Cold Spring Water (Cold Spring brewery)
Colony 13 (Pittsburgh Brewing)
Coney Island Beer (Heileman Prohibition Era)
Cool Colt Menthol (Heileman)
Colt 45 Double Malt (National)
Colt 45 Dry (National)
Colt 45 Malt Liquor (National)
Colt 45 Premium (Heileman)
Colt 45 Premium Light (Heileman)
Colt 45 Silver Deluxe (Heileman)
Colt 45 Stout Malt Liquor (National)
Colt Ice Malt Liquor (Heileman)
Columbia (Carling)
Continental (Heileman)
Cook's Goldblume Export—Prohibition) (Sterling/Associated)
Coney Island (Heileman)
Coqui 900 Malt Liquor (Christian Schmidt)
Country Cooler—Georgia Peach (Heileman)
Country Cooler—Wild Raspberry (Heileman)
Country Cooler—Orchard Citrus (Heileman)
Country Cooler—Garden Strawberry (Heileman)
Country Cooler—California Orange (Heileman)
Country Cooler—Fruit Punch (Heileman)
Crazy Horse malt liquor (contract brewing)
Culmbacher (Val Blatz brewery)
Culmbacher Dark (Val Blatz brewery)
Culmbacher Imperial (Val Blatz brewery)

D

Delight Near Beer (Heileman Prohibition Era)
Desire (Heileman)
Drewrys (Drewrys)
Drewrys Draft (Drewrys)
Drewrys Extra Dry (Drewrys)
Drewrys Old Stock Ale (Drewrys)
Drewrys Stout Malt Liquor (Drewrys)
Drewrys Malt Liquor (Drewrys)
Drummond Brothers (Falls City Brewing)
Duke (Christian Schmidt/Duquesne)
Duquesne (Christian Schmidt/Duquesne)

E

Edelweiss Light (Schoenhoffen/Drewrys/Associated)
Edelweiss Wheat Beer (Val Blatz brewery)
Eisenstarr (Heileman)
Emerald City Ale (Heileman/Rainier)
Erie (Christian Schmidt)

F

Falls City (Falls City Brewing)
Falls City Light (Falls City Brewing)
Fox Deluxe (Fox Head)
Fox Head Extra Dry Sparkling Malt Liquor (Fox Head)
Fox Head 97 Malt Liquor (Fox Head)
Fox Head 97 Stout Malt Liquor (Fox Head)
Fox Head "400" Draft (Fox Head)
Fox Head Bock (Fox Head)
Fox Head Old Waukesha Ale (Fox Head)
Fox Head Vat Age Lager (Fox Head)

G

Germanic Lager (Heileman)
Golden Leaf (Heileman 1900 and again in 1941)
GBX Malt Liquor (Grain Belt)
Grain Belt (Grain Belt)
Grain Belt Bock (Grain Belt)
Grain Belt Light (Grain Belt)
Grape Malt Duck (Carling)
Great Lakes Premium (Schoenhoffen/Associated)
Grenadier (Heileman Prohibition Era)
Gluek Finest Pilsener (Gluek)
Golden Velvet (Blitz-Weinhard)
G. Heileman's Export Beer (Heileman)

H

Hacker-Pschorr Dark (import—Germany)
Hacker-Pschorr Festbier (import—Germany)
Hacker-Pschorr Light (import—Germany)
Hacker-Pschorr Maibock (import—Germany)
Hacker-Pschorr Oktoberfest (import—Germany)
Hacker-Pschorr Pils (import—Germany)
Hacker-Pschorr Weiss (import—Germany)
Hauenstein (Grain Belt)
Heidelberg (Carling)
Heidelberg L.A. (Heileman)
Heidelberg Light (Carling)
Heileman's Bavarian Style (Heileman)
Heileman's Beer (Heileman)
Heileman's Cavalier Select Beer (Heileman)
Heileman's Delight (Heileman)
Heileman's Deluxe (Heileman)
Heileman's Export Lager (Heileman)
Heileman's Extra Pale Malt Syrup (Heileman)
Heileman's Famous Brew (Heileman)
Heileman's Keg Beer (Heileman)
Heileman's Lager Beer (Heileman)
Heileman's Mault-Beere (Heileman)
Heileman's Oktoberfest Brau (Heileman)
Heileman's Old Style Malt Tonic (Heileman)

Heileman's Old Style Picnic Beer (Heileman 1909 and again in 1933)
Heileman's Old Style Premium (Heileman)
Heileman's P & L (Heileman)
Heileman's Picnic Beer (Heileman 1890 and again in 1941)
Heileman's Wis (Heileman)
Heidel Brau (Kingsbury)
Heidel Brau Premium (Kingsbury)
Heileman's Alt-Lagern (Heileman)
Heileman Lager (Heileman)
Heileman Pilsner (Heileman)
Heileman Premium Light (Heileman)
Henry Weinhard Ale (Blitz/Weinhard)
Henry Weinhard Dark (Blitz/Weinhard)
Henry Weinhard Draft (Blitz/Weinhard)
Henry Weinhard Draft Light (Blitz/Weinhard)
Henry Weinhard Hefeweizen (Blitz/Weinhard wheat beer)
Henry Weinhard Private Reserve (Blitz/Weinhard)
Henry Weinhard Private Reserve Dark (Blitz/Weinhard)
Henry Weinhard Private Reserve Light (Blitz/Weinhard)
Henry Weinhard (Blitz/Weinhard)
Henry Weinhard Light (Blitz/Weinhard)
Henry Weinhard Root Beer (Blitz/Weinhard)
Henry Weinhard Ice Ale (Blitz/Weinhard)
Highlander (Rainier)
Hofbrau (Heileman)
Home Dry Lager (Atlas/Drewrys)

I

Iron City (Pittsburgh Brewing)
Iron City Cooler (Pittsburgh Brewing)
Iron City Golden Lager (Pittsburgh Brewing)
Iron City Light (Pittsburgh Brewing)
Iron City Special Dry (Pittsburgh Brewing)

K

Karlsbrau Old Time Beer (Duluth Brewing and Malting)
Katz (Schoenhoffen/Drewrys/Associated)
King of Clubs (Heileman Prohibition Era)
Kingsbury (Kingsbury)
Kingsbury Draft (Kingsbury)
Kingsbury Brew Near Beer (Kingsbury)
Kingsbury non-alcoholic Malt Beverage (Kingsbury)
Kingsbury Light (Kingsbury)
Kingsbury Pale (Kingsbury)
Kingsbury Red NA (Kingsbury)
Kingsbury Sparkling Malt Tonic (Kingsbury)
Knickerbocker (Christian Schmidt)
Koehler (Christian Schmidt)

L

LaCroix / water (Heileman)
LaCroix Lemon / water (Heileman)
LaCroix Lime / water (Heileman)
LaCroix Sparkling Citrus / wine cooler(Heileman)
LaCroix Strawberry / wine cooler (Heileman)
Lightship Light (Pittsburgh Brewing)
Lone Star (Lone Star)
Lone Star Bock (Lone Star)
Lone Star Dry (Lone Star)
Lone Star Light (Lone Star)
Lone Star Light Ice (Lone Star)
Lone Star Ice (Lone Star)
Lone Star L.A. (Lone Star)
Lone Star Natural Bock (Lone Star)
Lone Star Nonalcoholic Malt Beverage (Lone Star)
Lone Star 150 Private Stock (Lone Star)

M

Malta Hatuey (Duncan Brewing)
Maltbrau Nonalcoholic Malt Beverage (Champale)
Malt Duck Golden Apple (Carling/National)
Malt Duck Pink (Carling/National)
Malt Duck Red Grape (Carling/National)
Mc Sorleys (Christian Schmidt)
Mc Sorleys Ale (Christian Schmidt)
Mc Sorleys Double Dark (Christian Schmidt)
Mickey's Ice (Sterling)
Mickey's Ice Light (Heileman)
Mickeys Malt Liquor (Sterling)
Mickey's Red (Heileman)
Mickey's Stone Cold Beer (Heileman)
Mickey's Stone Cold Red (Heileman)
Midnight Dragon (Pittsburgh Brewing)
Milwaukee 1851 (Blatz)
Milwaukee 1851 Light (Blatz)
Milwaukee Weiss (Heileman/Val Blatz Brewery)
Moravia Super Premium (import—Germany)
Muenchener Draft (Val Blatz brewery)
Mr. Lager (Fox Head)
Mustang (Pittsburgh Brewing)

N

National Ale (National)
National Draft (National)
National Bohemian (National)
National Bohemian Bock (National)
National Bohemian Pale (National)
National Premium (National)
National Premium L.A. (Heileman)
National Premium Light (National)
New Style Lager Near Beer (Heileman Prohibition Era)
North Star (Schmidt)

O

Old Dutch (Pittsburgh Brewing)
Old German (Pittsburgh Brewing)
Old Heidelberg (Val Blatz brewery)
Old Heurich (Pittsburgh Brewing)
Old Style (Heileman)
Old Style Classic Draft (Heileman)
Old Style Classic Draft Light (Heileman)
Old Style Draft (Heileman)
Old Style Ginger Ale (Heileman Prohibition Era)
Old Style Grape (Heileman)
Old Style Ice (Heileman)
Old Style Lager (Heileman)
Old Style Lager Extra Light (Heileman)
Old Style Light (Heileman)
Old Style Light Ice (Heileman)
Old Style L.A. (Heileman)
Old Style Near Beer (Heileman Prohibition Era)
Old Style Malt Syrup (Heileman Prohibition Era)
Old Style Root Beer (Heileman Prohibition Era)
Old Style Royal Amber non-alcoholic (Heileman)
Old Style Special Dry (Heileman)
Old Style 2.2 (Heileman)
Old Dutch Brand The Good Beer (Old Dutch)
Old Times Lager (Heileman)
Oertel (Oertel)
Oertel's "92" (Oertel)
O'Keefe Ale (Carling)
Old Vienna (Canada—Carling)
Ortlieb's (Christian Schmidt)

P

Paul Bunyon (Duluth)
Pennsylvania Pilsner (Pittsburgh Brewing)
Pfeiffer Famous Beer (Pfeiffer)

Pfeiffer Premium (Pfeiffer)
Pioneer (Pioneer Brewing/Gluek)
Powermaster (Heileman)
Prager (Atlas/Drewrys)
Presidente Pilsener (import—Dominican Republic)

R

Rainier Beer (Rainier)
Rainier Ale (Rainier)
Rainier Bold Malt Liquor (Rainier)
Rainier Bold Malt Liquor Stout (Rainier)
Rainier Draft (Rainier)
Rainier Draft Light (Rainier)
Rainier Dry (Rainier)
Rainier Ice (Rainier)
Rainier Ice Light (Rainier)
Rainier Light (Rainier)
Rainier L.A. (Rainier)
Rainier Old Stock Ale (Rainier)
Rainier Peaks Nonalcoholic Malt Beverage (Rainier)
Rainier Premium Malt Liquor (Rainier)
Rainier Special Dry (Rainier)
Rainier Special Light Nonalcoholic Malt Beverage (Rainier)
Rainier Spur Stout Malt Liquor (Rainier)
Rainier Yakima Red (Rainier)
Reading (Christian Schmidt)
Reading Premium (Christian Schmidt)
Reidenbach Wisconsin Pale Dry (Kingsbury)
Red Cap Ale (Carling)
Red Top (Drewrys/Associated)
Red White and Blue (Pabst)
Red White and Blue Light (Pabst)
Regal (Duluth Brewing and Malting)
Reserve of Wisconsin (Heileman)
Rheingold (Christian Schmidt)
Rheingold Extra Light (Christian Schmidt)
Rheingold Extra Dry (Christian Schmidt)
Rheinlander (Rainier)
Rheinlander Light Pale (Rainier)
Royal 58 (Duluth Brewing and Malting)
Royal Bohemian (Duluth Brewing and Malting)

S

Sabinas (Heileman)
Sam Adams (brewed at Blitz/Weinhard for Boston Brewing, West Coast distribution)
Santa Claus Special (Heileman)
Schmidt's (Christian Schmidt)
Schmidt's Ale (Jacob Schmidt)
Schmidt's Dark (Jacob Schmidt)
Schmidt's Draft (Jacob Schmidt)
Schmidt's Draft Light (Jacob Schmidt)
Schmidt's Light (Christian Schmidt)
Schmidt's Light Ice (Jacob Schmidt)
Schmidt (Jacob Schmidt)
Schmidt City Club (Jacob Schmidt)
Schmidt Draft (Jacob Schmidt)
Schmidt Draft Light (Jacob Schmidt)
Schmidt Ice (Jacob Schmidt)
Schmidt Light (Jacob Schmidt)
Schmidt L.A. (Jacob Schmidt)
Schmidts Malt Liquor (Jacob Schmidt)
Schmidts Near Beer (Jacob Schmidt)
Schmidt Red Lager (Jacob Schmidt)
Schmidt Select Near Beer (Jacob Schmidt)
Schmidt Extra Special (Jacob Schmidt)
Select Brew (Heileman)
SGA (Associated)
SGA Light (Associated)
Special Export (Heileman)

Special Export Dark (Heileman)
Special Export Malt Lager (Heileman)
Special Export Malt Liquor (Heileman)
Special Export Light (Heileman)
Special Export EX (Heileman)
Special Export EX Light (Heileman)
Special Export EX Ice (Heileman)
Special Export EX Black Ale (Heileman)
Special Export Light Ice (Heileman)
Special Export Red Ale (Heileman)
Spike (Heileman)
St. Ide's (contract brewing)
St. Michaels (Pittsburgh Brewing)
Stag (Stag/Griesedieck Western/Carling)
Stag Bock (Stag)
Stag Extra Special (Stag)
Stag Light (Stag)
Stite Malt Liquor (Gluek)
Sterling Ale (Sterling)
Sterling Draft (Sterling)
Sterling Light (Sterling)
Sterling Premium (Sterling)
Sterling Pure (Sterling)
Storz Premium (Grain Belt)
Storz Triumph (Grain Belt)

T

Tempo (Blatz)
Tivoli (Val Blatz brewery)
Tropical Ale (Associated)
Trophy (Drewrys)
Tuborg (Carling)
Tuborg Deluxe Dark (Carling)
Tuborg Gold (Carling)

V

Valley Forge (Christian Schmidt)

W

Weber Private Club (Weber Waukesha/Fox Head)
Weber Special Premium (Weber Waukesha/Fox Head)
Weber Waukesha (Weber Waukesha/Fox Head)
Weiner (Heileman 1884/Blatz same era)
Wiedemann Draft (Wiedemann)
Wiedemann Fine Beer (Wiedemann)
Wiedemann Light (Wiedemann)
Wiedemann Genuine Draft (Wiedemann)
Wiedemann Bohemian Special Brew (Wiedemann)
Wiedemann Royal Amber (Wiedemann)
Wiener (Val Blatz brewery)
Windy City Amber Ale (Heileman)
Wisconsin Premium (Wisconsin Brewing / Fox Head)

Z

Zing Near Beer (Kingsbury)

NUMBERS

9-0-5 (Drewrys/Associated)
20 Grand Ale (Sterling)

Tracking a Can

In September 1981, the *La Crosse Tribune* published an extensive multi-page article that followed the life cycle of a can of Heileman beer. That article brought back childhood memories for me.

Before the days of federal safety restrictions, things were quite different for employees of the bottle house. They were allowed to drink as much beer as they wanted on the job, as long as they could perform their work. My father told stories of college students, hired as temporary help for the summer, who lost their jobs after one day because they took advantage of the free beer. Later the free beer was cut back and made available only in the break rooms.

In the 1960s, my father took me down to the brewery to pick up his paycheck when he was on vacation. I can still remember wet and slippery floors, broken bottles, the overwhelming smell of beer, and the deafening noise of the machines. He showed me each of the machines and explained how they worked, and I watched in fascination as a worker fed long tubes of can tops into a device that fastened them onto the full cans of beer. The highlight of the trip was being able to collect some bottle caps from all the different brands Heileman produced. Of course, the trip always included a stop in the break room, where my father drank a cold one before heading home.

The story of a can of Heileman beer began with the noisy machines that made the cans at Continental Can Company, located on the North Side of La Crosse. It took 25 minutes for a machine to take a huge roll of aluminum and bend it into two-inch tall cups. The cups were then stretched, shined, coated, and painted with the Heileman labels. Loaded onto pallets, they were then shipped to a warehouse at Heileman, where each day the La Crosse brewery used three million of them. Continental Can Company produced two million cans a day; one million more were provided to Heileman from other sources.

From the warehouse the cans were put on a conveyor belt that carried them 1,300 feet through an overhead walkway crossing Third Street. The cans came across seven or eight abreast, guided by air pressure, and were inspected by a worker using a giant mirror mounted above the conveyor. Dented or dirty cans were removed by the operator.

At this point they were separated into a single file, rinsed, and fed into a merry-go-round filler that poured 12 ounces of beer into each can, which was then sealed with a lid and flipped upside down to check for leaks. Any can not completely full was rejected by the machine and kicked off the conveyor belt into a waste bin. When the machine was running at full speed it was impossible to even see the cans being rejected.

Once they had been filled and inspected, other machines packaged the cans together either with plastic into a six-pack, or into 12-pack or 24-pack cases. Another machine packaged four six-packs into a cardboard box.

From there, the beer was piled onto pallets to be loaded onto the semitrailers that delivered beer to the distributors. Trucks heading to Chicago often left La Crosse by 3 A.M. and usually traveled in pairs in case of any problem. On the return trip, the trucks brought back empty half barrels to be refilled. In 1981, Heileman was delivering more than 600 million cans of Old Style a year just to Chicago.

—*Paul D. Koeller*

Chapter 22

Bread, Snacks, and More

HEILEMAN DID NOT LIVE BY BEER ALONE

Bread, snacks and other products were produced by Heileman-owned bakeries.

Heileman's first ventures outside the brewing industry were the result of being a good "corporate citizen" in La Crosse. It purchased companies in La Crosse that were for sale primarily to maintain local ownership. Bakeries, though, became a major part of the business.

In September 1967, Heileman purchased Machine Products, which was established in La Crosse in 1945 and manufactured airplane parts. In addition to its La Crosse facilities, there were warehouse operations in the area of Hartford, Connecticut, to support contracts with the Pratt Whitney Corporation. With Machine Products in La Crosse came the land that was used as the South Side Oktoberfest grounds. Agreements continued until 1989 to lease this area to La Crosse Festivals for that occasion.

In August 1970, Heileman bought another La Crosse firm, Nesco Sign Company. In this case, the company was purchased more to directly benefit business. In October 1986, Heileman sold what had become the Nesco-Briteway Sign Company to Everbrite Electric Signs Incorporated of Milwaukee.

Baking

In March of 1969, Heileman purchased Erickson Bakery of La Crosse and Federal Bakery of Winona, Minnesota, to be operated as a wholly owned subsidiary named Erickson Bakeries Incorporated. Ray Ping, formerly of Erickson Bakery, was named president of the subsidiary. The bakeries were in La Crosse and Winona, plus Baraboo, Wisconsin, and Red Wing, Minnesota. They employed 300 people and had annual sales of $6 million.

The purchase of Erickson Bakery was made primarily to keep the company in La Crosse, but Cleary quickly recognized parallels between the baking industry and the brewing industry. Small regional bakeries were increasingly being bought by larger regional or national bakeries, a trend similar to what was happening in the brewing industry. Heileman began to use the bakery distributors to sell high-priced regional specialty items nationally. For example, the Emrich Baking Company marketed a line of expensive Danish pastries that was originally distributed only in the Minneapolis area. Heileman was able to distribute the Danish pastries through all of its bakery distributors.

In April 1970, Heileman bought Holsum Bakery in Eau Claire, Wisconsin, and McGough Bakeries Incorporated of Rice Lake, Wisconsin. A year later, Colvin Baking Company of Janesville, Wisconsin, was acquired. Also, in September 1971, Heileman bought Gardner Bakery of Madison, Wisconsin, which operated bakeries in Madison and Janesville, Wisconsin. This bakery had 400 employees and sales of $8 million. Bernard Reese, president of Gardner Bakeries, was hired to oversee operations and became a Heileman executive.

By 1972, Heileman employed 181 people at Erickson Bakeries in La Crosse with a payroll of $1.7 million. It employed 134 more people at Machine Products with a payroll of $1.45 million, and 12 more at Nesco Signs with a payroll of $110,000.

In August 1976, Heileman expanded the bakery business into Iowa with the purchase of Trausch Baking Company of Dubuque. With the purchase of Trausch, the Heileman Bakery Division had a total of more than $40 million in sales. The Trausch bakery operated more than 100 routes in Iowa with major markets in Davenport, Cedar Rapids, Waterloo, Clinton, and Burlington. It also had routes in Rock Falls, Illinois, and Prairie du Chien and Monroe, Wisconsin. The bakery employed 350 people and had sales of about $12 million. Arthur Trausch Jr. remained as president and chief executive officer and replaced Reese within the next year as president of Heileman's bakery division, which had record sales of $38,699,000 in 1977.

Dick Brothers Bakery of Manitowoc, Wisconsin, was acquired in April 1978. It had been established in 1910 by the Dick family, which operated 60 bakery routes and had Wisconsin depot operations in Fond du Lac, Green Bay, Racine, Wabeno, and Wausau, as well as Escanaba, Michigan. The company employed 180 people and had sales of $6 million.

In July 1978, Heileman announced the purchase of Emrich Baking Company in Minneapolis. Started in 1919 by the Emrich family, it employed 160 people and marketed products under the Emrich and Egekvist labels. Annual sales were about $5 million. Sales for the Heileman bakery division were a record $48.69 million in 1978.

A year later, Heileman purchased Our Own Bakeries in Marquette, Michigan, originally opened in 1925. At the time of the purchase, it employed 140 people and had annual sales of about $6 million. The product was marketed under the Bunny label in the Upper Peninsula of Michigan and northern Wisconsin.

By 1980, rapid expansion was causing growing pains. The new corporate headquarters Heileman had built in the La Crosse Harborview was jammed, so the bakery division was moved to the old Ellickson Building in the 400 block of Cass Street.

In October, Heileman bought Bake-Rite Baking Company of Plover, Wisconsin, from the Mor-

America Financial Corporation of Cedar Rapids, Iowa. Bake-Rite was established in Stevens Point, Wisconsin, in 1923, and was best known for its Mrs. Carter's line of bread. The company employed about 300 people and had annual sales of about $14 million, with 93 wholesale bakery routes throughout Wisconsin. After this acquisition, baking operations accounted for nine percent of Heileman revenues.

Early in 1981, as a hedge against slowing growth in the beer business, Heileman expanded into yet another industry with the purchase of Barrel O' Fun snack foods—potato chips and popcorn—of Perham, Minnesota. At the time of the purchase, the company had $5 million in sales and employed 70 people. It distributed a full line of snacks via independent distributors in Minnesota, Wisconsin, North Dakota, South Dakota, and Montana. Barrel O' Fun had been established in 1973 by Kenneth Nelson, who continued on as general manager of operations after Heileman purchased the company.

Arthur N. Trausch Jr., head of Heileman baking, announced the Barrel O' Fun product line would be expanded to also include corn chip products and fried and baked cheese curls. After the purchase, Heileman took advantage of its network of 1,900 beer distributors to increase distribution of these snack products.

In May 1983, Heileman bought Red Seal Quality Foods Incorporated of Denver, Colorado. The 72-year-old company had sales of $12 million in potato and corn chips, primarily in Colorado, Montana, Wyoming, and New Mexico. Heileman retained all employees, including Earl Wilson, president, and Don Tideman, executive vice president.

Barrel O' Fun snacks sales surged from $5 million to $15 million, and in 1982 the bakery division had total sales of $87.4 million.

In July 1984, Heileman added Mrs. Howe's Food Products of Milwaukee, which produced potato chips, corn chips, popcorn, and corn snacks for the southeastern Wisconsin market and expanded that plant to produce Barrel 'O Fun snacks as well. Snack food sales were now bringing in about $40 million of Heileman's $1.3 billion in sales.

Heileman purchased the Federal Distributing Company of Milwaukee in early 1987 as a distributor for the Barrel O' Fun line of snacks, and moved the operation into the renovated Wonder Baking Company next to the Jaeger Baking Company and Val Blatz Brewery. The rest of the property was used for parking, storage, and future expansion of the brewery. Heileman called this complex "Heileman Hill" in a take-off on the term "Miller Valley," which was used to describe the Miller brewing complex in Milwaukee.

The baking division expanded again in June 1987 with a major growth of crouton manufacturing at the Erickson Bakery in La Crosse. More than $1 million was spent to automate the plant with state-of-the-art crouton-making equipment. The plant was operating 24 hours a day, five days a week to meet demand.

Heileman also established a new division that sold bakery products to airport food service operators and other large customers. In addition, the company also was a supplier for large national food industry customers, including Sara Lee, General Foods, McDonald's, and Quaker Oats.

Heileman Baking was given the Wholesale Baker of the Year Award by *Bakery Product Market* magazine and was featured in both the September and October issues of the magazine.

From modest beginnings in 1970, Heileman Baking grew to be the fifth-largest wholesale bread company in the United States. It employed 4,750 employees at 13 bakeries, four snack food plants, and 1,250 sales routes. Unfortunately, just as things were really going well, Bond corporation purchased Heileman and everything changed.

In February 1988, news surfaced that Heileman was negotiating with an undisclosed buyer to sell its Barrel O' Fun snack unit. Company officials claimed the sale had nothing to do with the recent takeover by Bond, but that it just lacked resources to pursue both the baking and snack food businesses. Michael Moon, president of Heileman Baking, said the snack foods had been a burden to management and it wanted to focus attention on the emerging snack cake business instead. In a related announcement, he said the baking headquarters staff of 35 people was moving back into the First Bank Place building from 334 Fifth Avenue South.

By early March, the sale of Heileman assets was in full motion and the company was seeking a buyer for the rest of Heileman Baking and also Machine Products. The two companies had 550 employees in La Crosse alone.

A management team headed by Michael Moon put in a bid for Heileman baking, but the offer was initially refused. In a letter to employees, Moon promised he intended to win the bid eventually. Analysts estimated the bakery had assets worth $120 million. Meanwhile, Joseph Webb, president of Machine Products, and Alex Skover, former president, announced they and a group of managers and investors had submitted a bid for the company. The investors included Russ Cleary and Heileman board member John Mooney.

The agreement between Heileman and Bond guaranteed these plants and jobs had to remain in Wisconsin for a period of at least three years. Initially, people thought Wisconsin law would also protect the sale of the assets, but the law only covered hostile takeovers, and once the Bond deal became a merger it no longer applied. Nevertheless, La Crosse Mayor Pat Zielke contacted Wisconsin Governor Tommy Thompson and asked for his assistance in keeping the jobs in La Crosse.

Bidding on the baking company and Machine Products continued until May, when Heileman suddenly surprised everyone by announcing that Heileman Baking Company assets had been sold to a Belgian sugar company, RT Holding SA. At the time of the sale, Heileman Baking had sales of almost $300 million and employed more than 4,700 people, including 1,225 in Wisconsin and 250 in La Crosse.

Initially things looked good for Heileman Baking, and it announced it was expanding the corporate headquarters staff of 32 in La Crosse by 12 more employees. But less than two weeks later, rumors were circulating that the Belgian company was negotiating with Metz Baking of Sioux City, Iowa, for a joint venture to run Heileman Baking. William Metz, chairman of Metz Baking, gave assurances nothing would change at the La Crosse operations, but he refused to comment on the future of the management or corporate staff working in La Crosse.

There wasn't much time to speculate on the future. The very next day Metz announced Moon and Steven Nett, executive vice president of Heileman Baking, were no longer with the company. The sale of Heileman Baking to Metz included the original Erickson Bakery in La Crosse, Wisconsin.

In 1993, Metz Baking was sold to Specialty Foods of Deerfield, Illinois.

Recycling

Heileman also was heavily involved with recycling in La Crosse. By 1976, all of the Heileman plants but Saint Paul were using aluminum cans. Heileman opened a new recycling center at the corner of Third and Market streets that initially accepted aluminum and steel cans, and later glass bottles. By February 1977, Heileman had recycled one million cans. Within a year, recycling had grown to more than four million cans. Each time Heileman recycled a million cans Cleary presented the person turning in the last can with a $50 savings bond.

Heileman moved the recycling center to Third and Jackson streets and announced a plan to donate 10 cents a pound of recycled aluminum to the Gateway Area Boy Scouts and Riverland Council of Girl Scouts. Since opening in 1975, the center had recycled 9.5 million cans. Originally, the recycled cans were sold to Reynolds Aluminum, but later they were sent to Continental Can Company in La Crosse, which made cans for Heileman.

Heileman hoped the recycling center would derail proposed mandatory deposit laws for cans and bottles. Such laws, already in effect in Michigan and Iowa, were having a negative affect on Heileman's sales and profitability there. Sales were down in Iowa as residents were crossing the border to avoid the mandatory deposit.

In the first 10 years of operation, the Heileman recycling program paid out more than $600,000 in La Crosse, and by April 1984 it celebrated 50 million recycled cans. In May 1985, Heileman joined with Riverfront Incorporated and Occupational Rehabilitation Center Industries to introduce a mobile recycling program.

In April 1990, Heileman began to recycle and reuse glass bottles at the Rainier and Henry Weinhard breweries in the Pacific Northwest.

BAKERIES

Bake Rite Baking Company
Milwaukee, Wisconsin

Colvin Baking
Janesville, Wisconsin

Dick Brothers Bakery
Manitowoc, Wisconsin (closed)
Green Bay, Wisconsin
Shawano, Wisconsin
Wittenberg, Wisconsin
Wausau, Wisconsin
Fond du Lac, Wisconsin
Escanaba, Michigan
Iron Mountain, Michigan

Emrich Baking
Minneapolis, Minnesota

Erickson Bakeries
La Crosse, Wisconsin
Winona, Minnesota (closed)
Tomah, Wisconsin
Rochester, Minnesota
Red Wing, Minnesota
Hayward, Minnesota
Mankato, Minnesota

Gardner Bakeries
Madison, Wisconsin
Milwaukee, Wisconsin
Baraboo, Wisconsin
Richland Center, Wisconsin
Platteville, Wisconsin
Beaver Dam, Wisconsin
Wausau, Wisconsin
Tomah, Wisconsin
Neenah, Wisconsin
Rhinelander, Wisconsin
Wisconsin Dells, Wisconsin
Plainfield, Wisconsin
Janesville, Wisconsin

Holsum Bakeries
Eau Claire, Wisconsin

McGough Bakeries
Rice Lake, Wisconsin (closed)
Minong, Wisconsin
Hayward, Wisconsin
Amery, Wisconsin

Mrs. Howe's Food Products
Milwaukee, Wisconsin

National Baking Company
Chicago, Illinois

New Process Baking Company Incorporated
Beloit, Wisconsin
Chicago, Illinois
Green Bay, Wisconsin
Highland, Indiana
Kenosha, Wisconsin
Milwaukee, Wisconsin
Watertown, Wisconsin
Wausau, Wisconsin

Oswald Jaeger Baking Company
Milwaukee, Wisconsin

Our Own Bakeries
Marquette, Michigan
Munising, Michigan
Newberry, Michigan
Sault Ste. Marie, Michigan
Manistique, Michigan
Escanaba, Michigan
Powers, Michigan
Iron Mountain, Michigan
Crystal Falls, Michigan
Ironwood, Michigan
Dollar Bay, Michigan
L'Anse, Michigan

Taystee Baking
Detroit, Michigan
Duluth, Minnesota (closed)
Kansas City, Missouri

Trausch Bakeries
Prairie du Chien, Wisconsin
Monroe, Wisconsin
Rock Falls, Illinois
Dubuque, Iowa
Clinton, Iowa
Davenport, Iowa
Burlington, Iowa
Ottumwa, Iowa
Waterloo, Iowa
Cedar Rapids, Iowa

SNACK FOOD MANUFACTURERS

Barrel O' Fun
Perham, Minnesota

Johnson Nut Company
Willmar, Minnesota

Willmar Cookie Company
Willmar, Minnesota

Mrs. Howe's
Milwaukee, Wisconsin

Red Seal
Denver, Colorado

BAKERY BRANDS

Autumn Grain
Better Way
Bunny
Country Hearth
D'Italiano
Dutch Maid
Egekvist
Emrich's
Gardners
Hillbilly
Hollywood
Holsum
Honey Meal
Hudson Bay Milling Company
Jaeger
Kappus
Less
Lumber Jack
Mrs. Carter's
Mickey's Snack Cakes
Olympic Meal
Our Own Brand
Peter Pan
Roman Meal
Sunbeam
Taystee
Weight Watchers

Heileman's air force

Throughout the 1970s, Heileman had a corporate plane piloted by Richard "Andy" Lamkin and copiloted by Larry Cain. By the late 1970s, the plane typically flew three to four days a week and often made eight to 10 stops a day at the Heileman bakeries. By the early 1980s, Heileman had three corporate planes and was flying hundreds of people in and out of La Crosse on as many as 5,000 flights a year.

In October 1992, after Heileman had moved its last remaining corporate jet to Chicago to serve the management team that had moved there, Heileman Air was sold to Tim and Debra Colgan and renamed Colgan Air Services.

Colgan had worked for Heileman for the previous 10 years and had managed Heileman Air for seven. The company had 20 full-time employees and owned eight airplanes, plus the Heileman hangar and a hangar previously owned by Trane Company. Heileman had bought the business in 1985 when it was known as Professional Aviation.

SNACK BRANDS

- Barrel O' Fun Potato Chips
- Barrel O' Fun Ripple Chips
- Barrel O' Fun Bacon and Sour Cream Chips
- Barrel O' Fun Sour Cream and Onion Chips
- Barrel O' Fun Barbeque Chips
- Barrel O' Fun Popcorn
- Barrel O' Fun Cheese Corn
- Barrel O' Fun Carmel Corn
- Barrel O' Fun Natural Corn Chips
- Barrel O' Fun Tortilla Chips
- Barrel O' Fun Tostadas Chips
- Barrel O' Fun Nacho Cheese Chips
- Barrel O' Fun Taco Chips
- Barrel O' Fun Baked Cheese Curls
- Barrel O' Fun Fried Cheese Curls
- Barrel O' Fun Hot Nibs
- Barrel O' Fun Salt and Sour Chips
- Barrel O' Fun Hot Chips
- Barrel O' Fun Hot Corn Chips
- Barrel O' Fun Deli Tostadas
- Barrel O' Fun Deli Tostadas Nacho Cheese
- Barrel O' Fun Deli Tortillas Nacho Cheese
- Barrel O' Fun Deli Dippers
- Barrel O' Fun Candy Corn
- Barrel O' Fun Assorted Jelly Beans
- Barrel O' Fun Deluxe Nacho Cheese Dip
- Barrel O' Fun Molasses Cookies
- Barrel O' Fun Oatmeal & Raisin Cookies
- Barrel O' Fun Salted Peanuts
- Barrel O' Fun Dry Roasted Peanuts
- Barrel O' Fun Honey Roasted Cashews
- Barrel O' Fun Party Peanuts
- Chicharonnes (pork skins)
- Gurley Nuts
- Hot Sauce
- Johnson Nuts
- Mrs. Howe's
- Red Seal Potato Chips
- Red Seal Tortilla Chips
- Red Seal Corn Chips
- Red Seal Krispuds
- Red Seal Sour Cream and Onion

Walt's Restaurant

Heileman bought Walt's Restaurant, 310 Mississippi Street, in 1981. Walt's had been in operation for more than 60 years, featured German-American food, and had real bullet holes in the bar. Originally owned by Walter Niggli, it was sold in 1946 to George Jones, who then sold the restaurant to Gerald F. Seymour and Borge "Bugsy" Knutson in 1958. Knutson eventually became the sole owner, but he sold the restaurant in 1969 to Richard Robinson and Vernon Dale. When Dale died in 1976, the restaurant became part of a trust and was operated by Glenn Addis, who already owned another La Crosse restaurant called the Mai Tai.

Walt's was purchased by Heileman from the estate of Vern Dale for $350,000. Rex Ritchie, a well-known local tavern owner who had most recently operated Rex's Corner in the Stoddard Hotel, was hired to manage Walt's.

The restaurant was closed on June 5, 1982, unable to make a profit because of the weak economy. A final celebration was held at Walt's on June 4, and featured music by Al Townsend and his Wonderful World Jazz Band. The building was turned into a tour center to accommodate the nearly 75,000 brewery visitors a year. The remodeled building featured a gift shop, a moderately priced German restaurant, and a theater showing a presentation of Heileman history.

Chapter 23

Turning Wine and Water into Profit

ALTERNATIVE PRODUCTS WERE ATTRACTIVE FOR A WHILE

"Finally . . . A light beer that deserves to be called special."

—ADVERTISING SLOGAN FOR HEILEMAN'S SPECIAL EXPORT LIGHT, INTRODUCED IN 1985

While the Schlitz and Pabst deals of the early 1980s were certainly major events, there were other big changes facing the brewing industry in the mid 1980s.

Opponents of alcohol were becoming more vocal about alcohol abuse, and the population was increasingly concerned with physical fitness and inclined to drink in moderation. Many states raised the legal drinking age from 18 to 21, and in just a few years, light beers had come from nowhere to taking over 20 percent of the beer market.

Heileman started developing a low-alcohol product in 1982 and by early 1983 had something marketable. However, government regulations prevented the use of the word alcohol on beer labels. Anheuser-Busch had solved the problem by using the letters L.A. (low alcohol). Heileman sought permission to do the same. In April 1985, Anheuser-Busch filed a lawsuit against Heileman and Stroh over the use of the letters L.A., saying it owned L.A., similar to a lawsuit that Miller Brewing lost several years earlier over the use of the term "light." The legal battles dragged on until January 1988, when Heileman and Stroh finally won against Anheuser-Busch.

Heileman already had three no-alcohol brands in Kingsbury Brew, Schmidt Select, and Zing. The brewery was the largest producer in the world of non-alcoholic beer. Heileman planned to introduce two new low-alcohol brands, Blatz L.A. and Black Label L.A., in the Midwest, and then expand them nationwide. The Blatz L.A. brand was favorably received. Initially in La Crosse, it was offered at the Alpine Inn on Grandad Bluff and at Shimshak's Tavern. Drinkers liked the taste and felt that it resembled beer more than other low-alcohol products. They also liked the reduced calories and not having to worry about drinking and driving.

Early sales of low-alcohol brands exceeded expectations and were followed by low-alcohol versions of Carling, Old Style, Rainier, Schmidt, and Lone Star. Cleary pointed out that the Heileman brands had only 73 calories, compared with 110 for the Anheuser-Busch product. He also claimed that the Heileman brands tasted better and challenged consumers to do their own comparison.

In response to increasing public concerns about alcohol abuse, Heileman made available a book that promoted responsible drinking and the benefits of moderate alcohol consumption. But it also quoted studies showing that beer could cut down on gallstones, contained lots of vitamins and minerals, and had a low salt content.

Heileman purchased the Cold Spring Sparkling Mineral water label from Cold Spring Brewery of Minnesota. This brand joined Heileman La Croix Sparkling Mineral Water. Heileman put La Croix water into cans for use on airlines and was introducing both lime and lemon flavors. A line of La Croix Sparkling Coolers, malt-based and available in strawberry and citrus flavors, was well received and Heileman was also test marketing wine served on draft in bars and restaurants.

Late in 1986, Heileman signed an agreement to purchase the Champale line of products from Champale Incorporated of Trenton, New Jersey. These products included sparkling extra dry, pink, and golden Champale, plus Champale coolers in a variety of flavors. The brands had sales of about 300,000 barrels and a loyal customer following. Analysts predicted the premium-priced brand could have a bigger financial impact for the company than either Special Export or Colt 45 malt liquor. The brand was being produced at a plant in New Jersey, but speculation was that Heileman would move production to its Belleville, Illinois, plant.

Beer on the Job?

As public awareness of alcohol abuse increased, concerns moved to the workplace, and brewers started to worry about employees drinking on the job while operating high-speed equipment.

For almost 100 years, employees of breweries had enjoyed free beer on the job. The first known reference to the practice was in 1887, when a Pabst union settled a strike for $60 a month salary and free beer. In 1984, most Heileman breweries still allowed free beer on the job, but at Miller the company had recently switched from free beer at work to three free cases a month to take home. Within a short time, Heileman also prohibited beer on the job.

Brewers were responding to the call for lower-alcohol beers, but at the same time imported beers were the fastest-growing segment of the industry. Heileman announced an agreement to become the sole importer for a Dominican Republic beer, Presidente Pilsner, a European-style lager, and hoped to market the brand in New York City and Boston.

Heileman Importers Limited which was already importing Beck beer, also made a deal to become the exclusive importer of Hacker-Pschorr beer from Germany. Heileman was to handle all of the Hacker-Pschorr brands, including Light, Dark, Pils, Maibock, Oktoberfest, Weiss, and Festbier. But in February 1986, a judge ruled Heileman couldn't distribute Hacker-Pschorr German beers in New Jersey and New England, since the Beer Import Company of Union, New Jersey, had been importing them for more than 40 years.

The next year, Heileman finalized an agreement with the 500-year-old Luneburger Kronen Brauerei in Hamburg, West Germany, to become the sole importers of its Moravia Super Premium beers. The deal included both the regular and dark brands and eventually the light and non-alcoholic brands.

August 1985 saw the introduction of Heileman's Special Export Light beer, and its advertising slogan: "Finally . . . A light beer that deserves to be called special."

In August 1985, Heileman President Russ Cleary and several other members of his management team met with Milwaukee Mayor Henry Maier. Cleary carried what appeared to be an architectural drawing as he entered the meeting. Neither party would comment on the purpose of the meeting, but they said an announcement would be made the next week. The rumor mill generated two possibilities:

1. Heileman would expand its recently acquired Oswald Jaeger Baking Company in Milwaukee.
2. A small brewery would be established to capitalize on the Milwaukee brewing heritage.

The next week Heileman announced its intention to build a new brewery in Milwaukee that would brew European-style beer in small quantities. The Val Blatz Brewery was intended to capitalize on the increasing popularity of import and specialty brands from microbreweries. The brands to be produced were from historic recipes brewed by the original Blatz brewery of Milwaukee: Old Heidelberg, Culmbacher, Blatz Private Stock, Tivoli, Wiener, and Muenchener Draft. The future included the possibility of brewing Weiss beer, German Alt beer, British stouts and ales, and special holiday brews. Initially the brewery only produced barrels of beer, although plans called for adding bottling and canning lines.

Building the new brewery, whose initial production was only 120,000 barrels, went against the nationwide trend. Only two other breweries had been built recently in the United States—by Anheuser-Busch in Saint Louis and by Miller in Ohio. The latter plant never opened because of declining demand. Even so, Cleary said Heileman might also build similar breweries on the East Coast and West Coast if the Val Blatz experiment was successful.

The new Milwaukee brewery tripled in size from original plans, and Heileman purchased another two acres of land nearby in anticipation of future expansion. Hans Kestler was named brewmaster at Val Blatz. He was a native of Ansbach, Germany, and had 25 years of brewing experience there and in the United States.

Observers felt that the new brewery was part of a bigger plan by Heileman to increase sales of Blatz in Milwaukee. In early September 1986 the new brewery was opened with a celebration including beer, food, music, and a demonstration by the Heileman Old Style skydiving team. The parade ended in Old Heidelberg Park in Glendale, since Old Heidelberg Private Stock was one of two brands initially produced at the brewery.

Mayor Maier took the opportunity to lash out at critics of the project, especially the *Milwaukee*

. . . From When the Earth Was Pure

In the summer of 1985, Heileman started to offer free water at a tap near the visitor center. This popular idea came from other breweries it owned.

Heileman had spent $500,000 a decade earlier to drill a 600-foot-deep well into the Mount Simon aquifer, to reach water which carbon dating tests showed to be 7,500 years old. It considered the pure water to be a key ingredient in a quality product with a consistent taste.

In 1985, when the free-water program first started, only 54 gallons of water per month were taken. By 1995 that volume had grown to 744,000 gallons a month.

During this period, concerns with contaminated water were becoming increasingly common in Wisconsin, Minnesota, and Iowa. Local residents liked the purity of the water and the lack of smell that they associated with city water. One hospital in Iowa even came and got the water for use on burn patients because it was so free from impurities.

The following sign hung above the Heileman water tap at Fourth and Mississippi streets:

> *More than 600 feet beneath this ground flows a stream of artesian water of exceptional purity. This pure natural artesian spring water, created by ancient snows and rains, has been stored in deep underground reservoirs protected by nature for thousands of years. Leading geologists have determined the age and origin of this water and consider it to be the purest known to man.*
>
> *To obtain this source of pure, perfect water, the House of Heileman has drilled deep beneath the Earth's surface to tap this pure water. No ingredient is more important in determining the quality and character of beer than the water used to brew it. We know of no finer or purer source of brewing water anywhere in the world.*
>
> ***Water From When The Earth Was Pure.***

In the spring of 1998, Stroh turned off the public water tap at the brewery in La Crosse for several months, prompted by abuse of the service by people hooking up hoses and filling large tanks and containers. During the closing, the tap was modified to prevent hose connections.

Journal, which had pooh-poohed the project for its small size. He told critics the size wasn't as important as the fact that Milwaukee had been able to attract the high-tech brewery in the first place, and challenged the newspaper to invest as much money in Milwaukee as the $6 million Heileman had spent to build the brewery. Early in 1987 Heileman Milwaukee Weiss, a wheat beer produced at the new brewery, won first place at the Great American Beer Festival among 120 beers in 12 categories.

In September 1988, Heileman announced a multimillion-dollar advertising campaign for the first domestic premium dry beer in America, Old Style Special Dry. The beer featured a crisper, livelier taste, with a distinctive dry finish obtained by a longer fermentation process. Dry beers were first introduced in

Japan in 1987 and quickly accounted for 40 percent of all beer sales there.

About a month after its introduction, Heileman reported that sales for Old Style Special Dry had exceeded all expectations, and production couldn't keep up with demand. The beer was originally introduced in Chicago, but was quickly expanded into the Milwaukee and La Crosse markets. It contained 139 calories, compared with 145 for Old Style, had the same alcohol content, and sold for about the same price. It didn't take long for Anheuser-Busch to challenge Heileman's product. Anheuser-Busch began test marketing Michelob Dry in five cities shortly after Old Style Special Dry was introduced.

Heileman and Anheuser-Busch claimed that dry beers would eventually account for 2 percent of all sales in the United States. However, industry observers disagreed, predicting that the market would falter, as it had for the low-alcohol beers several years earlier. Nevertheless, by March 1989, Heileman had introduced two additional dry brands, Rainier Special Dry and I.C. Special Dry.

In June 1989 a federal district court judge ruled that the law prohibiting disclosure of alcohol content on beer labels was unconstitutional. Heileman felt that would be helpful to the company's low-alcohol and no-alcohol brands. In April 1990 Heileman came out with strong support for a proposed law that would require labeling the alcohol content for any beer that had more than four percent alcohol content. In August that year, Washington became the first state to legalize alcohol content labeling on all malt beverages.

Val Blatz Brewery

An artist's drawing of the new Val Blatz Brewery showed it in the traditional German half-timber style. Plans were made to complete it by July 1, 1986. The brewery was built at 10th and Galena streets in Milwaukee on land Heileman had acquired as part of the purchase of the Jaeger Baking Company earlier in the year.

The new highly automated brewery cost about $4 million and was modeled after a recently opened brewery in the United Kingdom. Initial plans were to hire 12 to 14 people to run the entire brewery, with an additional 10 employees in each of the next two years. Additional employees were also hired to give tours and work at an accompanying gift shop that featured historic Blatz memorabilia.

Russ Cleary indicated that while Heileman could have built the brewery elsewhere, it felt it belonged in Milwaukee because of the rich brewing history there. Val Blatz, a Bavarian immigrant, had opened his brewery in Milwaukee in 1851. In 1875, it became the first brewery in the United States to bottle beer, and in 1876 a Blatz product won a gold medal at the Centennial Exposition in Philadelphia.

But there was another business reason for building in Milwaukee. Heileman management realized that the Pabst market in Milwaukee was up for grabs. It considered the investment in Milwaukee to be a good way to build goodwill and help capture some of that business.

Memories

Heileman bought its first corporate plane, a Piper Navajo, in 1967. But when Heileman bought Seattle-based Rainier in 1976, it still didn't own a plane capable of flying nonstop from La Crosse to Seattle.

Heileman was considering buying the latest Learjet when Russ Cleary and several other Heileman executives needed to fly down to Houston, Texas, for a national beer distributors convention. Cleary asked another executive to contact Learjet to see if they had one of the latest models available for a test flight. After a few quick phone calls, he was told a new Learjet, that had been built for another company, was up for a test flight. The pilot was directed to fly to La Crosse to collect Cleary and the other executives.

The Heileman folks were shocked to see a bright pink jet, which had been built for Mary Kay Cosmetics, rolling to a stop at the terminal in La Crosse. Several executives were horrified, but Cleary thought it was hilarious. When the plane arrived in Houston, Cleary recognized another arriving private jet owned by an executive from a competitor. The competitor prided himself on always having the latest and greatest jet. Cleary knew that for once he was flying on a newer and better jet.

He directed the pilot to park next to the other jet. As Cleary disembarked from the pink jet the competitor was just leaving his plane. He looked over at Cleary and remarked: "Russ, I always knew you were a maverick in the beer industry. However, I never thought I'd see the day when you flew on a pink jet."

—Memory submitted by Jerry Miller

Chapter 24

Politically Incorrect Brewing

POWERMASTER, CRAZY HORSE AND OTHER PRODUCTS BROUGHT CONTROVERSY: 1991–1995

To many employees and La Crosse residents these embarrassing episodes epitomized the problems at the company. Many felt those problems resulted from the loss of local control and lack of Midwestern ethics.

Powermaster, 5.9 percent alcohol content—1991

WHO OBJECTED

- The National Coalition to Prevent Impaired Driving and the federal Bureau of Alcohol, Tobacco, and Firearms asked Heileman to remove the word *power* from the label and advertising. It argued that the word *power* implied higher alcohol content and was therefore prohibited.
- Doctor Antonia Novello, the surgeon general, said Powermaster targeted blacks, particularly blacks ages 24 to 35, who had a higher rate of cirrhosis of the liver. The surgeon general called the product particularly irresponsible.
- A Baptist minister from Harlem, New York, launched a campaign to whitewash Heileman billboards advertising Powermaster.
- Black activist Dick Gregory and two Chicago priests, George Clements and Michael Pfleger, announced they were organizing a nationwide boycott and picketing of Heileman outlets and facilities. Members of the boycott included the National Association for the Advancement of Colored People and the Southern Christian Leadership Conference. A few days later, the priests appeared in La Crosse and demanded to see Heileman President Thomas Rattigan. They refused to leave the company's headquarters when they were told he was unavailable. The police were called, the two priests were arrested, and the event was featured on ABC's *Nightline* television show.
- Advertising executives from around the country called Powermaster the wrong product at the wrong time. But Lockhart and Pettus, a New York

agency that originated the advertising, was owned and run by blacks.

- John Convers Jr., a congressman from Michigan and senior member of the Black Caucus, along with five other congressmen and the governor of Illinois, all condemned the product.
- John Medinger, then a state representative from La Crosse, said the product was socially incorrect.
- The federal Bureau of Alcohol, Tobacco, and Firearms pulled the plug on Powermaster, ruling Heileman could not use the word *power.* Industry observers predicted the ruling was just the first against malt liquors with higher alcohol content. They didn't think they would be banned, but predicted advertising would have to be tamed. They noted Heileman's Colt 45 brand also had been criticized for advertising with a lightning bolt and the words, "It's got more."

WHAT HEILEMAN DID

Heileman donated $76,931 to the United Negro College Fund, and closed out the Powermaster brand. When the last of the product appeared in stores, can collectors rushed to buy them at inflated prices. A Milwaukee distributor charged retailers triple the normal price. Some people were paying anywhere from $4 to $25 for a single can. With the limited supply there was a huge demand for the last of Powermaster.

In La Crosse, employees were each allowed to purchase one case of Powermaster. People flocked to buy the product just to taste it and get one of the 16-ounce cans as a collector's item. Powermaster caps and advertising at the Heileman gift shop also sold well.

When a shipment of Powermaster arrived at a Philadelphia distributor, the Pennsylvania State Police, who claimed the label illegally advertised the alcohol content, confiscated two cases. The distributor agreed to sell all remaining inventory by midnight of September 6.

Before the whole Powermaster controversy could die down there was one last little fiasco related to it. As the court date for the trespassing charges against the two priests approached, Heileman decided it didn't want to press charges.

Unfortunately, it neglected to inform the judge or city attorney. As a result, the judge wouldn't drop the charges until Heileman submitted the request in writing. Eventually the company did so, finally bringing an end to the entire unfortunate set of events.

St. Ides malt liquor—April 1992

WHO OBJECTED

Black activists charged Heileman with using advertising themes aimed at black underage drinkers in the Milwaukee market.

WHAT HEILEMAN DID

Randy Smith, Heileman general counsel, pointed out that Heileman only brewed the product under contract with the McKenzie River Corporation, and had no role in its marketing.

Crazy Horse malt liquor, brewed under contract for the Hornell Brewing Company—April 1992

WHO OBJECTED

- The Oglala Sioux resented a connection between alcohol and the famous Indian chief. They were especially incensed by the fact the bottle resembled a whisky bottle.

- Surgeon General Antonia Novello sent a message to the alcohol industry that these products caused disease, disability, and addiction.
- About 20 activists from the American Indian Movement and the Wisconsin Greens, an environmental group, met in Riverside Park in La Crosse, where they picketed and dumped a 40-ounce bottle of Crazy Horse malt liquor into a toilet they had brought along. They called for a nationwide boycott of Heileman products, especially Arizona Iced Tea, another Hornell product. Simultaneous protests were also held at Heileman facilities in Chicago and Baltimore.
- Congress passed a bill that prohibited Hornell from using the Crazy Horse label. But in April of 1993 a U.S. district judge overturned the ruling, saying it violated the First Amendment.
- Arne Carlson, Minnesota's governor, signed a bill into law, effective August 1, 1994, that banned the sale of Crazy Horse malt liquor in Minnesota. The state of Washington also banned sales of the product, and in Nebraska the state's liquor control commission asked distributors to voluntarily refuse to sell Crazy Horse.
- In August 1995, an official of the U.S. Commerce Department denied Hornell a trademark for Crazy Horse Malt Liquor, saying the use of the Indian leader's name was particularly offensive and crass and undermined and demeaned his teachings and reputation.

WHAT HEILEMAN DID

The company initially responded that Crazy Horse, like St. Ides, was brewed under contract.

WHAT HORNELL DID

The product was not sold in states with large Indian reservations, such as South Dakota and Washington. It also argued the 40-ounce bottle was not intended to be a single-serving container, but a possible substitute for a bottle of wine in restaurants. It noted the product had half the alcohol content of wine and the container was attractive on a dinner table. Distribution was limited to the Northeast, and anything referring to American Indians was removed from the label.

Finally, a tribal judge from the Rosebud Sioux Court ruled that Seth Big Crow, a relative of Crazy Horse, could not punish Heileman for brewing Crazy Horse Malt Liquor, since the brand was not sold in South Dakota. However, it was ruled that he had the right to determine how his relative's name was used commercially within the reservation.

WHAT STROH DID

In April 2001, John Stroh III, chairman of SBC Holdings Incorporated (the former Stroh Brewing Company), settled with relatives of Crazy Horse. As a representative of the G. Heileman Brewing Company, he presented them with seven horses, 32 blankets, some tobacco and sweet grass and an apology at a ceremony attended by relatives of Crazy Horse and members of the Sioux tribe. For the Sioux, the apology was the most important part of the settlement, according to Seth Big Crow.

Colt 45 Premium malt liquor—May 1993

WHO OBJECTED

- The federal government accused Heileman of reintroducing the old Powermaster product under this new label.
- In Philadelphia, a coalition of community groups asked retailers to withdraw sales of Colt 45 Premium. They said the advertising phrase, "Be a Premium Player," was a reference to gang activity, sexual promiscuity, and sexual abuse of women.
- A February 1993 article appeared in the *Wall Street Journal* critical of Heileman's latest ad, which featured a black college graduate in shirt and tie sitting on a front porch drinking a Colt 45. The dialogue identifies him as the first college graduate in his family, and he is saying that he hopes the brothers in the neighborhood will follow in his footsteps. Critics of the advertisement felt the message was directed at underage black drinkers.
- Local people and special interest groups asked why Heileman continued to produce malt liquors and other controversial products. Russ Cleary said malt liquor sales were skyrocketing, and had a high profit margin. For Heileman, malt liquor sales represented almost 20 percent of its total volume at that point. Smith said malt liquor production was saving jobs, especially at the Heileman breweries in Baltimore and Portland. It was still being sold when the company was sold to Stroh.

Old Style—June 1993

WHO OBJECTED

Mayor Richard Daley of Chicago asked Heileman to remove 15 Heileman advertising billboards that featured the late gangster Al Capone and the slogan, "In 1929 Al persuaded all his friends to try Old Style." The ads were part of a new campaign linking historic Chicago residents to Old Style. Daley considered the billboards to be in bad taste and felt it created a poor image for Chicago. He worried about the reaction from foreign visitors coming to the city for the upcoming World Cup soccer games.

WHAT HEILEMAN DID

The billboards were replaced with ones that featured University of Chicago nuclear physicist Enrico Fermi.

A version of Special Export called "EX" —1995

WHO OBJECTED

The Minnesota Medical Association argued the ads appeared to be targeted at adolescents and sent a not-so-subliminal message that linked beer and sex. It was being marketed using slogans such as, "The joy of Ex," "Men think about Ex 100 times a day," and "Practice safe Ex, don't drink and drive."

WHAT HEILEMAN DID

Lou Lowenkron, Heileman's chief executive officer, refused to pull the ads.

To many employees and La Crosse residents these embarrassing episodes epitomized the problems at the company. Many felt those problems resulted from the loss of local control and lack of Midwestern ethics.

Chapter 25

Ask for the Beer of the Grenadier

ADVERTISING OVER THE YEARS

Old Style Lager "stands for all that's good and pure in beer . . ."

—HEILEMAN AD FROM 1903

In 1900, Old Style Lager's unique bottle label was the creation of the marketing genius of E.T. Mueller. He said the predominately green Old Style Lager label, with its many interesting caricatures, illustrated the history of brewing from ancient Teutonic times through the monasteries of Europe to modern day. On June 25, 1907, Heileman registered the famous "monk brewing" picture as a trademark.

Mueller was responsible for all sorts of marketing initiatives supporting Old Style Lager. "The beer with the snap to it" was one of his early advertising themes. A caricature of a grenadier became associated with the brand, as were unrelenting messages espousing the superiority and exclusivity of the product. Fat grenadiers, predecessors to the more commonly known and normally proportioned grenadier, were used with a variety of jingles.

An advertisement that appeared in the *La Crosse Leader and Press* on July 25, 1903, featured a biblical scene that proclaimed: "It needs no Daniel to interpret the handwriting on the wall!" The ad also indicated that Old Style Lager: "Stands for all that's good and pure in beer, Bringing to partakers Health and Happiness, Comfort and Good Cheer. It brings the roses to pale cheeks, And drives dull care away. Do not wait, do not delay, But order a case today."

The wit and wisdom of Mueller was clearly evident when he wrote

Heileman cone-top can featuring "monk brewing" picture from about 1935.
FROM THE COLLECTION OF PAUL D. KOELLER.

the following for an advertisement which appeared in *Nord Stern,* published in La Crosse on April 10, 1908. The translation from the German text is as follows: "Produced at a brewery with unmatched exclusivity and staffed with a packaging department of heart filling, yes even homesickness quality. The original Old Style Lager. There are beers and there are beers in the world but only one Old Style Lager. Whether civilization followed beer or beer followed civilization, one thing is for sure; that the establishment of civilization would be pretty lean where Old Style Lager was not served. Obviously one who goes to Rome wants to see the Pope, and obviously one who comes to La Crosse definitely wants to see the unique and outstanding brewery where beers are made of hops and malt with just a touch of kindness and poetry and God's promise to preserve. God Preserve Heileman's brewery."

A newspaper ad on August 4, 1908, referred to Germany as one of the healthiest nations and stated that in Munich the consumption of beer was more than two pints per day for every man, woman, and child. The ad included sketches of famous German artists, musicians, scientists, military leaders, writers, and government leaders as evidence of the benefits of beer drinking. People were encouraged to drink beer with every meal because "there's health in every drop."

An advertisement in the July 2, 1910, *La Crosse Tribune* states: "HURRAH FOR US. There's an individuality about the American way of doing things that puts our country in the lead of all nations. There's an individuality about the 'Heileman way' of making beer that puts *Old Style Lager* 'The Beer with a Snap to it' in the lead of all beers. No other beer excels in taste or purity. **It has no superior.**"

A *Minneapolis Journal* ad on August 23, 1911, promoted Old Style Lager with an interesting twist in pre-Prohibition days—"Old Style Lager appeals to the particular man and the discriminating physician. Intelligent persons of this class well understand that the small percentage of alcohol in Old Style Lager will act as a tonic which will develop and strengthen the body and brain."

By the early 1940s, Heileman had changed the Old Style themes to "Sign of a Friendly Host" and "America's Quality Beer."

In 1944, Heileman issued a paperback cookbook, *The Sportsman's Way—How to Prepare Wild Game & Waterfowl.* In addition to numerous recipes for venison and more common game, it contained recipes for things as exotic as raccoon, possum, and buffalo tongue. Of course, the booklet also featured advertisements for Old Style and encouraged cooks to always serve Old Style. The back cover featured two sportsmen enjoying an Old Style as they admired their guns, with a deer head mounted on the wall behind them.

The next year, Heileman issued *The Sportsman's Way—How to Prepare Fish and Seafood Cookery,* which covered a wide variety of seafood and fish. An appendix listed all of the world records for each variety of fish. Old Style was suggested to be the perfect beverage to be served. The back cover featured an advertisement of two men in a rowboat enjoying an Old Style while they fished.

A *La Crosse Tribune* ad on May 12, 1945, contained a coupon offer for a free *Better Homes and*

Gardens Vegetable Garden Guide presented by Heileman in the interest of "Food for Victory." Heileman's slogan was that Old Style Lager was "Proud to be part of La Crosse" and "It's America's Quality Beer."

In the early 1950s the first television commercials were produced promoting Old Style Lager. The lyrics of the "Heileman Waltz" beckoned, "Ask for the beer of the grenadier . . . Heileman's Old Style Lager." Several commercials showed actors actually drinking beer in a bar scene, something that has long since been prohibited by the brewers' advertising code. The script included the theme, "Aged far, far longer than any other premium beer," and clocks were used to symbolize aging. Two commercials were cut specifically for sponsorship of the television programs *Racket Squad* and *Hollywood Showcase*.

Soon a likable cartoon character, the Little Professor, came upon the Old Style Lager television commercial scene. In a German accent, the Little Professor asked rhyming questions put to music about Heileman's spring water, malt house, aging process and the resulting tempting stein of beer, to which a chorus would respond. These jingles were clever and became quite popular. The first Little Professor commercials were in black and white. Color was added in the mid-1950s.

In 1955, Heileman issued a 45 rpm record of "Heileman's Old Style Lager Song" to the tune of "Schnitzel Bank Song," and "The Heileman's Waltz." A schnitzel bank is the bench that a cooper straddles as he shapes the wooden staves for a beer barrel.

A new sales pitch in 1957 proclaimed that there are two kinds of people in the world, those who think that Old Style is the world's finest beer and those who haven't tasted it yet. This theme was promoted through newspapers, television, radio and billboards. The Little Professor was joined on TV by George Stone, a well-known Chicago television and radio personality. Heileman's new advertising agency explained that the commercial's focus was to help create appetite appeal such as in scenes where beer was shown being poured. The theme became "Aged longer than any other beer."

By 1958, Old Style television commercials featured a group of singers who encouraged viewers to "drink to the new style of Old Style." Commercials featured the new packaging that included flattop 12-ounce cans, 12-ounce returnable bottles and 8-ounce returnable bottles called juniors. All the containers sported the Old Style shield. In January 1958, Heileman began sponsoring the new television show *Sea Hunt,* which was seen throughout most of Wisconsin, Illinois, and parts of Iowa. The show was the No. 1-ranked half-hour television show in Chicago by 1959.

In the late 1950s, Heileman took an entirely new approach to advertising. The familiar Heileman Grenadier and the Little Professor were given only minor roles in the new advertising, which focused on the beer and the water used to brew the beer. The goal was to convince buyers that Heileman products were of the highest quality and worth the extra money, a direct response to the trend toward lower-priced brands introduced by some of the national breweries.

To capitalize on new brands, the company introduced a new corporate trademark in 1963, a black shield and eagle symbol with the words "House of Heileman." The shield and eagle had been used as symbols of the brewery for many decades.

In 1965, Heileman introduced a new Old Style advertising campaign based on the "Pure Brewed" theme. In 1966, the theme was expanded to "Twice brewed, Pure Brewed . . . Heileman's Old Style . . . The light likable beer that is easy to stay with glass after glass."

In 1970, "Old Style, the singular beer . . . from God's Country" was aimed at potential customers in Chicago and other large metropolitan areas.

Heileman dramatically increased spending on advertising to almost $14 million for 1977. Old Style touted the themes of: "Brewed In God's Country Slowly and Naturally," "Kraeusening," and "Sparkling Pure Wisconsin Spring Water." The company also introduced the first formal Special Export advertising campaign: "Special Export—You can travel the world over and never find a better beer." Schmidt was advertised as "the beer that grew with the Great Northwest" and Rainier as "mountain fresh." Wiedemann claimed "A naturally better beer."

Blatz, sold in 35 states, was the closest thing Heileman had to a national brand, and was being marketed as "America's Great Light Beer." Blatz sales were up due to hidden camera taste comparison commercials, which featured consumers comparing Blatz with several national brands, including Budweiser, Pabst, and Schlitz. Some breweries and consumer agencies complained the participants weren't told they were being videotaped. However, Heileman had cleared all objections and hurdles and came out with an honest and candid comparison.

During the mid-1980s, Heileman needed new ideas to increase sales. It rapidly introduced new products, businesses, promotions and advertisements

Brewed in God's Country

In 1805 Zebulon Pike explored the Upper Mississippi
When he reached this valley he wrote . . .
A man can expect to enjoy such a prospect but twice or thrice in his life.
I left this valley when I was young. Only recently have I returned.
I stood where Pike had stood, and wondered
Why had I ever left! This is La Crosse, Wisconsin.
Where the Mississippi and Black and La Crosse and Bad Axe rivers form God's Country.
La Crosse is the home of Heileman's Old Style.
Old Style is pure brewed, double brewed.
Naturally brewed. The only beer that truly is.
Consider: if you lived here, wouldn't you take the extra time and effort
To make the finest beer possible, just so you could stay?
Try some pure, genuine Old Style.
The singular beer—from God's country.

The proposition is simple.
You live here. And you like living here.
It's God's Country.
You'd like to stay. So, since you brew beer for a living,
You try and brew the best beer in the world.
The beer is called Heileman's Old Style. It's pure brewed,
Twice brewed with only sparkling pure spring water.
Yes they brew their Old Style as carefully
As if their whole way of life depended on it.
If you lived here . . . Wouldn't you?

—Text of God's Country television commercials aimed at potential customers in large cities.

to try to deal with nationwide beer sales that had declined for the first time since 1957.

In 1979, Heileman had opened the "Heileman Haus" beer pavilion at the Wisconsin State Fair, and in 1983 it reached an agreement to sell Old Style beer at Milwaukee Brewer baseball games. The announcement was met with anger by the unions in Milwaukee, who were outraged that Milwaukee-made beer wasn't being sold.

By the end of 1984, Old Style was served at all Green Bay Packer, Milwaukee Brewer, and Milwaukee Bucks home games. Heileman also had contracts with the Minnesota Twins and the Chicago Cubs for beer sales at those stadiums. Heileman produced 40,000 banners and 40,000 posters for the Chicago Cubs in preparation for the National League playoff games. The company hired a former Milwaukee Bucks basketball player, Wayne Embry, who had previously done marketing for Coke and Pepsi, as special marketing consultant.

Heileman sponsored the Old Style Stock Car Racing Circuit for the Central Wisconsin Racing Association, offering an $8,000 point fund for the top 20 drivers and special "Old Style Dash For Cash" races with the winner of each race receiving $1,000. An Old Style Sky Diving Team was formed and thrilled audiences with daring dives and precision landings. There was an Old Style stage at Milwaukee Summerfest for the first time. The stage featured a new 50-foot-high illuminated sign designed by Nesco signs of La Crosse.

A giant motorized can of Old Style beer was unveiled at the Oktoberfest parade in La Crosse

Old Style Lager fishing warden bar sign from the 1940s.
FROM THE COLLECTION OF GARY SCHULTZ

in 1983. It had been obtained from Blatz four years earlier and repainted as a can of Old Style. Jay Hintzke and other employees of the plant services department took turns driving the can in parades and other events.

At the 1984 Milwaukee City of Festivals parade, Heileman led the parade with a new corporate float, "Tribute to America's Space Program." Astronauts Deke Slayton and James Lovell served as honorary parade marshals. The float, 70 feet long and featuring a futuristic-looking spaceship, was built by Chicago's To-Di Trucking Company, which also built floats for the Rose Bowl parade and other celebrations. The float, powered by a 20-year-old Jeep, had a stereo system that played music from the movie *2001: A Space Odyssey.*

Late that year Heileman changed advertising themes. Ads continued to focus on the water used to make Old Style, but stressed that the water was thousands of years old. The ads featured dramatic scenery from Wisconsin, Alaska and Montana. Television ads were set to music from the Academy Award-winning film *The Chariots of Fire.* The familiar voice in the ads belonged to Hal Riney, who had been featured in ads for Gallo Wines and in Ronald Reagan's presidential re-election ads.

In September 1985, Jimmy's Bar in Bangor, Wisconsin, was the site for the filming of a new Heileman television commercial that used 11 local residents along with seven professional actors. The scene supposedly was a bar in Chicago in which a diehard

La Crosse Interstate Fair Advertising booth during Prohibition.
PHOTO COURTESY OF MURPHY LIBRARY,
UNIVERSITY OF WISCONSIN-LA CROSSE

Budweiser drinker was persuaded to try Heileman Old Style and became a convert. During the day of the filming of the commercial, the tavern was closed. The next day, lost sales were made up by the best single-day ever at Jimmy's Bar.

A second Heileman commercial was filmed at the experimental forest near Bangor. The commercial showed Russ Cleary driving a team of horses pulling a Heileman beer wagon that passes a team of Budweiser-like Clydesdales. The Budweiser look-alike horses were actually a team of Clydesdales owned by Dan Jones of Bangor. Later, at a horse show, Jones showed a picture from the commercial to a genuine Budweiser Clydesdale driver, who looked puzzled and said he couldn't remember ever filming the commercial.

Another commercial, filmed on the front porch of Zabolio's General Store in Genoa, Wisconsin, showed a group of diehard Budweiser drinkers being introduced to Old Style and finding it better. They calculated that they had made 8,808 past mistakes drinking Budweiser, and they were determined to make up for those mistakes by drinking an equal number of Old Styles.

In December, Heileman celebrated the 130th anniversary of the Schmidt brewery in Saint Paul. The company bought time on 130 radio stations across Minnesota which simultaneously played a birthday salute to Schmidt. Minnesota Governor Rudy Perpich, and more than 1,700 Minnesota residents with the last name of Schmidt, were sent invitations to attend the largest birthday party in Minnesota history.

Ads featured black-and-white film clips of old James Cagney movies in 1986. In one, the Cagney character muscled into a bar to persuade the owner to stock Heileman products.

That fall, four new television commercials were filmed in La Crosse. About 120 local residents were paid $100 each to play the role of extras in the commercials. The first ad featured a wedding reception and was filmed at the Eagles Club, Fifth Avenue and King Street. Local residents Cheri Wilhelm and Bruce Parr played the roles of bride and groom, while other residents played the role of the priest and polka dancers. The Colonial Plowboys, from Coon Valley, Wisconsin, provided the polka music.

Another ad featured many local residents lined up across the Heileman parking lot waiting to get free water from the Heileman artesian well. In the ad, a couple of local retirees asked what the holdup was and the response came back that the couple at the head of the line had 23 jugs to fill. The other two ads didn't feature many local extras. One featured the Heileman good old boys from previous ads standing in awe in front of the Giant Old Style Six-Pack. The final commercial featured brewmaster Hans Ruether in front of the copper brewing kettles inside the brewery.

To increase sales in the summer of 1986, Heileman began a more aggressive advertising campaign. The new ads featured everything from a model in a bathing suit praising the qualities of bread to a standup comedian pitching the Barrel O' Fun potato chips. A new in-store campaign known as "Heileman Summer Supply Headquarters" featured Heileman bread, buns, snacks, and beer. The campaign was especially successful in the Midwest, and even in Denver, Colorado, where Heileman products were less well-known.

Heileman New Style Lager advertising from Prohibition era.
PHOTO COURTESY OF CLEARY-KUMM FOUNDATION

In 1988, advertisements for Old Style began to reflect the aggressive marketing of the Alan Bond era. To an original score by Glenn Fry, former member of the Eagles, the ads stressed that hard work and dedication lead to the realization of dreams. The first ad showed a baseball pitcher who, after practicing in frigid Midwestern conditions, finds glory in the big leagues.

Heileman sponsored rock concerts in Wisconsin, and the nation's richest walleye fishing tournament was held in La Crosse in the fall of 1988. A $3 million budget helped sponsor events such as a Minnesota Twins towel giveaway, Seafair in Seattle, Bite of Seattle, Taste of Chicago, the Illinois State Fair, Summerfest Amphitheater in Milwaukee, the Milwaukee Wave soccer team, County Zoo Terrace in Milwaukee, and a variety of other minor events.

Throughout the 1970s, Heileman had used an advertising approach that featured the product as the hero. But by the 1990s, it relied on humor, famous people, and a more aggressive approach to marketing its products. The rules had changed and Heileman had proved that it too could change with the times.

However, the big question remained: Was the new approach an example of too-little, too-late in a fast-changing beer market?

Chapter 26

We're Not Alone Here

HISTORY OF OTHER LA CROSSE BREWERIES BEGINNING IN THE 1850s

A perfect beer; a tonic that promotes the health and longevity of men and women.

—ADVERTISING DESCRIPTION OF JOHN GUND BREWING COMPANY'S PEERLESS BEER

Heileman was neither the first nor the largest La Crosse brewery in pre-Prohibition days. Both the Gund and Michel breweries were larger. The Heileman and Michel breweries were the only ones to survive Prohibition, and Heileman was the only one to become nationally known.

In 1900, the five La Crosse breweries had more than 900 employees earning $900,000 in wages. More than half a million dollars was reportedly paid to farmers for grain that year.

The brewing industry in La Crosse peaked in 1918, just before Prohibition, when brewers were employing about 1,640 people earning $1.2 million. The breweries also paid more than $3 million in rent, taxes, repairs, advertising, travel expenses, freight, and cereals used in the manufacture of their products.

Breweries in La Crosse's history include:

Nicolai/Nicolai & Franz Brewery

The Nicolai Brewery, in business from 1854 to 1857, was located on the north side of Pearl Street between Second and Third streets. Sometimes referred to as the Nicolai & Franz Brewery, this entity was owned by Dr. Gustavus Nicolai and Jacob Franz. The owners hired young Gottlieb Heileman as a foreman one month before the business dissolved. The Nicolai Brewery was the first to sell beer in Prairie La Crosse.

City Brewery of Prairie La Crosse

City Brewery of Prairie La Crosse in Wisconsin was John Gund's chosen name for his first brewery, which operated from August 1854 until 1858. This brewery, the first built in La Crosse, was actually a log cabin standing on the southeast corner of Front

This old sketch purportedly shows the log building that served as the Gund brewery.
PHOTO COURTESY OF LA CROSSE COUNTY HISTORICAL SOCIETY

and Division streets. After selling his property to C.L. Coleman in 1858, Gund partnered with Gottlieb Heileman to found the City Brewery. In 1872, Gund left the partnership and started his own Empire Brewery.

John Gund Brewery

The John Gund Brewery was built at the corner of Ninth Street and South Avenue (south and somewhat east of the current Lutheran Hospital), at a cost of $250,000, using limestone quarried from the bluffs surrounding La Crosse. Gund's brewery was one of the first in the United States to be electrified. The brewery thrived and by 1880 was producing 9,000 barrels per year and doing a large export business. That same year the business was incorporated and the name changed to the John Gund Brewing company. Beer was being shipped to Wisconsin, Minnesota, Iowa, North Dakota, South Dakota, and elsewhere. The brewery employed 25 people with an annual payroll of $15,000. Production went from 9,000 barrels per annum in 1880, to 43,000 in 1890, and to 94,000 by 1900.

On September 23, 1897, the Gund brewery was destroyed by fire. Gund had rebuilt the brewery by May 1899 and was back in business. In 1900, Gund won a medal and diploma for its Peerless Beer at the Paris Exposition. Peerless was extolled as "a perfect beer; a tonic that promotes the health and longevity of men and women."

Gund's beer was supported with very sophisticated and classy lithography pieces and advertising. In 1902, Gund purchased the assets of the Plank Road Brewery after George Zeisler's death. The Gund brewery operated until 1920, when it was closed by a labor strike and Prohibition. Much of the brewery property was purchased by G. Heileman Brewing Company in 1941. The malt house was used by Heileman for many years thereafter. After Prohibition, the Peerless brand was produced by La Crosse Breweries Incorporated until that company closed in 1956.

John Gund brewery on South Avenue in La Crosse about 1900. COURTESY OF MURPHY LIBRARY, UNIVERSITY OF WISCONSIN–LA CROSSE

Eagle/Franz Bartl/Kunz/Ziegler Brewery

Jacob Franz, partner with Nicolai in their previously unsuccessful Nicolai Brewery venture, struck out on his own in 1857 and established the Eagle Brewery at 1201 La Crosse Street. In 1862, Frederick Mueller joined Franz as a partner and the two of them operated the Eagle Brewery together until Franz left La Crosse and moved to Sioux City, Iowa. It then became the Kappes and Mueller Eagle Brewery.

In 1870, John Hofer replaced Frederick Mueller, and the brewery was renamed the Kappes and Hofer Eagle Brewery. In the mid-1870s, John Hofer assumed sole ownership of the brewery. Hofer added a beer garden that he called the Park Saloon and Garden. In 1886, he sold the brewery to Franz Bartl. Franz Bartl was born in Bohemia in 1838, came to the United States in 1868, and moved to La Crosse in 1874. He had worked in the brewing industry since he was 14 years old, and had been previously employed by the Plank Road, Gund, and Peter Bub (of Winona, Minnesota) breweries.

When Bartl bought the brewery he dropped the Eagle name. Early brands were Matchless and Premium Brew. A new bottling plant was constructed about 1900. The company incorporated as the Franz Bartl Brewing Company in 1904. A July 18, 1910, advertisement in the *La Crosse Tribune* offered Premium Brew and High Grade in bottles and Bavarian Brau Lager (presumably keg) beer. Another brand was Bartl Bräu. Franz Bartl's sons, Joseph and Frank, ran the company following his death on October 5, 1914.

During Prohibition they manufactured cereal beverages and bottled soda drinks. The business was sold in 1933 to George Kunz, and reopened the following year as the George Kunz Company. In September 1934, Kunz was forced out of the company and replaced by Theodore J. Molzahn. The plant was enlarged and modernized and was producing about 10,000 barrels per year of mainly Hofbrau and Queensbury beer. LaX Club was a brand it marketed in 1935.

The brewery operated until 1937 and remained closed until 1948. At that time, the Louis Ziegler Brewing Company of Beaver Dam, Wisconsin, reopened it as Ziegler's Old Fashioned Brewery. During this time, the plant produced about 2,000 barrels of Old Fashioned Lager each year before closing in 1950. Much of the brewery's equipment was later dismantled and the building became a soda pop factory.

La Crosse/C&J Michel/ La Crosse Breweries Incorporated

Charles Michel moved to the United States in 1848 and settled in Philadelphia, where with his brother, John, he opened a contracting business. In 1849, the two brothers were drawn to California by the Gold Rush, but eventually returned to Philadelphia and from there moved to Chicago in 1856. They disliked Chicago and decided to head up the Mississippi River to Saint Paul. Along the way their route was blocked by ice and they ended up spending the winter in La Crosse. They decided to stay in La Crosse and started a contracting business and built several houses. The La Crosse Brewery opened for business on December 24, 1857, at the southeast corner of Third and Division streets.

In 1858, the Michel brothers hired a new brewmaster, Gottlieb Heileman, who had just lost his foreman position due to the Nicolai Brewery's cessation. Charles Michel brought two La Crosse brewing families together by marrying Louise Gund, daughter of John and Louisa Gund, in 1872. By 1880 the La Crosse Brewery was one of the largest in La Crosse, producing more than 7,000 barrels of beer per year. In 1882, the brewery's name was changed to the C&J Michel Brewing Company, and by 1889 the brewery buildings covered more than five acres. The plant included a brewhouse, malt house, elevator, ice houses, bottle house, cooper shop, engine house, and stables.

By 1893, the brewery had a successful export business and was shipping beer to Wisconsin, Illinois, Iowa, Minnesota, Nebraska, North Dakota, and South Dakota. On December 8, 1894, the brewery suffered significant loss due to a fire. In 1907, most of the brewery was moved to the west side of Third Street and significant additions were made at a cost of $1 million. The company's brands included Elfenbrau and Perfection. In 1919 the brewery's name was changed to the La Crosse Brewery, and a year later brewing operations ceased due to Prohibition.

Carl F. Michel reopened the brewery after Prohibition as La Crosse Breweries Incorporated and purchased the Peerless trademark and label rights from the defunct John Gund Brewing Company. The brewery operated at 700 and 718 South Third Street and produced Elfenbrau and Wisconsin's Best in addition to Peerless. L.J. Roberts managed the brewery until 1944, when he was replaced by Michel.

Michel remained in control until 1955, when W.E. Fantle took over. When this brewery closed, in March 1956, Heileman was left as the only brewery in La Crosse.

Plank Road Brewery

In 1867, George Zeisler and Otto Nagel opened the Plank Road Brewery at 718 North Third Street (Third Street between Grove Street and the La Crosse River). The original building was three stories high and built of stone at a cost of $25,000. It had a capacity of about 1,000 barrels per year.

Zeisler was born in Bavaria in 1825 and in 1853 settled in Monroe County in Pennsylvania. He came to La Crosse three years later and worked for the C.L. Coleman Company for five years before buying a copper still for making malt whiskey. He was in the whiskey business for six years and then ran a butcher shop on Main Street for a year and half before opening the brewery.

In 1869, Zeisler took sole ownership of the brewery and operated it until 1902. On December 14, 1873, a fire destroyed the brewery. It was rebuilt in the spring of 1874, but again was beset by fire on July 4, 1874. Finally reconstructed in the summer of 1875, the main building was a four-story stone structure. The cost of the rebuilding effort was said to be $35,000. In 1880 the brewery was producing 2,800 barrels of beer per annum. By 1890 Zeisler's two sons, George Jr. and Leonard, had joined the business, which was incorporated that year as Geo. Zeisler and Sons Brewing Company. The company's beer brands were called "Gambrinus Beverages." George Jr. in 1884 married Emma Heileman, daughter of Gottlieb and Johanna Heileman. Following Emma's death in 1926, he married another Heileman daughter, Jenny.

George Zeisler Jr. was elected to the board of directors of G. Heileman Brewing Company in 1892. Apparently in disfavor at Heileman, he was removed as a director and stripped of his Heileman stock on October 17, 1899. But on February 2, 1902, he again was elected to the Heileman board. In February 1905, he became a vice president and served as president of the company during Prohibition (1929–1933). George Zeisler Sr. passed away on August 14, 1902.

On October 5, 1902, the two sons sold the brewery to the John Gund Brewing Company for $125,000. The deal included between 20 and 30 saloons that the Plank Road Brewery controlled at the time. The brewery was thereafter closed and the tied-house saloons immediately became purveyors of Gund's beer.

Voegele/North La Crosse/North Side/ Monitor Brewery

The North La Crosse Brewery, owned by George F. and John Voegele, was built at 210 Mill Street (now Copeland Avenue) and operated from 1888 to 1920. In 1893 the ownership was changed to Voegele Brothers, but it was still called the North La Crosse Brewery. On April 2, 1900, the business was sold at a foreclosure sale to Jacob L. Erickson, son-in-law of John Voegele, and the name changed to the North Side Brewery. In 1901, Erickson again changed the name, this time to the Monitor Brewery.

George Neukomm, former head brewmaster at the Heileman brewery, became the Monitor Brewery's brewmaster, making Monitor Lager. The Monitor Brewery was the only brewery operated by non-Germans in La Crosse, since Erickson was born in La Crosse in 1864 to Norwegian immigrants. The Monitor Brewery closed with the advent of Prohibition in 1920. It reopened briefly in 1934, but closed the same year.

The Berlin Weiss Brewery

From 1868 to about 1900, Gustav Carl bottled soda and beer and imported wines and liquors. Originally he operated his business at 77–79 South Third Street, but later moved to 510–520 South Third Street. He bottled soda water, mineral water, champagne cider, sparkling Catawba, lager beer, seltzer water, ginger beer, lemon beer, and weiss beer.

About 1897, he hired Warninger and Houthmaker (first names not available) to operate the soda water factory. From 1897 to 1906, Warninger and Houthmaker operated the La Crosse Bottling Works and Berlin Weiss Beer Brewery.

The Bluff Brewery

Not much is known about the Bluff Brewery, which was in operation from 1856 until perhaps the 1870s. The small brewery was owned by Fritz Diefenthaler, and its location was described as "on the South Salem Road, Highway 16, opposite Keppel's farm." Keppel's farm is the current site of Bittersweet Flower Market along Highway 16. Diefenthaler also operated a dance pavilion and a summer garden that were said to be located somewhere in the woods near the brewery.

The Emil G. Kohn Brewery

The Emil G. Kohn Brewery, 1896–1897, was located between 14th, 16th, and Barlow streets. Only two batches of beer were brewed. The first was a success, but someone allegedly put bread crumbs in the second and spoiled it. In addition to this venture, Kohn and four other men ran the Onalaska Brewing Company until 1902, when it was converted to a pickle factory.

Other Breweries

Ignatz Furst also ran a brewery in the 1850s, but little other information is available.

PART III

People

Louis Armstrong, right, provided the big-name entertainment for the 1964 Oktoberfest in La Crosse. The reigning Miss Oktoberfest from 1963 was Mary Kay Knudson, and Roy Kumm, second from left, was festmaster of the 1964 celebration.
PHOTO COURTESY OF CLEARY-KUMM FOUNDATION

The employees are the secret ingredient
in Heileman's success,
every one of them proud to be
part of the Heileman family.

RON FISHER, HEILEMAN'S LA CROSSE PLANT MANAGER, IN 1984

Chapter 27

The Beer Barons of Heileman

LA CROSSE'S BREWERY THRIVED UNDER LOCAL LEADERSHIP

More than 160 carriages were in the mourning procession at the funeral of Gottlieb Heileman.

Gottlieb Heileman

Gottlieb Johann Heilemann was born to Johann Casper and Maria Friederica (Majer) Heilemann on January 6, 1824, in the town of Kirchheim unter Tech, in the province of Wuerttemburg, Germany. Caspar Heilemann was a baker as was Gottlieb's maternal grandfather in Germany. As a young man, Gottlieb received training in both the baking and brewing trades.

PHOTO COURTESY OF DAVID DELANO

To escape the political and economic turmoil in Germany, Gottlieb Heilemann came to America in 1852 and at some point Americanized his name to Heileman. He lived for about a year in Philadelphia before moving to Milwaukee, where, after unsuccessfully seeking employment at a brewery, Heileman and a fellow German immigrant, Gottlieb Maier, started a bakery.

The Heilemann/Maier bakery was located on the northeast corner of Reed and Oregon streets (now South Second Street). Milwaukee County real estate records reveal that Heilemann and Maier purchased that property on March 17, 1856, for $2,550. The young Germans quickly proved to be shrewd businessmen. On April 1, 1857, only a year after taking out their three-year mortgage, they were able to pay it off in full.

Six months later, on October 1, 1857, Heileman sold his share of the bakery business to his partner for $1,525 cash and made the move to fulfill his American dream. Venturing west to La Crosse, he procured work a month later as a foreman at the brewery of Dr.

Gustavus Nicolai, which failed and ceased operations suddenly only a month later. Heileman then took a job with the Michel brewery, but he had other plans as well.

PHOTO COURTESY OF LA CROSSE COUNTY HISTORICAL SOCIETY

In the summer of 1858, he returned to Milwaukee and on June 28 married Johanna Catharine Bandle. She was born August 31, 1831, in the German province of Wuerttemberg to Ludwig and Cathrina (Sigel) Bandle. She immigrated to America in 1852, where she lived with her brothers in New York City for four years before moving to Milwaukee. She met her future husband there, and was employed as a domestic servant in the household of a brewing family.

Gottlieb and Johanna raised a family of eight children: Louisa, Carolina, Emma, Minnie, Pauline, Henry, Ida, and Jennie.

Heileman was described as a man of genial manner and kindly disposition, with many friends. He lived a quiet contented life with his wife and eight children. He was respected in the business community as a man of his word, a good employer and an outstanding citizen of La Crosse who always did more than his share for the community.

His obituary stated that "his honesty and fairness in all transactions were unimpeachable, and with these characteristics as a solid foundation, he built a business which extended over a vast territory." His funeral at the German Lutheran Church was one of the largest ever to take place in La Crosse, with more than 160 carriages in the mourning procession. Pallbearers were fellow La Crosse brewers Charles and John Michel, John Hofer, George Zeisler, John Legler, and Franz Bartl, and a large group of family and friends were present as he was laid to rest in Oak Grove Cemetery.

John Gund

John Gund was born October 3, 1830, in Schwetzingen, Germany, a village between Heidelberg and Mannheim on the Rhine River. After serving a two-year apprenticeship at a cooperage (barrel-making facility) in Germany, he immigrated to the United States in 1848 and joined his family in Freeport, Illinois. Upon the death of his parents from cholera in 1850 he moved to Galena, Illinois, and found work in a brewery. There he met and married Louisa Hottman, who eventually bore five children: Louise, George, Henry, John Jr., and Emma.

PHOTO COURTESY OF LA CROSSE COUNTY HISTORICAL SOCIETY

In 1852 the couple moved to Dubuque, Iowa, where he worked for a short time at the Anton Heeb Brewery before returning to Galena where he and a man named Wetzel operated another brewery. In 1854 the Gund family moved up the Mississippi River to La Crosse. There, in a log cabin on Front Street and Cameron Avenue, Gund opened his own brewery, which he named City Brewery of Prairie La Crosse. He was aced out of the honor of having the first brewery open for business in the village by the Nicolai brewery, which opened just two weeks earlier. The story goes that Gund would have been the first had someone not sabotaged his first brew with sawdust.

Following the coin toss that dissolved the Gund-Heileman partnership, Gund decided to build his own brewery. In 1873 he started construction on his new Empire Brewery in La Crosse, near Mormon Coulee Road and Ninth Street, at an eventual cost of $250,000. Throughout the 1870s, Gund continued to expand and improve his brewery, until on May 1, 1880, the John Gund Brewing Company was reorganized with Gund and his two sons, George and Henry, as owners (by this time his sons were much involved with the business). That brewery burned to the ground on September 23, 1897. Gund's last brewery was rebuilt on the same site and was completed on August 16, 1898.

The John Gund Brewing Company became the largest brewery in La Crosse, and was an enormous operation by the standards of the day with 450 employees and production exceeding 94,000 barrels annually by 1900. However, a few years later Gund Brewing ceased operations, beset by labor problems and the coming of national Prohibition.

John Gund died at the height of his success on May 7, 1910, and is buried a short distance from Gottlieb Heileman in Oak Grove Cemetery in La Crosse.

Roy E. Kumm

Roy E. Kumm was born on October 12, 1912, in La Crosse, one of seven children of German and Finnish descent. He held his first job at the age of 12, working as a butcher after school and on Saturdays. Following graduation from La Crosse Central High School, he graduated from the Wisconsin Business University in La Crosse with a major in accounting. His first full-time job after college was as manager of the retail store and warehouse for the Firestone Service Store in La Crosse, and after that at the Recreation Bowling Alley.

One of Kumm's first loves was the Mississippi River. He owned a canoe and used it to court a local girl named Lillian (Hope) Staats, whom he married on July 21, 1932. They had one daughter, Joanne (Gail), who married Russell Cleary.

PHOTO COURTESY OF THE CLEARY-KUMM FOUNDATION

In April 1933, at the age of 20, Kumm began his career at Heileman as an accounting clerk. By 1937 he was the company's chief accountant, and he became comptroller in 1943. In 1949, he was named to the board of directors and became treasurer of the company. He became president of Heileman in 1957.

Kumm knew that the company needed to expand to survive. Heileman needed other brands to complement its premium beer, Old Style Lager, and its super premium brand, Special Export, in the marketplace. He also recognized the importance of distributors in reaching new markets. Kumm led Heileman into an unprecedented period of growth through the purchase of other regional breweries, acquiring additional labels to fill out Heileman's product line and the distributors and market to expand sales of the existing Heileman brands.

Kumm was also a leader in the city of La Crosse, volunteering both his time and money. He served as president of the board of Western Wisconsin Technical College and became a member of the board of governors in 1949. The school's health-sciences building was named for him in 1970.

Kumm and his wife, Hope, were both licensed pilots, and were instrumental in helping to establish the La Crosse Chapter of the Civil Air Patrol. He served as one of its first officers in 1942.

He also served as president of the Greater La Crosse Area Chamber of Commerce and was named Man of the Year by that group for 1969. He was chairman of many divisions of the La Crosse Area United Fund and was president of La Crosse Redevelopment Authority, serving on the board of directors from 1962 to 1971.

Kumm was involved in the Gateway Area Boy Scouts and served as chairman and a national representative for the Boy Scouts. Kumm also contributed his efforts as chairman of fund-raising for Holy Cross Seminary, and helped raise money to aid developmentally disabled children, the Boy Scout building fund, Viterbo University Fine Arts Center, YMCA-YWCA, and the Lutheran Hospital Building Fund. He was fundamental in the acquisition of the Girl Scouts' Camp Ehawee.

Around 1960, Kumm visited Germany, where he attended an Oktoberfest celebration. He came back to La Crosse and was one of the original organizers of the La Crosse Oktoberfest celebration. He was one of the early Oktoberfest festmasters and served as a trustee for La Crosse Festivals Incorporated. He was also actively involved with the Interstate Fair and served on the Fair Board. He and Heileman also played an important role in supporting the La Crosse County Fair.

Kumm's employees remember him as a caring, personable boss who interviewed and personally approved every person hired to work in the office during his tenure.

Outside of La Crosse, he was a member of the Governor's Board of Economic Development as well as numerous other committees on welfare, tourism, alcoholism, and safety. In 1965, he was given the Eagle Club's statewide Civic Service Award for outstanding community service. In 1970, he served as chairman of the State Cancer Crusade and was a member of the National Advisory Committee on Crime and Delinquency.

Kumm loved deer and duck hunting, fishing, golfing, curling, and poker, but his favorite leisure activity was cruising the Mississippi River in the family houseboat, which he built. He later replaced his homemade boat with a much larger one christened the *Hi Hope.* The large houseboat had living quarters and was docked within view of the brewery. When he needed to relax or mull a difficult decision, he often chose to go there. Many nights were spent on the boat playing poker with the boys, and it was also used to entertain wholesalers and other business associates.

Kumm's employees remember him as a caring, personable boss who interviewed and personally approved every person hired to work in the office during his tenure. He had a tradition of going to the Bier Stube with office employees for a beer after work, and on special occasions would bring along a bottle of whiskey to share with them. At Christmas, Roy and Hope would make holiday drinks and serve them to the employees at Christmas parties held at their home. As the brewery grew, the tradition moved to the brewery or some off-site location.

Kumm personally knew many of the workers in the plant. Once, walking down the street with a group of dignitaries, he noticed Paul E. Koeller, a bottle house employee, leaving work. Kumm called him over and introduced him to the governor of Wisconsin.

Kumm died of cancer at his home on March 18, 1971, at age 57. Following his death he was honored by numerous eulogies from Heileman employees, local and state officials, and many other individuals and organizations.

Pallbearers at his funeral included Quincy Hale, Lynden Gjerde, Newell Holley, Ray Ping, C.B. Goes, and Russell Smith. In addition there were numerous honorary pallbearers, including past Festmasters Donald Rice, John Coleman, Jack Martin, John Thomas, John Hans Zoerb, Lincoln Neprud, and Carlton F. Prinz. Other honorary pallbearers were: State Senator Milo Knutson, Rector of Saint Joseph the Workman Cathedral Rt. Rev. Msgr. John Paul, Dale Snyder, John Sleik, Harold "Pete" Isenman, Glenn Gilbertson, Charles Parrott, and Charles Richard.

Russell Cleary

Russell Cleary was born in Chippewa Falls, Wisconsin, on May 22, 1933. He lost his parents when he was young and was raised by his aunt, Mabel Halseth, his mother's sister, in La Crosse. He attended Franklin Elementary School, Logan Junior High School, and Logan High School, graduating in 1951. He was ranked at the top of his class, was editor of the yearbook, *The Winneshiek*, was president of the student council, and was known for his debating ability.

PHOTO COURTESY OF THE CLEARY-KUMM FOUNDATION

His wife, Gail Kumm, went to La Crosse Central High School. They met during their junior years on a field trip to Washington, D.C. They were married on January 8, 1955, and had two daughters: Kristine, a lawyer who graduated from Marquette University, and Sandra, a CPA and an accounting graduate of Hamline University in Saint Paul.

After graduation from the University of Wisconsin–Madison with a law degree, Cleary intended to buy into a practice in Reedsburg, Wisconsin. Instead, he returned to La Crosse where he became involved in real estate, teaching some classes in the business at the technical college and managing Hoeschler Realty Company. As Heileman started to make acquisitions, his father-in-law, Roy Kumm, asked him to do some of the real estate work for the brewery. He joined Heileman full time in 1960.

He was known as a shrewd, competitive businessman with strong marketing talents who ruled the brewery with an iron hand in a velvet glove. Cleary encouraged Heileman employees to call him by his first name. They were very loyal, and turnover was low. It was almost impossible to find anyone in La Crosse who had a bad word to say about Cleary, although he was basically shy and not totally at ease in social settings. He admitted that a cocktail party and small talk were not his idea of an enjoyable evening.

Heileman employees were some of the highest paid union workers in La Crosse, and when Cleary took control of the company he brought an end to the frequent labor strikes that had plagued the company until then. Ron Buschman, secretary-treasurer of the brewery workers union, called Cleary a tough but fair negotiator. Buschman joined Heileman in 1960, the same year as Cleary, and knew him to be a man who personally returned calls, whose door was always open to employees, and whose word was always good.

Cleary was known nationally as a powerful business leader. His trademark was his integrity, and he was a dynamic leader known for taking the company into battle with the giants of the industry.

Heileman was known as a very down-to-earth, no-frills company. The office buildings and advertising were simple and straightforward, bordering on Spartan. Cleary had no chief operating officer and no public relations department, and pretty much ran things with the help of his secretary, Louise Bruring, a 45-year Heileman veteran.

In 1985, there were 512 union members of Teamsters Local 1081 at the brewery in La Crosse. Many of them knew and respected Cleary, a local boy who had gone to grade school and high school with some of them. Unlike many company executives, Cleary never expected to be treated like royalty. He personally knew many of the workers, mingled with them at company picnics, and would stop by a tavern and buy a round for the employees. Pictures of Cleary standing side by side with union representatives and company workers celebrating some milestone in company production are numerous.

James G. Skoy, president of the union, said a key to the successful labor relations at Heileman was open communication between management and the union. He noted that while the workers worked hard, they knew that Cleary typically worked 10-hour to 12-hour days, six days a week, to make Heileman successful. Thomas Howe, a 35-year union member, credited Cleary with bringing the union employees and management together as the Heileman family.

In a 1984 interview, Ron Fisher, the plant manager in La Crosse, called the employees the secret ingredient in Heileman's success, every one of them proud to be part of the Heileman family. He said Cleary personally cared for them as family, and praised them as the most dedicated, loyal, and hardworking employees in the industry. He had nothing but respect for them and continually credited the success of the company to them.

Cleary never forgot his roots as his career soared. Roger Ferris, another 1951 Logan graduate and local shoemaker, remembered him as always having time to stop by to take him out for coffee or a beer. He said that Cleary eventually got too busy to help plan class reunions, but he was still willing to donate beer, name-tags, or anything else to make the party a success.

Cleary was known nationally as a powerful business leader. His trademark was his integrity, and he was a dynamic leader known for taking the company into battle with the giants of the industry. In 1980, he was named Executive of the Year by *Corporate Report Magazine*. In 1983 he was named best chief executive officer in the brewer/distillers category by *The Wall Street Transcript*, and in 1985 he received the Bronze Award from *Financial World* for Top Performance in the Beverage Industry.

Cleary was very active in civic affairs and served as a director for other companies. He was a director and festmaster of Oktoberfest USA, director of the Greater La Crosse Area Chamber of Commerce, chairman of the La Crosse Condemnation Commission, a director of the La Crosse chapter of the University of Wisconsin Alumni Association, president of the United Fund, and president of the La Crosse Interstate Fair Association. He also served as a director for the Protection Mutual Insurance Company, the Illinois–Wisconsin Advisory Board of American Mutual, Trane Company, the Ninth District Federal Reserve Bank of Minneapolis, Ecolab, A.O. Smith, Kohler, Soo Line, and Wisconsin Alumni Research Foundation.

The Clearys also were known as strong supporters of the city of La Crosse.

They enjoyed cruising the Mississippi River on their Skipperliner houseboat. After his retirement in 1989, he started Cleary Management Corporation, a family business, to focus on business consulting and management of real estate investments and other investments of the Cleary and Kumm families.

Russ Cleary died on May 1, 1997, following heart surgery. At his funeral, Wisconsin Governor Tommy Thompson eulogized Cleary as having three loves in his life—"his family, the city of La Crosse, and G. Heileman Brewing Company—and may the Lord help anyone who messed with them."

A HISTORY OF THE COMPANY'S CHIEF EXECUTIVE OFFICERS

City Brewery

John Gund & Gottlieb Heileman
1858-1872, Partners

Gottlieb Heileman
1872-1878, Sole Proprietor

Johanna Heileman
1878-1890, Sole Proprietor

The G. Heileman Brewing Company
(incorporated 1890)

Johanna Heileman
1890-1917, President

Emil T. Mueller
1917-1929, President

George Zeisler
1929-1933, President

G. Heileman Brewing Company Incorporated (new corporation 1933)

Albert C. Smith
1933, President

Harry Dahl
1933-1936, President

Albert J. Bates
1936-1944, President

Nordahl Nustad
1944-1947, President

Richard Macalister
1947, President

Nordahl Nustad
1947-1951, President

Ralph T. Johanson
1951-1956, President

Roy E. Kumm
1957-1971, President and chairman

Russell G. Cleary
1971-1988, Chairman and chief executive officer

Murray S. Cutbush
1988-1991, President and chief operating officer

Thomas J. Rattigan
1991-1994, Chairman and chief executive officer

Richard F. Gaccione
1994, President and chief executive officer

William J. Turner and Russell G. Cleary
1994-1995, Co-chief executive officers

Monroe L. "Lou" Lowenkron
1995-1996, President and chief executive officer

Chapter 28

Get Your Beer Here

DISTRIBUTORS AND WHOLESALERS WERE A COLORFUL BUNCH 1880s–1990s

Russ loved to sell beer around the smokestack.

—DAVID MAHONEY, HEILEMAN SALESMAN, DESCRIBING RUSS CLEARY'S DETERMINATION TO SELL BEER CLOSE TO HEILEMAN'S BREWERIES

In the early years beer was transported between the brewery and La Crosse saloons via horse-drawn beer wagons. The Heileman brewery maintained a stable of horses and a fleet of beer wagons for this purpose.

The range of the beer wagon was limited, however, and management realized that in order to increase market share significantly, new markets beyond the reach of the La Crosse-based beer wagons would have to be explored. In 1885 the first brewery-owned "distributing station" was opened in Glencoe, Minnesota. Distributing stations became known as "agencies" and soon many other Heileman agencies were established in South Dakota, Minnesota, Wisconsin, and Illinois.

Beer was transported via railroad to these agencies, where a local manager and staff would take possession and redistribute the product to local establishments. Heileman's largest agency was in Chicago, Illinois, a harbinger of the tremendous business the brewery would generate there many years later. But even in pre-Prohibition days more than 50 employees were on the Heileman payroll to handle distribution in the Windy City.

A secondary group of independent distributors also became a factor. As their name implies, "carload distributors" bought railroad cars of beer. This kind of distributorship evolved after the successful introduction of Old Style Lager in 1902, which was originally produced only in bottles and, packed in wooden cases, could more easily be shipped long distances than keg beer. Heileman's carload distributors were located in many large cities, including: Milwaukee, Springfield, Indianapolis, Chattanooga, Toledo, Des Moines, Denver, Boston, Omaha, San Francisco, Portland, Seattle, Lexington, Atlanta, New Orleans, Saint Louis, Houston, Jacksonville, Memphis, and Charleston.

Edward A. Maurer drives a Heileman delivery team and wagon in the early 1900s. George Smith recalls that his grandfather, John H. Smith, sold this team of horses to the brewery. John Smith had taught the horses, when they were colts, to run to him for treats when he whistled. One day he happened to be in downtown La Crosse when the team was making a delivery. He whistled, and they came running, to the deliverymen's amazement. PHOTO COURTESY OF MURPHY LIBRARY, UNIVERSITY OF WISCONSIN–LA CROSSE

In the decade prior to Prohibition, Heileman shipped railroad cars of Old Style Lager to just about any customer who came up with the cash to pre-pay it. Beer was even sent to Puerto Rico and Canada, and by 1916 a total of 3,998 straight railcar shipments had been delivered. Almost all of the agency and carload distributor business came to an end, however, when Prohibition became the law of the land in 1920.

Following the 13 bleak years of Prohibition, a new set of rules was established with the federal Beer-Wine Revenue Act of 1933. This act imposed a federal excise tax of $5 per barrel of beer and gave much authority to the states for regulating the terms and conditions of the sale of alcoholic beverages within their borders. A three-tier beer distribution system (brewer, wholesaler and retailer) was established to control taxation and legal sales of beer. When the production and sale of beer resumed, Heileman was dealing with a new set of rules that would dramatically affect how business was conducted.

Heileman's branch office in Chicago about 1906.
PHOTO COURTESY OF MURPHY LIBRARY, UNIVERSITY OF WISCONSIN-LA CROSSE

Heileman reorganized following Prohibition and the new management was eager to re-establish wholesaler accounts. In most states, brewers authorized wholesalers to sell specified Heileman beer in specific territories. The agreement that formalized the brands, territories and other conditions of sale was known as the Heileman Wholesaler Appointment Agreement. As wholesaler ownership changed, or additional brands or territories were added or modified, each Wholesaler Appointment Agreement was amended as appropriate. With the number of Heileman wholesalers growing rapidly, this became a formidable task to manage.

Heileman's initial wholesaler network following Prohibition was fairly small and regional, covering Wisconsin, Minnesota, Iowa, the Dakotas, Illinois, and a few other states. The distribution area grew gradually, but significant change did not occur until Heileman began acquiring other breweries. Salesmen were hired in key markets such as Chicago, Wisconsin, and Iowa to call on local distributors. When the greater expansion began, it was determined that a better organized sales management force would be necessary to coordinate the sales and marketing efforts of the wholesaler network.

Heileman hired Dale D. Snyder as a salesman in 1952, and by the time the acquisitions had begun he had become director of sales. As the field sales staff increased, so did the sales management staff in La Crosse. Ray Flower and Ed Bloedorn were salesmen

Bill Schirmang Sr., right, chats with Heileman President Russ Cleary and Heileman Director of Sales Dale Snyder, left, during this meeting in Chicago. The gathering was held to observe Snyder's 1977 retirement.
PHOTO COURTESY OF SKOKIE VALLEY BEVERAGE COMPANY

hired by Heileman in the 1960s who served in various capacities for many years. Flower recalled that as a young man in the late 1940s he saw Heileman truck drivers carrying large sums of cash and drinking beer. He immediately determined that this was the business for him. Many new faces joined the Heileman sales team following the Blatz acquisition in 1969, including Wally Lorenz, Stan Just, and Ron Drout, all of whom enjoyed long careers with Heileman.

Heileman's acquisition of new brands and breweries also increased the number of wholesalers. Typically, when Heileman acquired a brewery, wholesalers already assigned territories with the acquired company were allowed to continue to sell under those same conditions.

John S. Pedace was born in 1926, the youngest in a family of 11 children in Norwich, Connecticut. He started his career in the beer business working for a beer wholesaler and soon found his way to employment at the Piel's brewery of New York.

Surviving a number of buyouts, Pedace was working for the Associated Brewing Company in 1972 when Heileman acquired Associated. Russ Cleary and Snyder interviewed him and offered him a management job at Heileman, and in 1976 Pedace was promoted to vice president of sales and marketing, presiding over what would become a 200-person Heileman sales and marketing division.

Pedace was a good fit with Cleary's management style. Both were tough-minded, intensely committed individuals who commanded respect. Their relationship with the wholesaler network was a key factor in developing the loyalty and dedication that so many distributors felt for the Heileman brewery. Cleary and Pedace understood the difficulty of competing with the giants of the industry, but they had a great faith in Heileman's many powerful regional brands and encouraged the wholesaler network to take advantage of regional selling.

By the mid-1970s, Old Style sales had increased so dramatically that several Chicago-area wholesalers sold more than one million cases per year. These wholesalers were recognized by Heileman as members of the "One Million Case Club." Jerry Campagna, owner of C&K Distributors Incorporated, was a charter member of the club and became Heileman's

Jerry Campagna, owner of C&K Distributors in Chicago, relaxes with a cigar in his Chicago office about 1980. His company sold more than 7 million cases of beer in a single year.
PHOTO COURTESY OF *LA CROSSE TRIBUNE*

largest wholesaler during the late 1970s. At its peak in 1981, C&K Distributors sold more than 7 million cases of Old Style beer in a single year.

Campagna became somewhat of an icon of success stories amongst Heileman wholesalers. A large man who constantly smoked a cigar, Jerry had a classic beer baron physical resemblance to E.T. Mueller, who ironically also smoked cigars. From humble beginnings, Campagna parlayed his venture of becoming a Heileman wholesaler into considerable wealth. He was born on Napoleon Bonaparte's birthday, and he considered Napoleon to be his hero. His entire office was a tribute to his other hero, El Cid.

Campagna's office walls were covered in red plush material, and on these walls hung a portrait of El Cid and a collection of 20 antique military swords. A full suit of medieval armor, sporting an Old Style cap and mace in hand, completed the decor.

He had a flare for the dramatic, which was quite appropriate for a major combatant in the battle for market supremacy in Chicago. Campagna encouraged his well-paid delivery drivers to build huge floor displays with Old Style beer, which left little room for competitive products on the retailer floors. During a 1979 blizzard, the worst storm in a century, his aggressive employees sold more beer than during the previous summer. Campagna's classic instructions to his sales force were: "Bring me the head of (name of competitor)."

As the acquisitions of the 1970s added volume, the best of the sales personnel from the breweries acquired were added to the Heileman payroll. David Mahoney

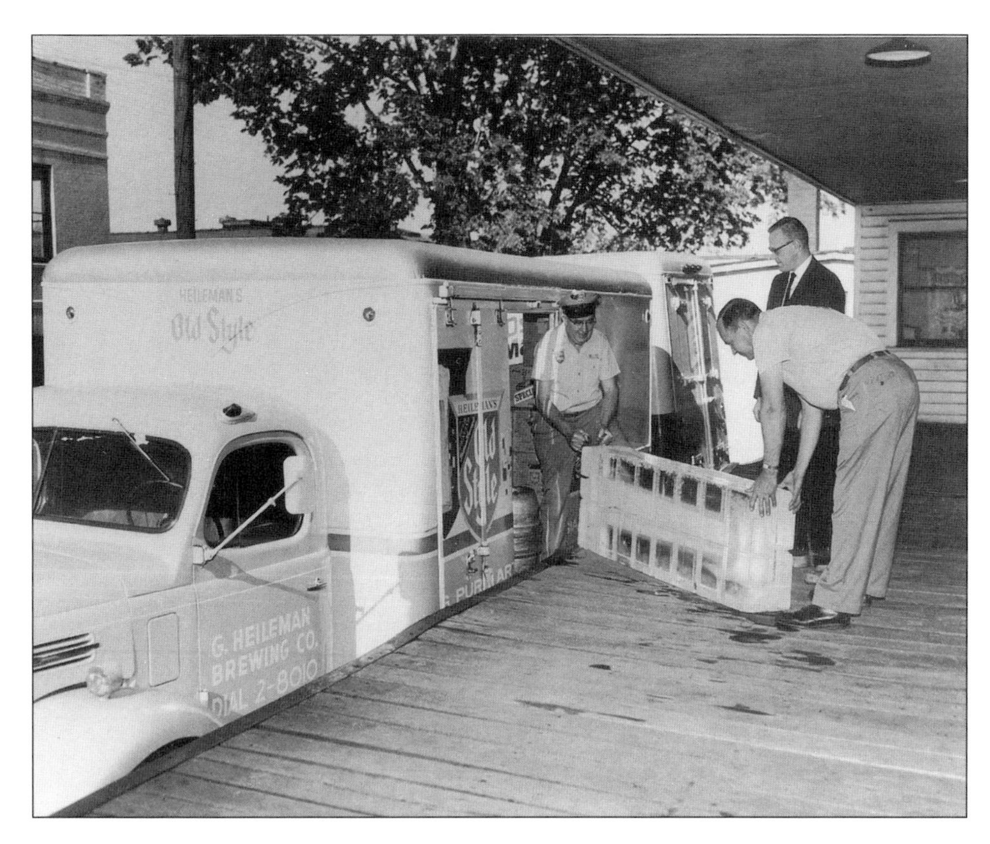

Bill Kane, left, Bob Young (bending over) and Ralph Horn on the loading dock.
PHOTO COURTESY OF MURPHY LIBRARY, UNIVERSITY OF WISCONSIN–LA CROSSE

was typical of the dozens of salesmen who brought their expertise to the House of Heileman. Working for Carling-National when Heileman acquired it in 1979, Mahoney was excited about joining the Heileman sales team, which had a proven track record in marketing regional beer brands. Mahoney remembered how much Cleary and Pedace were respected in the beer industry and how impressed he was with their ability to listen to other perspectives on marketing regional brands. "Russ loved to sell beer around the smokestack," recalled Mahoney, meaning Cleary wanted to sell most of his beer close to the brewery.

Another Carling-National salesman who joined Heileman was Art Westbrook, who recalled how close Heileman management was to its sales staff, frequently dining out with the salesmen and their wives. He also recalled Cleary's annual "state of the industry" speeches, where the brewery president would give candid analysis of the various companies competing for business in the brewing industry, often with accurate predictions of mergers and future business trends. Westbrook also recalled the effectiveness of the wholesaler panel meetings, often attended by both Cleary and Pedace, which were designed to encourage dialogue and marketing feedback from the wholesalers.

By the 1980s, Heileman's diverse wholesaler network had grown to more than 2,500, by far the most of any brewer. A few of the larger Heileman wholesalers exclusively sold Heileman beer, while the great majority sold other brands as well. Some wholesale operations were enormous while others were more "mom-and-pop" size, but the great majority genuinely enjoyed their relationships with Heileman, which always tried to hire salesmen who could relate to the wholesalers.

The office staff was professional and progressive, and the company offered a great variety of quality beers. By the 1980s, Heileman wholesalers generally offered retailers a full line of products—premium beers, light beers, popular-priced beers, near beers, low-alcohol beers, malt liquor, imported beers, mineral water and more. Being a full-line supplier allowed Heileman products to occupy a high percentage of retailer shelf space, an effective marketing concept that the La Crosse brewer pioneered.

Many wholesalers also owned shares of Heileman stock, which made them feel like part of the Heileman family and, therefore, they put forth greater sales effort to ensure their mutual success. It was this dynamic business atmosphere, created in the late 1970s and early 1980s, that made the beer business fun for Heileman salesmen and wholesalers.

Skokie Valley Beverage of Wheeling, Illinois, started doing business with Heileman in 1946, with three generations of the Schirmang family taking part in the Heileman saga through the good years and the bad. Bill Schirmang Sr. recalled his fleet of semis with the "God's Country" theme painted brightly on their sides, rolling billboards in great numbers, hauling oceans of beer up and down Interstate 90.

Don Lewis Sr. of L&V Distributing, Crystal Lake, Illinois, was another longtime Heileman wholesaler who remembered how much fun it was to come to La Crosse for the annual sales meetings, where he and fellow wholesalers were treated like royalty. Lewis recalled that Cleary's fiery speeches were always the highlight of those gatherings.

Don Morello started Beloit Beverage Company with his father in Beloit, Wisconsin, in 1960. He talked about the tremendous loyalty the wholesalers had for the Heileman brewery throughout the Kumm and Cleary eras. Morello also recalled how Cleary inspired confidence within the wholesaler network by initiating direct communication and promoting a feeling of one big family—the Heileman brewery and Heileman wholesalers.

Donna Colberg purchased a small Schmidt wholesaler business from her father in 1966. Chisago Lakes Distributing Company of Chisago Lakes, Minnesota, grew with Heileman over the years. Colberg felt that her company received solid support from Heileman corporate and field sales staff. The employees of Chisago Lakes Distributing, who saw to it that Heileman products were aggressively purveyed within their territory, reciprocated that support. Colberg said she liked Cleary's "down-to-earth" style and his commitment to the business. She enjoyed going "toe-to-toe" in a tough business dominated by males and considered Cleary to be a role model.

From the wholesaler's perspective, there wasn't much not to like about Heileman during the Kumm and Cleary eras, when the brewery was a financially sound supplier with a highly successful acquisition trail. The company offered high-quality beer, hard-hitting advertising, innovative packaging and a profit margin for the wholesalers that allowed many of them to make a lot of money. Heileman's breweries were geographically located to allow wholesalers competitive shipping rates, and the Heileman support staff was friendly to wholesalers and committed to excellence.

When Pedace retired in 1985, business had begun to stagnate, and with the Bond corporation's purchase of Heileman in 1987, the gung-ho attitude of many of the wholesalers began to fade. No longer having partial ownership or the relationship which Cleary and Pedace had provided through the years, wholesalers were dismayed as they saw the Bond corporation stumbling and about to fall. With Bond's financial situation deteriorating, advertising dollars once spent in copious quantities to promote Heileman beer began to dry up, further contributing to sales erosion and a continuing downward cycle.

This combination of events had a snowballing effect on wholesaler morale. Some sought competitors' brands to regain volume lost by sliding Heileman sales, and many simply lost faith in the company. In the years following the Bond demise, desperate Heileman management attempted to squeeze wholesaler profit margins, and this met a predictable response from the already disillusioned distributors. The magic that once existed between Heileman and its mighty wholesaler network had vanished, leaving only bittersweet memories.

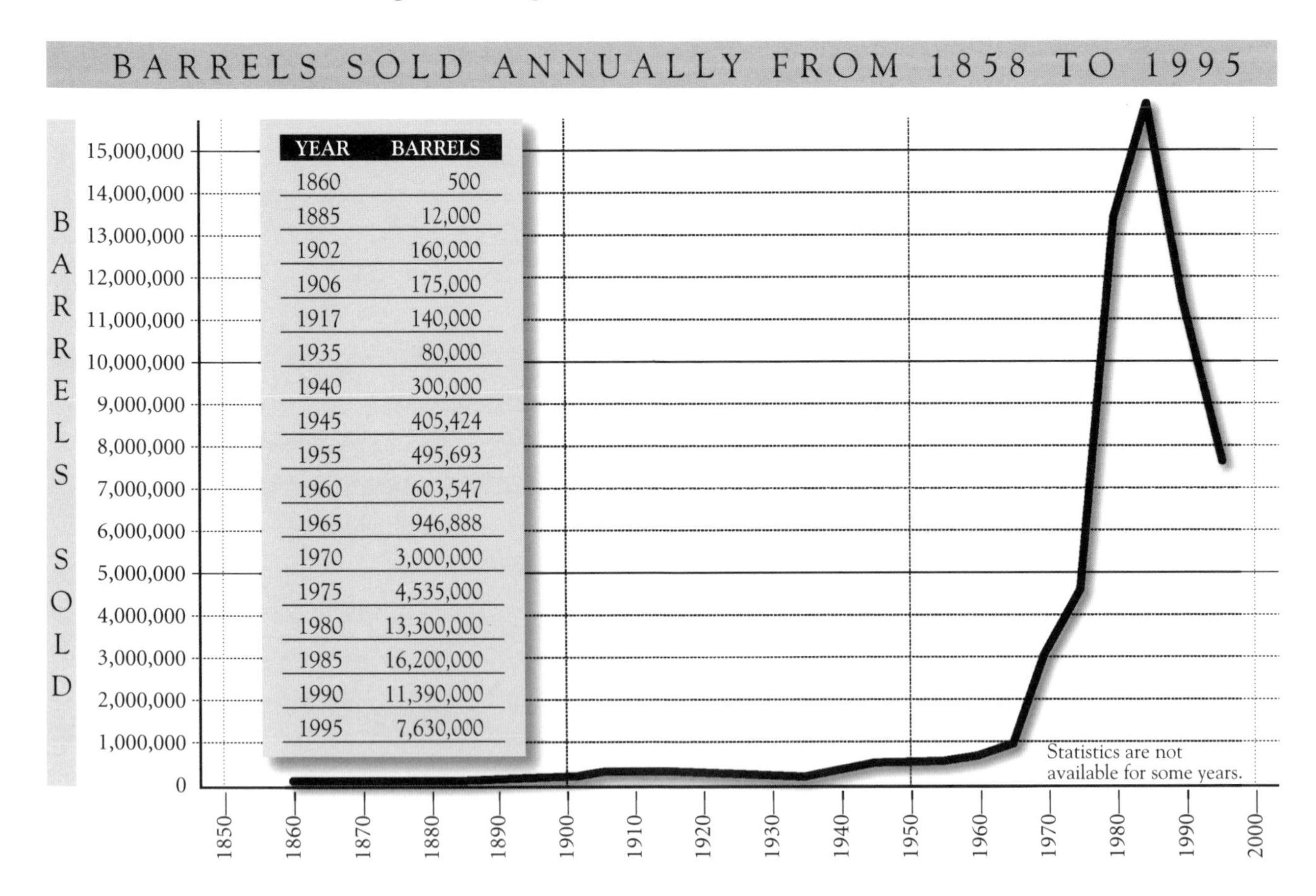

YEAR	BARRELS
1860	500
1885	12,000
1902	160,000
1906	175,000
1917	140,000
1935	80,000
1940	300,000
1945	405,424
1955	495,693
1960	603,547
1965	946,888
1970	3,000,000
1975	4,535,000
1980	13,300,000
1985	16,200,000
1990	11,390,000
1995	7,630,000

Chapter 29

The Bean Counters

OFFICE STAFF GREW ALONG WITH THE BREWERY 1863–1990s

"Heil-e-man's."

—THIS CHEERY SINGSONG TELEPHONE GREETING WAS A COMPANY TRADITION FOR ALMOST 50 YEARS.

While the principal mission of the Heileman brewery from the beginning was focused on brewing and marketing quality beer, it also became necessary very early in the company's existence to keep accurate accounting records.

In 1863 the United States government passed a law that required brewers to pay an excise tax on beer sales at a rate of $1 per barrel. The purpose of the new tax, according to its proponents, was to finance the Union army's Civil War effort. As the Civil War came to an end in 1865, politicians found other uses for the money generated from the beer tax, and their promises to sunset the brewers' excise tax were soon forgotten. The federal government had established a lucrative new revenue enhancement program, which would increase manyfold in the years ahead.

Brewers quietly passed the cost of the 1863 federal excise tax on to their customers by incorporating it into their cost structure and thus increasing the price to the consumer. Bookkeepers (which they were called in those days, rather than accountants) were employed to attend to the detail of the excise tax, and the brewery office came into being. A fairly accurate knowledge of Heileman's annual sales from the early years is probably the ironic offshoot of the bookkeeping required to calculate excise tax payments due the federal government.

E.T. Mueller's formal training at business school concentrated in bookkeeping, and thus he soon assumed the responsibilities of Heileman business manager in the early days. Throughout the 1880s and 1890s, Mueller personally, in beautiful and stylish handwriting, maintained the general ledger in which accounting transactions were recorded in huge (approximately 15 inches by 20 inches) leather-bound books. Although somewhat difficult to understand when reviewed 100 years after they were created, these books contain detailed numbers for purchases, expenses, payroll information, inventories, accounts receivable and payable and, of course, sales and production numbers.

A small office staff was in place at the turn of the 20th century to assist with the record keeping and order taking of the growing Heileman brewery. The office was housed in a quaint European-style building on the east side of Third Street, where the giant six-pack currently stands. This building also housed the early bottling facility. But, as business increased in the first decade of the 20th century, the bottle house was moved to the west side of Third Street adjacent to the brewhouse and other brewery buildings. The Heileman office building, as it became known, was built with a Germanic flair which included a stork positioned on top of the roof. The stork, a symbol of fertility, was a Teutonic custom going back to the Middle Ages. This building was in use until fire destroyed it on December 19, 1959.

When Heileman brewery workers elected to unionize in 1904, office staff was not included with the collective bargaining employees. They continued as salaried and hourly employees until the corporate office was dissolved by Stroh in 1996.

Other bookkeepers joined Heileman as business expanded in the early 1900s. Leo Schroeder became chief accountant, Herman Jahn procured orders and issued invoices to customers, and Emil "Mouse" Horn manned the order desk before, during, and after Prohibition. In those days the federal excise tax was collected via federal tax stamps, which were sold in denominations according to the volume of the container of beer. They were perforated with the date when the product left government bonded brewery premises. The stamps were then glued to beer cases or the keg itself. One of Horn's jobs was attending to the purchasing detail of the federal excise tax stamps. The office staff, which had grown to about 15 people in the prosperous pre-Prohibition period, was greatly reduced as Prohibition became the law of the land in 1920.

When the company reorganized, following Prohibition, fresh faces were brought into the Heileman office. Several of those would have a significant impact on the course the brewery would follow over the next several decades. Among those hired in the 1930s were Roy Kumm, Linden "Lindy" Gjerde, Glenn Gilbertson, and Paul Voelker.

Kumm started his career at Heileman as a bookkeeper, became office manager, comptroller and visionary president of the company.

Gjerde began his Heileman career as a bookkeeper and later became general credit manager and office manager. He was instrumental in hiring hundreds of office workers (author DeLano included) in a career that spanned 42 years. Gjerde also served as company historian for many of those years. Much of the information regarding the company's formative years, including a significant contribution to the pages of this book, is available because Gjerde kept historical documents and appreciated and maintained the rich history of the company.

Gilbertson was a member of the Heileman Lagers football team, starting his Heileman career as an auditor and later becoming comptroller. Voelker played quarterback for the Heileman Lagers before accepting a job as chemist at Heileman in 1937. During his 38-year career at Heileman he

Wayne Ruppel, left, and Paul Voelker work in the foreground of the Heileman quality assurance lab in the late 1960s.
PHOTO COURTESY OF MURPHY LIBRARY, UNIVERSITY OF WISCONSIN-LA CROSSE

established the quality assurance laboratories and became chief chemist.

Other longtime office employees who were hired in the 1930s were: Lucille Rheinhard, Walter Patterson, Clarence Koelbl, Hazel Brown, Lucy Ryan, Pete Tanke, and Violet Hayes.

In the 1940s Jim Beranek and Ralph Horn began long careers. Beranek worked as a cost accountant and later as a production planner. Horn's career spanned 38 years, which included service as accountant, chief accountant, assistant treasurer and assistant controller, and eventually vice president and controller.

Heileman's main telephone operator in the 1940s was Dorothy Reed, and she became known for answering the telephone with a cheery, singsong "Heil-e-man's." This tradition was later passed on to Lola Green-Fry, and the sung greeting became a trademark of the company for almost 50 years. Louise Bruring was hired in 1943 as a secretary, starting a 45-five year career in which she served as executive secretary to Kumm and later Russ Cleary.

Fortunately, no one was hurt when the office building was destroyed by fire in 1959, and almost all of the important office paperwork was recovered from a fireproof vault. The destruction of the office, however, created havoc for dozens of office employees. Following the fire, they were relocated in the Heileman and Mueller houses in the 900 block of South Third Street. A corridor was constructed to connect these buildings, but there was still insufficient space for the entire office staff.

Early in 1960, plans were made to construct a warehouse-type building toward the back of the Heileman house in the former location of the horse stables. This building was created to house the majority of the office staff, although the Heileman house continued to serve as executive offices. A large green carpet was laid on the floor of the new building, and it became known as "Green Acres." The Mueller house was eventually razed in the 1970s, but the Heileman house continued to house executive offices. It was also in the 1960s that the Heileman office entered the age of the computer. Staff was added to run the computers, which would eventually replace many of the manual tasks previously handled by bookkeepers.

In the 1960s and into the 1970s the company began to experience growth from sales of Old Style and also from acquisitions. Typically, as Heileman purchased the brands and breweries of other companies, many of their office functions became redundant and were soon consolidated under the roof at Green Acres.

Some of the people hired during this period and who enjoyed long office careers were: George Dahnke, Gary Stelzig, Sandy Gilbertson, Robert Bush, Jim Thompson, Dennis Larson, Thelma Severson, Walter Baltz, Jerry Miller, Audrey Brye, Terry Christopherson, Don Westphal, Jim Kennedy, Wayne Ruppel, and Cleary. Baltz became the company historian in the 1970s in addition to his responsibilities as credit manager and political liaison. Kennedy headed the order-expediting/production planning department. Ruppel joined the company as a chemist, eventually becoming vice president of quality assurance, and Miller negotiated labor contracts. Cleary began his career in the Heileman office in May 1960 and became president of the company in 1971.

In the 1970s and 1980s, continued growth and acquisitions necessitated the hiring of a large number of (mostly) young employees too numerous to detail in this book. There was always a lot of camaraderie in the Heileman office, but the hiring of a large number of young employees gave it a special reputation for being a fun place to work.

One of its benefits was the availability of free beer in the company bier stube after work. Located in the basement of the Heileman house, the bier stube was supposed to have been at one time the wine cellars of Gottlieb Heileman. On Friday nights the house would provide sausage and cheese trays, and usually a game of cards or a dice game known as "shut box" would spring up. Ralph Horn was especially famous for his incredible luck in such games of chance.

Green Acres and the Heileman house were filled to the brim with office employees by the late 1970s due to continued expansion, most notably the Carling-National acquisition. Contemplating a site for a new building to house the corporate staff, Cleary decided to take part in an urban renewal project taking shape in downtown La Crosse. He chose a site at 100 Harborview Plaza, directly north of a Radisson hotel project and only a couple of blocks away from the La Crosse Center. A three-story building was built and occupied in 1980. This building was able to house almost all of the corporate staff, but continued acquisitions in the 1980s meant yet more employees. They were accommodated in offices leased on the top floor of the new 10-story U.S. Bank building across the street and the old W.A. Roosevelt building on the northeast corner of Second and State streets. The latter was purchased, refurbished for offices, and called the Corporate II building.

Heileman office workers were known not only as a congenial bunch, but also for their dedication and efficiency. An example of the latter was the Heileman PreAuthorized Clearing (HPAC) Service, which was initiated by the Heileman Credit Department in 1980. HPAC was a revolutionary change from the way conventional business was conducted at the time. HPAC allowed Heileman to initiate preauthorized checks (later, electronic fund transfers) against wholesalers' accounts in compliance with the terms and conditions of the sale. It proved to be an extremely efficient means of conducting business, and before long all other major American breweries had cloned HPAC.

Such systems are widely used today not only in the beer business but also in hundreds of other applications. Another example of Heileman efficiency was a highly sophisticated computer communication system with the wholesaler network called BREWNET. Initiated in the late 1980s, BREWNET allowed the brewery and wholesalers to electronically exchange orders, retail sales numbers, inventories, promotional and account status information.

With the numerous acquisitions that Heileman made during this period, management had many opportunities to compare the practices of the Heileman office staff to those taken over, and the Heileman office staff always compared very favorably. Departments that functioned at the Heileman office in the 1980s included office services, tax, accounts payable, engineering, payroll, legal, information systems, sales, credit, accounting, purchasing, traffic, operations/distribution planning, insurance, marketing/advertising and human resources.

As Bond Corporation Holdings Limited completed its acquisition of Heileman in 1987, business had begun to fizzle and the need for corporate support staff declined. Layoffs and terminations increased toward the end of the 1980s and into the early 1990s, and Heileman's 1991 bankruptcy sent many office employees looking for employment elsewhere. The offices in the bank building and Corporate II were abandoned and the remaining staff retreated to the Heileman Corporate Center until the end came on June 30, 1996, when the business was sold to Stroh.

At that time almost all of the remaining office jobs, which at one time numbered close to 300, were taken over by Stroh and transferred to Detroit. Only a handful of office employees were offered and accepted positions in Detroit.

Memories

In 1969, when Heileman bought Blatz from Pabst, the La Crosse-based brewer not only obtained the label but also some delivery trucks.

At the time there was a lot of animosity between Heileman and Pabst. Some people even were afraid there might be violence when Heileman went to get the trucks. To solve the problem, Roy Kumm devised something that came to be called "Operation Snatch."

He organized a group of office employees, and they drove to Milwaukee in the middle of the night. They knew that nobody would be around at 4 A.M., which is when they slipped into about 40 delivery trucks and began driving them back to La Crosse.

—Memory submitted by Jerry Miller

Chapter 30

Heileman Teams Had a Ball

FROM FOOTBALL TO KITTEN BALL, THE BREWERY SPONSORED THEM ALL

The Old Style Lagers opened their regular season against the Green Bay Packers in 1935.

Over the years, as part of its overall marketing efforts, Heileman sponsored football, kitten ball, baseball, bowling, golf, fishing, boating, and marathon running teams.

Football

Thomas Skemp organized the Old Style Lager professional football team in 1933 and coached it for four years. After 13 years as head football coach at Saint Mary's College in Winona, Minnesota, he had resigned and asked Harry Dahl, Heileman chief executive officer, to sponsor a professional team. Dahl agreed and provided money for uniforms and equipment.

Some people called it a pro team and some called it semipro. Players were paid about $100 for the entire season. Tickets for the games at Memorial and Swanson fields in La Crosse cost $5 for the whole season. For $7.50 you could have a sponsor's season ticket. A typical game brought in about $100 in gate receipts.

In its initial 1933 season in the Tri-State League, the team out-scored its opponents 261 to 46, defeating the Tomah Veterans, Milwaukee Schlitz, Dubuque Bulldogs, New London Bulldogs, Austin Bluejackets, Spring Valley Huskies, Wisconsin Rapids, Minnesota All-stars, and the Chippewa Marines.

In 1934, the team played the Chicago Bears in Winona in a preseason battle. It cost the team $1,500 to bring the Bears to Winona, but the stands were packed and the game, which the Bears won, 25–0, generated more than $3,000 in gate receipts.

Though they lost the game, the Lagers were surprisingly competitive with the pro team. One of the local team's best players was Clyde "Swede" Gallup, whose strength was legendary among fans and La Crosse tavern patrons alike. A graduate of Carroll College with a degree in philosophy, Swede had

The Old Style Lagers football team posed for this picture in the 1930s.
PHOTO COURTESY OF MURPHY LIBRARY, UNIVERSITY OF WISCONSIN-LA CROSSE

had a tough time finding work, and so was delighted to take a job delivering Heileman beer to La Crosse taverns. On one occasion he rolled a beer barrel into a saloon and asked the bartender where he wanted it. "Why don't you put it up here?" the bartender joked, pointing to the bar top. Swede promptly immortalized himself by bear-hugging the full wooden barrel and placing it as directed.

In 1935, the Lagers opened the regular season against the Green Bay Packers. Members of the 1935 Old Style Lagers included: Thomas Skemp (coach), Tom Skemp Jr. (mascot), Clayton Biddle (guard), Val Pralle (equipment manager), Paul Marcou (assistant coach), Harvey Boldt (end), Santo Curro (back), Clint Riebeth (back), Bob Culp (back), Ed Knapp (tackle), Jim Christie (back), Paul Voelker (quarterback), Paul Wuest (back), Solly Kramer (back) Ed Lynch (end), Glenn Gilbertson (end), Harry Klawitter (center), Earl Lower (tackle), Joe Kurth (end), Lambert Duresky (center), Francis

Members of the 1933 Old Style Lagers football team had a well-attended 30th reunion in 1963.
PHOTO COURTESY OF MURPHY LIBRARY, UNIVERSITY OF WISCONSIN-LA CROSSE

Billock (tackle), and Tony Prelesnik (guard). The Packer lineup included such great players as Buckets Goldenberg, Don Hutson, and Arnie Herber, while the Lagers were led by ex-Packer Johnny Blood. The Packers won the game 49–0. The Lagers also twice played the Chicago Cardinals, who were training in La Crosse. The Lagers lost both games, 41–0 and 20–0.

After three years in the Tri-State League the team switched to the Northwest League, which included Des Moines, Madison, Rock Island, Ironwood, Duluth, Saint Paul, and Minneapolis. During one memorable game, the Lagers defeated Madison 100–0. When asked about the score, Skemp said Madison didn't belong in the league and he wanted to force them out.

During a trip to play a game in Minneapolis, the team was involved in an auto accident, which killed fullback Russell Cycmanick and seriously injured a guard named Herman Gay.

Members of the Heileman kitten ball team in 1938 were, from left: back row—Jul Kriese, Clarence "Crotch" Pinker, Paul "Pip" Wuest, Bobby Bendel, Sig Wateski and Erwin "Petsey" Voss; second row—Clarence "Swish" Beranek, George Mekvold, Clair Raith, George "Nook" Riese, Frankie Smith, and Fritz Raith; front row, Robert "Buck" Tanke (batboy), Howie Voss (mascot) and Francis Krueger (official scorekeeper).

PHOTO COURTESY OF ADELINE KRIESE

Skemp said he believed the Lagers fielded their best team in 1935.

In 1963, the Old Style Lagers football team held a 30th anniversary reunion in La Crosse that was attended by: Ed "Bucko" Lynch (end), Ambrose Liskovec (tackle), Irv Pincsak (back), Lambert "Pie" Duresky (center), Clyde "Swede" Gallup (tackle), Earl "Sparky" Lowe (tackle), Harold "Nook" Blank (end), Ralph Watson (end), Carl "Bumps" Moe (end), R.H. Pearse Sr. (director), Thomas Skemp (coach), Robert Culp (back), Jim Christie (back), Paul "Pip" Wuest (back), Joe Weber (back), Paul Voelker (quarterback), Joe Abraham (back), Paul Marcou (assistant coach), and Francis Grenison (director).

Kitten ball

Heileman was also famous for its kitten ball (softball) teams. The 1938 Heileman Old Style Lager kitten ball team included Jul Kriese, Clarence "Crotch" Pinker, Paul "Pip" Wuest, Bobby Bendel, Sig Wateski, Erwin "Petsey" Voss, Clarence "Swish" Beranek, George Mekvold, Clair Raith, George "Nook" Riese, Frankie Smith, Fritz Raith, Robert "Buck" Tanke (batboy), Howie Voss (mascot), and Francis Krueger (official scorekeeper). Other members who joined the team later included Richard "Hooks" Koeller, Jack Grosskopf, Bob Coorough, George Halverson (business manager), Ben "Mooney" Vondrashek, George "Yip" Christopher, Emil "Punts" Temp, Charlie Mahlke, and Al Joren.

Members of this Heileman softball team from the late 1950s included, from left: back row—Leo Davis, Ken Ingham, Bill Dowell, Don Miller, Norm Hanson and Charlie Hastings; front row—Tom Pretasky, Bob "Hummer" Olson, Larry Schoen, Armin Wehrenberg, and Joe Gilles. Bob Hastings is the batboy in center.

PHOTO COURTESY OF MARIAN PRETASKY

One of the many sports teams Heileman sponsored over the years poses in front of the Heileman office building before boarding their bus in the 1940s.

PHOTO COURTESY OF MURPHY LIBRARY, UNIVERSITY OF WISCONSIN-LA CROSSE

After World War II the team played games in honor of former member Clair Raith, who was killed while serving in the Navy. A Clair Raith memorial trophy was awarded to a current softball player each year. The games were played at the West Avenue Diamond in Powell Park. In the 1950s, a best-of-five series against Ed's Tavern drew 3,200 spectators for each game. The team played a 1953 benefit game to raise money for a former member, Tanke, who was hospitalized with heart problems.

Bowling

Heileman also sponsored several bowling teams, and starting in 1958 they were made up entirely of Heileman employees. The teams wore matching shirts with the words "House of Heileman" and, in later years, the trademark black eagle insignia across the back.

In 1959 the following teams were sponsored by Heileman:

Classic League—Les Betthauser, Verd Grabinski, Paul E. Koeller, Ray Soller, Ed Troyanek and Ed Ziesler.

Heileman Exports—Lynn Burbach, Reno Ekern, Ralph Hauser, John Jefson, and Dick Olson.

Heileman Juniors—Gil Campbell, G. Gilles, Don Houlihan, A. Miller, and Ray Schmit.

Office team—James Beranek, Alan Bjerstedt, Ralph Horn, Les Jensen, Gene Lehman, Earl Patterson, and Bill Ritter.

Three unidentified duck hunters and their dogs pose with their bounty in this early 1900s photo. Note the wooden Old Style Lager beer case being favored at left by one of the dogs.

PHOTO COURTESY OF MURPHY LIBRARY, UNIVERSITY OF WISCONSIN-LA CROSSE

Malt house team—Victor Haas, Lester Jensen, Joe Gilles, Willard Manske, Joe Papacek, Harold Strittmatter, and Ervin Strittmatter.

Golf

Golf was another sport that was sponsored by the company, which organized clubs for both men and women. In 1958, the following individuals were given awards in the company golf tournament:

Bill Kato—Winner of championship flight and longest drive.

Frank Liberte—Runner-up championship flight.

Ken Ingham—Winner of first flight and most 6s.

Jim Breiden—Runner-up first flight.

Jim Shoger—Winner of second flight.

Cully Johnson—Runner-up second flight and most 7s.

Chester Covey—Best average.

Ray Baily—Most 5s.

Howard Scharpf—Highest score on a hole.

Rudy Todt - Youngest man present.

Boating

The Old Style Boat Club was organized in 1958 and had various outings on the river, including overnight camping trips. The club also taught water safety and worked to promote better boating facilities in the La Crosse area. There were three different groups divided up into small, medium, and large crafts. Club officers were Frank Liberte (president), Reno Ekern (vice president), and Carl Johnson (treasurer). Lester Johnson, Pete Jehlen, Tom Kessler, and Charles Hastings served as club directors. The club had a big end-of-the-year party with dancing to music by Jack Hefti's Orchestra.

In 1960, the company published a boating guide for employees, which included all of the Wisconsin laws regarding boating and detailed maps of the Mississippi River from Red Wing, Minnesota, down to Guttenberg, Iowa.

Roy Kumm and Russ Cleary were both avid boaters, and the company owned a houseboat, the *Hi Hope,* which was frequently used for employee outings and to entertain visitors to Heileman.

Fishing

With the Mississippi River literally in the brewery's backyard in La Crosse, fishing also was an important pastime. The company often sponsored fishing tournaments for employees with prize categories for pan fish, bass, trout, walleye, northern pike, and rough fish. The monthly prize was a case of beer, and there were bigger annual prizes. The company also sponsored ice-fishing contests.

Running

In April 1988, Heileman announced a three-year, $3.9 million contract to sponsor the Chicago Marathon and rename it the Old Style Marathon —Chicago. The race had been canceled the previous year after its corporate sponsor backed out. Cleary pointed to this as an example of Heileman's new focused marketing strategy as well as the deeper pockets of Bond Corporation Holdings Limited, new owner of Heileman.

But when October rolled around, problems arose. The race lacked any big-name runners because the New York City Marathon, scheduled just one week later, offered appearance fees and long-term contracts. Still, Heileman officials were confident their race would be a success and hoped the recent entry of British Olympian and a team of seven Soviet runners would add some luster to the event.

Loren Wardwell, manager of training and development at Heileman, organized a team of 60 runners who had been training together as part of a Heileman team. It included Jack Isherwood, a senior vice president and veteran of 28 previous marathons, seven women, 15 first-time marathon runners, and Bart Bardwell, an accomplished wheelchair athlete.

• • •

Heileman employees were most noted for making and selling beer, but they also were involved in football and fishing, bowling and boating, baseball and softball, and many other activities. Clearly, Heileman employees both worked hard and played hard.

This Heileman-sponsored softball team captured the city championship in 1981. Team members celebrating at Erickson Field in La Crosse include: front, Coach Gary Michaels; first row, from left, Sandra Cleary and Barb Michaels; second row, from left, Mary Kitzke, Anita Althoff, Joan Hansen, Karen Nedvidek, Pam Sidie and Connie Michaels; back row, from left, unidentified, Rose Hehn, Kim Subbert, Lisa Gilbertson and Brooke Prinsen.

Chapter 31

Let's Get Organized

UNION ROOTS GO DEEP AT HEILEMAN 1902–2004

Brewery workers were reminded they needed "to be willing to give in order to get something in return."

—UNION OFFICER ADDRESSING 1943 MEETING OF LOCAL 81

On September 2, 1943, a meeting of La Crosse Local 81 Brewery Worker's Union was held in the La Crosse Labor Temple. The featured speaker for the day was an elderly man named Charles Nickolaus, one of the senior officers of the International Union of United Brewery, Flour, Cereal, and Soft Drinker Workers of America. He recounted some memories of the brewing unions over the years, and paid tribute to the brave American brewery workers who first organized in the late 1880s.

He likened the union to pioneers crossing the American West in wagon trains. Those pioneers quickly discovered their need for strength in numbers to defend themselves against hostile Indians. In the same way, a union of workers could resolve its grievances with a company more effectively than an individual, Nickolaus said. He implored the workers to support the union and urged younger members to fight to sustain and improve working conditions in the breweries. He also reminded them they needed to be willing to give in order to get something in return. That meant they owed the company good service and eight hours of hard work, and in return they could expect improved working conditions.

He reminisced about his first trip to La Crosse. The year was 1898, and Michel's Brewery of La Crosse was in the middle of a labor strike. Nickolaus met with the owner of the brewery, and offered to organize the workers and negotiate a settlement to the strike. He was told to leave the owner's office and never return. Four months later, however, Nickolaus was back in that office and finalized a contract between the workers and the company. This was probably the start of organized labor in the breweries of La Crosse.

At Heileman, the union was first chartered on October 14, 1902, as Local 81, International Brotherhood of Brewery Workers, a union that also represented workers at the other breweries in La Crosse.

Workers assemble Old Style Lager cartons, probably 1950s.
PHOTO COURTESY OF MURPHY LIBRARY, UNIVERSITY OF WISCONSIN–LA CROSSE

On October 17, 1921, during Prohibition, Local 81 merged with Flour and Cereal Workers Local 95 to form the International Union of Brewery, Flour, Cereal, and Soft Drink Workers of America. That union had jurisdiction over workers in those industries as well as the production of malt, yeast, vinegar, commercial alcohol, cider, and mineral water. Union members were referred to as "brothers" in all union activities.

Following Prohibition, Heileman and La Crosse Breweries were the two primary breweries represented by Local 81. The union briefly represented workers at Kunz Brewery and Ziegler's Old Fashioned Brewery in La Crosse, as well as workers at breweries in Hillsboro, Baraboo, and New Lisbon.

The number of brewery workers grew during the late 1930s and early 1940s, but union leaders wanted to enlist even more members. In late 1942, they proposed having two union groups, an "A" group limited to 250 members and a "B" group consisting of mostly seasonal workers. Workers belonging to the union prior to February 1, 1941, would be part of the "A" group, and the company was asked to discharge anyone not unanimously accepted into the union.

The breweries rejected this idea and eventually a single union evolved. To deal with seasonal summer work, the company was allowed to hire temporary workers who received significantly less in pay and benefits than union members. College students and seminarians were often hired to fill these jobs in La Crosse, then laid off in the fall before they had worked long enough to join the union. But many students worked several summers, eventually earning that right and a full-time job.

In 1939, the Teamster's Union set its sights on brewery workers, and disputes between the two

Employee picnics were a tradition for the last 100 years.
PHOTO COURTESY OF MURPHY LIBRARY, UNIVERSITY OF WISCONSIN–LA CROSSE

unions became common. There were reports of Teamsters following Heileman delivery trucks into taverns and warning the owners they would be picketed if they accepted beer from Heileman union drivers. The disagreement escalated throughout 1941 and into 1942. A tentative resolution of the dispute between the Teamsters and the International Brewery Workers was reached in Cincinnati, Ohio, in March 1942, but rumors of more trouble persisted. Finally, more than 30 years later, the Teamsters won the battle. On November 29, 1973, Brewery Workers Local 81 became Teamsters Local 1081. Local 1081 still represents union workers at City Brewing Company in La Crosse.

Union positions included officers, various committees, and special members originally known as shop delegates and later as shop stewards. Union officers and officials were brewery workers who also were paid a salary for their union work. Officers of the international union were full-time paid employees of the union.

There was a strong German heritage in the early days and it wasn't until 1942 that union bylaws were changed to no longer require officers to have a command of the German language. In early years, the local officers conducted most of the union business, but later, a full-time business agent was hired. Committees conducted the business of contract negotiating, dealt

Ladies of the G. Heileman Brewing Company Worker's Union after Labor Day Parade sometime befoe 1910.
PHOTO COURTESY OF MURPHY LIBRARY, UNIVERSITY OF WISCONSIN–LA CROSSE

with issues of safety, sent representatives to other labor organizations, and provided entertainment.

The shop steward represented union members in most day-to-day disputes with the company. A member with a complaint or situation was not allowed to go directly to the company. Instead, he reported to the shop steward, who then met with management to seek a resolution. In the early years, each brewery had only one or two shop stewards, but by the 1970s Heileman had shop stewards for each shift in the bottle house, the brewery, the malt house, and the delivery departments. If the shop steward and company officials couldn't resolve a situation, union officers became involved. If the issue still couldn't be settled, it might be sent to arbitration.

From the beginning, members paid dues to the union, which, in the days before the company provided benefits, were used for that purpose. In 1921, when union member Adolph Lux was hospitalized, the local paid his hospital bills, and until the 1940s union dues also provided sick pay. Members were encouraged to visit brothers who were sick or elderly, a tradition continued into modern times. Members would also take up a Christmas collection for sick or elderly retired brethren. In the 1930s, the union collected a death-benefit fee of $1 from each worker for the widow or the estate of members, as well as sending floral bouquets and a representative to the funeral.

Members needing money could approach the union for a loan, and in November 1940 this evolved into a proposal to establish a credit union, which members voted, 95–47, to support. Len Killian was the first chairman of the credit union. Serving as board members were Joe Gillis, Cliff Bakkum, John Schoen, William Bedessem, Al Brietzke, and Richard Zeisler.

Deposits in the credit union were more than $3,000 by the end of 1941, and on January 15, 1942, the first cash dividend of 4 percent was paid to each member.

The union had a seniority system that basically determined that workers with the most years at the brewery were the last to be laid off. Workers transferring between breweries were also protected. In 1941, as Heileman was growing and La Crosse Breweries was in decline, the union was successful in transferring 10 workers to Heileman. In 1956, when La Crosse Breweries closed, some workers with the most seniority there were again transferred to Heileman.

Following World War II, the union negotiated the rehiring of returning servicemen, who were given priority to return to their old jobs and seniority credit for the years they were in the service. Similar benefits were granted in the Korean and Vietnam wars, and in 1982 members diagnosed with Vietnam Veterans Syndrome were awarded sickness and accident benefits.

Of course, work hours and pay were always major topics of negotiation between workers and the company. The union was largely responsible for negotiating pay increases, but didn't necessarily always get them. In 1922, the union offered to take a $1.50-a-week pay decrease to help the company survive Prohibition. The company made a counteroffer of a $3-a-week decrease and members voted to accept it.

During contract negotiations, the union often compared its pay with brewery workers in Milwaukee, Minneapolis, Cincinnati, Chicago, and Saint Louis. But by 1956, company officials had made it clear they could not compete with the major breweries on wages and benefits. Heileman told union employees their wages represented 95 percent of the pay at the large national breweries, making local members some of the highest-paid laborers not only in La Crosse but also in the entire Upper Midwest.

In 1939, the union negotiated contract clauses limiting working hours to a maximum of 16 hours within a 24-hour period, and was urged by the international union to try to get a contract for a 30-hour work week—five workdays of six hours. During the 1930s and 1940s a workweek of 48 hours was common. In November 1945, 123 union members met in a special session to complain about sometimes being required to work nine-hour days seven days a week. They were able to eventually negotiate a 40-hour week that paid a premium for night shift work, time and half for Saturdays, double time on Sundays and overtime pay for more than an eight-hour day. There also were other limitations on the amount of overtime, which members could accept or decline based on seniority.

As early as 1941 the union was investigating group insurance for workers. It was negotiating for hospitalization and surgical insurance by 1945, and was seeking family insurance by 1950. In order to provide coverage for their families, at least 70 percent of the members needed to participate in the program. In 1953, $2,000 of paid life insurance was added to the benefits.

In 1941, the union tried to negotiate seven paid holidays and two weeks of vacation, eventually settling for one week of paid vacation and seven paid holidays. In 1944, however, the company agreed to the second week of paid vacation for employees with more than five years of seniority, and by the 1970s a worker with more than 25 years of seniority was allowed seven weeks of paid vacation. Until then, vacations had to be taken in full weeks, but eventually single days were allowed. Most vacation was taken during the winter months, when production demands were lower, to help the company avoid layoffs.

A committee was formed to begin the discussion of pension alternatives in 1952. Finally, in 1958, Local 81 and the company negotiated the first Employees' Pension Plan, which paid union employees $2.10 a month for each year of service up to 35 years ($73.50 a month). Employees could retire with full pension at age 68 with 15 years of service, or take early retirement at age 65 with reduced benefits. The plan also included a provision for total disability retirement at age 60.

Through the years, the union became increasingly concerned with health and safety issues, asking Heileman to provide safety glasses for bottle house workers as early as 1939. In 1942, the Wisconsin State Industrial Commission was asked to inspect the Heileman pitch yard and fermenting cellars for safety violations and working conditions, and in 1944 a permanent safety committee was established.

On numerous occasions the union complained to the company regarding fumes from the various machines and ventilation concerns in the bottle house. When forklifts became popular, union leaders asked for safety lanes to be painted on the floors, and requested fans and air conditioning to make the summer heat more tolerable. In 1946, an elevator was installed in the malt shop to reduce stair climbing for workers. The union pressed the company hard on many of these issues, but also warned members it would not stand behind those who did not adhere to safety regulations.

Safety and health issues were increasingly influenced in the 1980s by Occupational Safety and Health Administration requirements and the workers' desire for a healthier lifestyle. The federal administration mandated beard shrouds, safety glasses and earplugs on many jobs, and there was increased concern about the misuse of alcohol and tobacco.

A time-honored tradition at Heileman was free beer for workers, but by the early 1980s workers were requesting the alternative of low-alcohol beer in the lunchrooms. The practice of allowing workers to drink during working hours finally came to an end on April 15, 1987, about the same time that lunchrooms became smoke-free. In 1986, union and company officials discussed mandatory drug testing for workers.

The union served as a strong advocate for workers in disputes with the company, but it didn't stand by its members unconditionally. In 1921, a worker walked off his job and went home after refusing a job order. The union voted 37–0 that he was wrong and refused to support him. On other occasions, the union refused to go to bat for members who were

Heileman employees on the keg line.
PHOTO COURTESY OF MURPHY LIBRARY, UNIVERSITY OF WISCONSIN-LA CROSSE

fired for being drunk on the job, habitually late or absent, or for fighting at work.

Throughout its history, Local 81 was a strong supporter of other unions. When Heileman needed to hire painters, plumbers, steamfitters, or other outside workers, Local 81 ensured that union workers were employed. If another union went on strike, it could count on support from the Heileman union—strikers at Trane Company, Norplex, Pepsi Cola, Hillview Homes, and other companies were supported with cash, as well as product, over the years. In 1937, three cases of Heileman beer were sent to striking workers at the Hackner woodworking company, 32 cases went to striking workers at the Electric Auto-Lite Company plant in 1958, and two half-barrels of beer were given to strikers at the La Crosse Cooler Company in the 1970s. Union solidarity could also extend to boycotts, such as the one in place against certain grocery stores in the La Crosse area during a meat-cutters' strike. Subscriptions to the *La Crosse Union Herald* newspaper assisted members in understanding the local labor scene.

For the families of brewery workers, no event was more memorable than the annual employee picnic, which also generated income for the union. A band was featured at the Heileman Family Day Picnic in 1902. The earliest picnics were held at Oehler's Cave south of La Crosse, and the gatherings later moved to other locations, including Tauscher's Farm and Veteran's Memorial Park. The picnic always included a meal and lots of cold beer, and it was said that Special Export beer was first brewed for one held at Oehler's Cave in the 1930s. By the late 1950s, the picnic had expanded to include lots of rides for the children, like a merry-go-round, kiddie cars, ponies or, better yet, the 40 et 8 locomotive from the La Crescent American Legion.

The union also provided entertainment for the workers. For example, there is a 1902 photograph of the annual Heileman Stag Party after a day of fishing. Union member John Mehren organized a stag picnic in 1941. A ticket cost $1.50 and members were allowed to bring a friend.

Another time-honored tradition was to hold "smokers," opportunities to get together and drink beer, smoke, play cards, and fraternize with fellow workers. Smokers also were held to celebrate contract settlements, as going-away parties for brothers headed for service in the nation's military forces, or as a way to raise funds for union activities. Typically these events were held at Bohemian Hall, the American Legion, or in later years, the Baus Haus.

From the earliest years the union was a strong supporter of sporting events for workers. The union was sponsoring several bowling teams by the late 1930s, for which it also purchased shirts and paid entry fees for local, state, and national tournaments. Softball and baseball teams, as well as golf and fishing tournaments, also were underwritten.

The union had a long history of political involvement. In 1922, it received and officially accepted a letter from the Socialist Party requesting a delegate, and in 1936 members were told they could join the Farmer Labor Progressive Party if they desired. In later years the union was primarily associated with the Democratic Party, and from the 1960s to 1980s was a strong supporter of Gaylord Nelson and William Proxmire, the United States senators from Wisconsin. The union made donations to candidates, and members attended political events and held fund-raisers. In 1968, Nelson toured the plant and a dinner was held in his honor. Candidates for local and state elections often addressed union meetings, and members were encouraged to support those who supported labor.

Local 81 also was active in lobbying issues of alcohol use and regulation. In 1922, members were encouraged to write to the House Ways and Means Committee urging it to end Prohibition and support bonuses for returning soldiers. They also wrote to officials in La Crosse, encouraging them to support the sale of beer and light wine. In 1924, members were required to donate 25 cents to a political action committee.

In 1939, members were fighting to stop a law to prohibit beer advertising on the radio. Members wrote to their congressmen and senators in 1942 and asked them to allow beer at Army and Navy camps. For Heileman, this paid off handsomely by allowing the introduction of Old Style beer at Camp McCoy in Sparta, Wisconsin. Petitions were circulated at local taverns urging legislators to fight against a return to Prohibition. In 1956, union officials signed affidavits for the National Labor Relations Board confirming they were anti-Communist, presumably a concomitant of being pro-beer.

In 1945, when the breweries needed more workers because so many men had gone off to war, wives, mothers, and daughters of union workers were given preference for those jobs, and the union fought for equal pay, benefits, and protection for those women. However, after the war the union negotiated for men to replace the women as they returned from war.

In general, relationships between Heileman and the union were respectful and fairly amicable. But strikes occurred when a contract couldn't be settled. The most notable were in 1948, 1962, 1966, and 1969. A particularly bitter strike in 1972 lasted eight weeks and included the arrests of union members for vandalism and threats of violence. Russ Cleary had just taken over the company and needed a dedicated and cooperative work force. To get rid of the us-versus-them mentality following that strike, he vowed to ban lawyers from future bargaining sessions and to settle contracts without hired outsiders. After that, there was never another strike at the House of Heileman, and on one occasion, Cleary was asked to be parade marshal of the annual Labor Day parade.

During the 1980s, union and management established several traditions. Each time they entered negotiations, the union presented management with a bottle of ketchup to remind them that workers in La Crosse were paid less than those at Anheuser-Busch and Miller and needed about $2.50 an hour more to "catch up." In turn, the company presented the union with a beef tongue and heart, symbolic of the union having talked management to death with its "bull," and wanting to tear the "heart" out of the company. At the end of successful negotiations, union and management teams traditionally dunked each other in a swimming pool, a symbolic way to wash away any hard feelings.

Both Roy Kumm and Cleary personally knew many of the union workers. In the small town of La Crosse, if Cleary saw one of them out for dinner he would generally send a beer over. With that kind of close contact, Heileman workers were apt to respect and like both Kumm and Cleary. When Kumm died in 1971, union members took up a collection for a gift to honor his memory, and when Cleary stepped down in 1989, they contributed more than $700 for a retirement gift— a plaque at the brewery and a cell phone for his houseboat. Perhaps they were hoping he would not be too far out of contact in the days to come.

Throughout Heileman's long history, its union played a critical role, providing numerous benefits to its members and a dedicated work force recognized as one of the finest in the brewing industry. The House of Heileman enjoyed this key advantage over its competitors for as long as it stayed in business.

Prohibition . . . Again?

By 1939, the brewery workers union was worried about increased activity favoring a return to Prohibition. A national meeting was held in October, at which five mandatory items for unionists were formulated:

1. Work for temperance as opposed to prohibition.
2. Educate the public on the health benefits of beer.
3. Combat legal restrictions on beer.
4. Propose legislation favorable to the brewing industry.
5. Oppose legislation that would allow prohibition at a local level.

They helped make the union go and grow

It would be impossible to list every person who ever was employed by Heileman in La Crosse, or who was in some way involved in the history of the company. The following is a selected list of union officers and other individuals who played a role in the history of the union. Exact dates for each individual are difficult to obtain. However, for each person a general era or year is indicated when they in some way contributed to the history of the union. This material was obtained from records from 1920 to 1990 and therefore are not complete. Much of this material was obtained from hand-written meeting minutes. Spellings and dates may not be exact.

Name	Role	Approximate Years or Era
Akright, William	Contract committee, business agent, secretary/treasurer	1971 - 1981
Albitz, Don	Executive board	1970 - 1971
Albitz, John	Shop steward drivers, contract committee	1942 - 1946
Allen, James	Brewery steward, trustee	1971 - 1974
Allen, Fred	Shop steward, vice president, executive board	1979 - 1990
Arttus, Bill	Shop steward	1987 - 1989
Bain, William	Labor council	1935
Bakkum, James	Auditor, shop steward	1971 - 1989
Bakkum, Clifford	Labor council, entertainment and auditing committees, finance secretary	1939 - 1968
Banasik, Stanley	Shop steward (Michel's), safety committee	1938 - 1946
Bantle, Bill	Shop steward	1957 - 1970
Basset, Bill	Shop steward	1989 - 1990
Becker, Bill	Shop steward	1985
Bedessem, William	Financial secretary, auditing committee, treasurer, trustee of labor council, executive board	1943 - 1958
Belinger, Frank	Shop delegate	1926
Benrud, Darrel	Malt house steward	1970 - 1980
Beranek, George	Entertainment committee, executive board	1941 - 1948
Beranek, Clarence	Shop steward brewery, executive board	1942 - 1975
Beranek, William	Trustee	1975 - 1978
Berger, Clifford	Shop steward (Ziegler's Brewery)	1946 - 1950
Bettin, John	Sergeant at arms, executive board	1945 - 1960
Bey, Frank	Sergeant at arms	1946 - 1949
Biche, Joe	Contract committee	1926
Bishop, Ed	Executive board, entertainment committee, shop steward brewery (La Crosse Brewery)	1938 - 1946
Boeck, Henry	Shop steward bottle house, executive board, contract committee	1952 - 1962
Brazda, William	Vice president	1920s
Breidel, James	Shop steward	1967
Brintnall, Archie	Shop steward mechanical, safety committee	1942
Buchmann, August	Finance committee, correspondence secretary, treasurer, trustee	1921 - 1945
Buelow, Henry	Recording secretary, safety committee	1933 - 1950

Burand, Adolph	Trustee	1920s
Burrow, Fred	Shop steward brew house (La Crosse Brewing)	1953 - 1955
Buschman, Ronald	Brewery steward, contract committee, trustee, president, secretary/treasurer, executive board	1971- 1990
Byer, William	Labor council	1936
Carrier, Banner	Trustee	1920s
Carroll, Tim	Shop steward	1985 - 1987
Check, Paul	Shop steward	1987 - 1989
Collins, Dave	Shop steward	1972
Conrad, Dale	President, executive board	1971 - 1978
Coughlin, William	Shop steward drivers, executive board, vice president, shop steward drivers, president	1938 - 1952
Covey, Chester	Shop steward	1963 - 1969
Cozy, Brian	Shop steward	1983
Crandall, Mike	Shop steward	1984 - 1989
Culp, Robert	Shop steward delivery	1942 - 1943
Duermeyer, Carl	Finance committee	1938
Duresky, Lambert	Stop steward delivery, safety board	1940 - 1942
Eckert, Frank	Shop steward	1963
Emerson, Russ	Bottle house steward	1973
Erlewein, Henry	Vice president	1938
Feltes, Bill	Shop steward, executive board	1989 - 1990
Ferrier, Clarence	Warehouse steward, executive board	1971 - 1990
Finn, James	Executive board	1960 - 1965
Fontish, Clarence	Shop steward mechanical (La Crosse Brewery)	1943 - 1953
Fried, Chut	Shop steward drivers	1944
Friese, Emil	Trustee	1936 - 1937
Fuchs, John	Executive board, shop steward bottle house, recording secretary (Michel's La Crosse Brewery), sergeant at arms, contract committee	1938 - 1952
Feuling, Martin	Trustee, shop delegate machine shop, shop steward mechanical (La Crosse Brewery / Heileman) executive board, safety board, contract committee	1934 - 1944
Gallup, Clyde	Shop steward delivery	1943 - 1957
Gautsch, Arthur	Shop steward	1959
Genz, Earl	Shop steward mechanical	1946 - 1949
Gilbertson, Clarence	Entertainment committee	1945 - 1947
Gilles, Joseph	Executive board, recording secretary, shop steward brewing, president, financial secretary	1943 - 1962
Gleason, Harry	Membership committee, shop steward	1947 - 1973
Glennie, John	Shop steward	1971 - 1972
Gmeiner, Joe	Shop steward bottle house, contract committee, labor council	1933 - 1946
Goede, Otto	Vice president	1932 - 1937
Good, Alvy	Sergeant at arms	1942 - 1943
Gorske, Henry	Guard	1940
Grabinski, Verdon	Auditing committee	1946 - 1957
Graves, Sidney	Mechanical steward, executive board, trustee	1967 - 1975

Greener, Frank	Shop steward mechanical department, vice president	1941 - 1944
Griffel, Frank	Trustee	1922
Grosch, Frank	Shop steward	1959
Grosskopf, Arthur	Corresponding secretary	1921
Gruley, Paul	Labor council	1933
Hammes, Sylvester	Shop steward malting	1943
Hanifl, Kenneth	Shop steward	1971
Harkness, Don	Executive board	1972
Hanson, Pete	Shop steward	1984
Harris, Guy	Executive board, shop steward mechanical (Michel's La Crosse Brewery)	1938 - 1941
Haskness	Executive board	1974
Hastings, Charles	Executive board, shop steward mechanical	1954 - 1970
Hauser, Ralph	Executive board	1967
Hawley, Henry	Entertainment committee	1942
Hefty, Frank	Trustee	1921
Herlitzka, Clarence	Shop steward brewhouse, executive board	1950 - 1963
Hess, Louis	Contract committee, executive board	1950 -1963
Hess, Robert	Shop steward	1960
Hetznecker, Joe	Shop steward (Kunz Brewery)	1936
Hickey, George	Executive board	1971 - 1973
Hiekel, Emil	Trustee	1921
Hillyer, Walter	Trustee, labor council, executive board, guard, representative at state convention	1935 -1946
Hinze, Les	Shop steward	1975
Hole, Ron	Shop steward, executive board	1975 - 1985
Hottinger, Frank	Contract negotiating, membership and safety committees, shop steward bottle house	1943 - 1960
Houlihan, George	Finance and auditing committees	1943-1945
Howe, Tom	Vice president, contract committee, executive board	1960 - 1989
Huber, Gile	Shop steward	1969
Huska, Frank	President	1933
Ingham, Ronald	Executive board	1960
Jiracek, Joe	Shop delegate	1933
Johnson, Conrad	Safety committee	1941 - 1942
Johnson, S. A.	Vice president of Labor Temple Association	1922
Kaatz, Larry	Mechanical department steward	1975 - 1978
Kabat, Emil	Labor council, clerk, executive board	1943 - 1946
Kabat, Victor	Membership and contract committees	1946 - 1952
Kaiser, Leo	Recording secretary, entertainment and contract committees, safety board	1938 - 1945
Kane, William	Business agent, attended international conventions, auditing and finance committees, president, contract committee	1943 - 1963
Kato, William	Contract committee, executive board	1950 - 1958
Kerska, David	Shop steward	1972
Kessler, Bill	Shop steward	1984 - 1985
Killian, Leonard	Shop delegate bottle house, labor council, president, safety and contract committees	1936 - 1950
King, George	Labor council	1943

Kleinpeter, Florian	Heileman shop delegate	1923
Klug, Clarence	Shop steward delivery (La Crosse Brewery)	1940 - 1941
Knebes, John	Recording secretary	1943 - 1946
Knox, J.O.	Treasurer of Labor Temple Association	1922
Koeller, Paul E.	Contract committee, bottle house shop steward day shift, executive board.	1950s – 1970s
Koenen, LuVern	Corresponding secretary (Michel's), executive board, business agent, labor council, contract committee	1938 - 1957
Kostecki, Frank	Shop steward night shift	1943
Kowalke, Otto	Corresponding secretary, legislature committee	1921 - 1923
Kriese, Jules	Executive board, contract committee	1943 - 1971
Krugel, Clarence	Executive board, shop steward mechanical	1942
Kruger, Steve	Shop steward	1990
Larkin, Mike	President	1967 - 1969
Lawrynk, Dale	Shop steward, business agent	1984 - 1987
Lennartz, Theodore	Vice president, shop steward mechanical department (La Crosse Brewing)	1938- 1948
Lepsch, Emil	Recording secretary	1941
Lepsch, Charles	Shop steward bottle house (La Crosse Brewing)	1953
Leske, William	Member	1925
Leske, Harry	Trustee, labor council, shop steward brewery, executive board, representative at state convention, and finance, education, auditing and contract committee	1937 - 1948
Liberte Frank	Executive board, bottle house steward	1958 - 1975
Linberg, William	Vice president	1942 - 1944
Linhart, Frank	Shop steward brewery (La Crosse Brewing)	1944 - 1949
Liston, Jerome	Bottle house steward	1971
Luedke, Adolph	Shop steward	1928 - 1933
Lusk, Matt	Vice president, attended state and national conventions, contract and safety committees, business agent, shop steward	1948 - 1963
Lynch, Edward	Executive board, secretary, shop steward delivery, contract committee, recording secretary	1940 – 1975
Majerle, William	Executive board, recording secretary, finance committee, labor council, shop steward brewing	1941 - 1943
Malin, Ray	Shop steward	1984 - 1990
Mauer, Edward	President	1923 - 1926
Mauer, Bud	Trustee	1922
May, Milton	Contract committee	1952 - 1954
McGinnis, Edgar	Shop steward bottle house (La Crosse Brewery)	1948
Mehren, John	President	1934 - 1945
Miller, Donald	Bottle house steward day shift	1964 - 1972
Miller, Louis	Executive board, president, contract committee	1934 - 1940
Miller, Lutz	Finance committee, trustee	1938 - 1939
Miller, Oscar	Recording secretary, Heileman shop delegate, joint board, executive board	1922 - 1938
Minor, Ken	Shop steward brewery, executive board, contract negotiating committee	1960 - 1970
Mitby, Walter	Auditor	1967
Morton, Ralph	Financial secretary	1965 - 1972

Mueller, Thomas	Shop steward	1968
Muenzenberger, Paul	Shop steward	1986 - 1990
Nack, John	Trustee	1931 - 1933
Neihesel, Erwin	Contract committee	1926
Netzer, William	Recording secretary, president, labor council, executive board, business agent, finance and contract committees	1922 - 1946
Nickelatti, Tom	Shop steward	1987 - 1990
Niedbalski, Kenneth	Bottle house steward, executive board	1971 - 1974
Oelke, Harold	Shop steward	1967
Oliver, Jeff	Shop steward	1984 - 1985
Olson, Edward	Entertainment committee	1946 - 1947
Olson, Elmer	Entertainment committee	1946
Olson, Robert	President, vice president	1954 - 1964
Opitz, Gregory	Executive board	1951 - 1955
Papacek, Joseph	Shop steward malt house, executive board	1938 - 1948
Papenfuss, Albert	Shop steward (La Crosse Brewing)	1953
Paul, Carl	Trustee, finance committee, treasurer	1936 - 1943
Peterson, Art	Executive board, vice president, shop steward (La Crosse Brewing), contract negotiating and education committees	1941 - 1948
Peterson, Oscar	Shop steward brewery (Michel's)	1938 - 1939
Pierce, George	Shop steward mechanical	1934
Pierce, Roy	Shop steward	1950
Pischke, Joe	Shop steward	1934
Pitz, William	Finance and contract committees, vice president	1928 - 1934
Platz, Henry	Marshal	1921 - 1922
Poellinger, Frank	Shop steward	1927
Polkowski, Joe	Labor council	1935 - 1936
Pretasky, Tom	Vice president, president, executive board	1953 - 1966
Petrowski, Ed	Safety committee	1946
Pust, Albert	Recording secretary	1921
Quarstad, Orvall	Shop steward bottle house (La Crosse Brewing)	1949 - 1950
Rahnenfuehrer, Walt	Shop steward brewhouse (La Crosse Brewing), safety committee	1941 - 1943
Raith, Joe	Finance committee, corresponding secretary, executive board, labor council	1921 - 1938
Rand, Tim	Shop steward	1986 - 1989
Raymond, Charles	Heileman shop delegate	1923 - 1925
Richert, Tom	Audit committee	1972
Reid, Al	Sergeant at arms, bottle house steward	1972 - 1977
Reisman, Alvin	Shop steward brewhouse (La Crosse Brewery)	1946 - 1948
Richmond, Ed	Shop steward malting plant	1945 - 1946
Ristow, Henry	Entertainment committee	1946
Rohleder, Elmer	Sergeant at arms	1938 - 1950
Roraff, Joseph	Vice president, shop steward delivery department (La Crosse Brewing), executive board	1949 - 1954
Rounds, Melvin	Labor council	1942

Name	Position	Years
Sagen, L. John	Shop steward, executive board, contract committee	1971 - 1990
Saley, Roger	Shop steward	1985 - 1987
Schams, Gene	Shop steward	1983 -1989
Schaumberger, Fred	Shop steward drivers (La Crosse Brewing)	1947 - 1948
Schiessl, Joe	Corresponding secretary, shop steward bottle house, executive board, and finance, entertainment, and contract committees	1938 - 1948
Schlict, Irvin	Bottle house shop steward night shift, contract committee, business agent	1953 - 1972
Schlifer, Doug	Shop steward	1980
Schmalz, Jim	Recording secretary, executive board	1984 - 1990
Schmidt, Joseph	Member	1925
Schmidt, Ray	Sergeant at arms	1967
Schmidt, Harry	Shop steward	1948
Schmitt, George	Sergeant at arms	1942 -1943
Schnell, Fred	Finance secretary, legislature and contract committees	1921 - 1932
Schnick, Reinhold	President	1922 - 1923
Schock, Arden	Trustee, shop steward	1978
Schoen, John	Recording secretary, executive board, president, labor council, and finance, education, auditing, and contract committees	1934 - 1949
Schoen, Hilary	Sergeant at arms, vice president	1960 - 1970
Schoenfeldt, Ben	Vice president	1923
Schroeder, David	Finance secretary, treasurer	1972 - 1973
Schubert, Joe	Finance committee	1920s
Schuelke, Henry	Entertainment committee, executive board	1943 - 1949
Schultz, Donald	Shop steward mechanical department	1945 - 1953
Schumacher, Dennis	Shop steward, executive board	1984 - 1987
Schuttenhelm, John	Finance committee	1922
Schwarze, Arnold	Executive board	1963 - 1964
Schwaergerl, Andrew	Clerk	1946
Severson, Conrad	Labor council, sergeant at arms, entertainment committee, vice president	1942 - 1948
Shimshak, Ed	Contract negotiating committee (La Crosse Brewing), shop steward	1944 - 1951
Sieger, Russ	Vice president	1944
Skoy, James	Bottle house steward, contract committee, recording secretary, president, executive board	1973 - 1990
Skoy, James	Shop steward	1951
Smith, Frank E.	Entertainment committee	1945 - 1947
Snyder, Leo	Contract committee	1949
Soller, Ray	Auditor	1963
Soller, John	Heileman shop steward, contract committee	1923 - 1934
Spika, Robert	Shop steward	1947
Stanke, Fritz	Finance committee	1922
Stenberg, David	Power plant steward	1973
Stonedahl, Cliff	Labor council, finance committee, shop steward (La Crosse Brewery), executive board	1938 - 1956
Starch, David	Shop steward, trustee	1978

Strasser, Matt	President (Michel's), labor council, executive board, education committee	1938 - 1953
Streck, Theodore	Shop steward bottle house night shift, contract committee	1946 - 1954
Strehlow, Mike	Entertainment and safety committees, shop steward	1943 - 1949
Strittmatter, Harold	Malt house steward	1946 - 1967
Sullivan, Paul	Shop steward	1972
Swertfeger, Fred	Shop steward delivery (La Crosse Brewery)	1955
Tanke, Robert	Delivery steward, bottle house steward	1960 - 1983
Tanke, Gus	Vice president	1927 - 1929
Temp, Albert	Executive board, vice president, shop steward, sergeant at arms	1940 - 1965
Temp, Walter	Executive board	1942 - 1949
Terry, Walter	Executive board, recording secretary, entertainment committee	1939 - 1942
Thaldorf, Andy	Labor council, shop steward bottle house	1940 - 1943
Thomas, Stan	Bottle house steward night shift, president, trustee	1967 - 1975
Thompson, David	Malt house steward	1968 - 1970
Tikal, Frank	President	1920s
Tischer, Gerald	Brewhouse steward-cellars	1965 - 1973
Todt, Rudolph	Entertainment committee	1943
Tooke, James	Sergeant at arms, shop delegate bottle house	1936 - 1938
Townsend, Errol	Entertainment and contract committees	1947 - 1950
Tracy, John	Guard, labor Council	1941 - 1943
Treakle, Roy	Shop steward malting plant, entertainment committee	1939 - 1963
Troyanek, John	Contract and finance committees, shop steward	1925 - 1933
Troyanek, George	Shop steward bottling department (La Crosse Brewing)	1945
Ulrich, Fredric	Vice president	1971 - 1974
Verchota, J.J.	President of Labor Temple Association	1922
Verse, John	Shop steward bottling	1942
Weber, Jack	Contract committee, executive board, business agent	1951 - 1969
Wehrenberg, Harold	Shop steward delivery department	1945
Weibel, Matt	Shop steward mechanical	1941
Weinsberger, Tom	Executive board	1971
Wells, Tim	Shop steward	1970
Wells, F. O.	Secretary of Labor Temple Association	1922
Wester, John	Trustee	1924 - 1925
Whipple, Weldon	Executive board, shop steward (Michel's), safety committee	1939 - 1942
Wiemerslage, Paul	Sergeant at arms, financial secretary	1955 - 1959
Williams, Les	Finance committee, vice president, president, shop delegate	1925 - 1944
Wiltinger, Leo	Trustee	1920s
Wise, William	Contract committee	1926
Wojahn, Robert	Mechanical department steward	1973 - 1974
Zahn, John	Treasurer, legislature committee	1921 - 1928
Zanter, Joseph	Shop steward brewhouse, executive board	1943 - 1953
Zeisler, Erwin	Membership committee	1946
Zeske, Harry	Shop steward brewery	1936

Chapter 32

Steins Marked the Years

COLORFUL HEILEMAN MEMORABILIA IS PRIZED BY MANY

The first stein, issued in 1979, is generally regarded as the hardest to obtain because just 2,000 were made.

Beer steins, each with different designs and themes, were issued to Heileman employees every year from 1979 through 1996. The steins were popular with brewery workers and wholesalers immediately, and many now are highly prized by collectors of memorabilia from the brewing industry.

Details about the steins include:

1979—The first stein in the Heileman series was produced in West Germany by the BMF company. There are no dates or numbers on these steins, which feature the House of Heileman logo and the brewery's motto: "We don't aim to make the most beer, only the best!" The clear-glass stein is 7.5 inches tall from its base to the tip of its lid. Heileman had five breweries in 1979, and they are recorded near the base: La Crosse, Wisconsin; Newport, Kentucky; Saint Paul, Minnesota; Evansville, Indiana; and Seattle, Washington. Just 2,000 of these steins were produced, the fewest of any year in the series.

The first stein
FROM THE COLLECTION OF PAUL D. KOELLER

1980—Heileman's expansion is reflected in this stein, which recognizes the brewery's addition of three plants: Baltimore, Maryland; Frankenmuth, Michigan; and Phoenix, Arizona. Heileman's brewery in Belleville, Illinois, is curiously absent from this stein. Pictorials of the eight breweries are framed with grain stalks on the sides of the stein, which is made of opaque white glass trimmed in yellow. The Heileman motto is wrapped around the base, and the seven-inch-tall stein has a silver-plated lid sporting a white circular inlay containing the Heileman logo adorned with grains. There were 5,000 of these steins produced by BMF.

1981—Expansion again is the theme, as the Belleville plant has been added. Pictorials of the nine Heileman breweries are displayed on the opaque white glass stein. House of Heileman logos made of metallic gold are placed between the pictorials, and the motto can be found under the pictorial of the La Crosse brewery. This pot-bellied stein stands six inches tall, including the silver-plated lid, and is trimmed in brown. It was made by BMF, and 5,000 of them were distributed to employees and wholesalers.

1982—A pictorial of a mug of beer is featured on this stein, which also shows King Gambrinus, the Heileman motto and a map of America indicating the locations of the Heileman breweries, which now total 10. The company's latest addition, in Auburndale, Florida, has been added to the display. Wrapped around the bottom of the stein are representations of cans of the company's core beer brands. BMF made 6,000 of these 7.5-inch-tall steins.

1983—King Gambrinus, the patron saint of brewing, is featured on this stein. To the king's right is a United States map disclosing the cities where Heileman breweries were located. Hops and grains, the main ingredients that go into beer, are shown to the left of the king, who is standing against the backdrop of a waterfall. The 7.5-inch-tall stein is again made of opaque white glass trimmed in brown. There were 6,000 of these steins produced by BMF.

1984—This year's stein shows a river scene, King Gambrinus, the Heileman logo and motto and a United States map featuring brewery locations. The map reflects the addition of Heileman plants in Portland, Oregon; San Antonio, Texas; and Perry, Georgia. The brewery in Auburndale has now been closed, and it is not represented on this stein, which stands seven inches tall and is made of opaque white glass trimmed in blue. BMF made 7,000 of these steins.

1985—This stein features four scenes: barley and hops; King Gambrinus; the House of Heileman logo beneath the company's motto; and a flowing river. Listed in the frames of the scenes are the locations of 11 Heileman breweries. A notation that states "founded 1853" actually gives an incorrect year. This clear-glass stein stands six inches tall and is distinguished by the words "seventh edition 1985" placed on the inside of the lid. This year marks the first time dates are associated with the series, and 1985 also is recorded in Roman numerals on the stein. There were 7,000 of these steins produced by BMF.

1986—The Heileman motto centered below the House of Heileman logo is featured on this seven-inch-tall stein, which is made of opaque white glass trimmed in blue. A pictorial of the Old Style marketing campaign of 1986—"brewed with water from when the earth was pure"—flanks both sides of the logo and motto. The 11 cities containing Heileman breweries are listed around the stein's base. BMF made 7,000 of these steins.

1987—A map of the United States, with Heileman logos marking the locations of cities containing company breweries, is featured on this stein. A 12th brewery, in Milwaukee, was added to the Heileman roster, and the stein, this year. This seven-inch-tall stein again was made of opaque white glass trimmed in blue. BMF made 7,000 of the steins, which were the last produced by the German company for Heileman.

1988—This year's stein is beige ceramic and features a gold metallic Heileman logo and a map of the United States. The stein lists the 12 Heileman breweries, six to the left of the map and six to the right. A red banner displaying the Heileman motto is wrapped around the nearly eight-inch-tall stein, which was the first in the series to be numbered individually. Ilka Ceramics of Beloit, Ohio, made 7,000 of the steins.

1989—Gottlieb Heileman, one of two German immigrants who founded the La Crosse brewery in 1858, is featured on this stein. His portrait is below a gold House of Heileman logo and is flanked to the left by a scene of Gottlieb examining a brew sample and to the right by a horse-drawn Heileman beer wagon. The ceramic stein, primarily tan colored with brown bands, stands 10 inches high and was designed by a Heileman staff member for the first time in the series. An inscription again incorrectly states the company was established in 1853. Ilka Ceramics made 2,550 of these steins.

1990—"A Tradition of Brewing Excellence" is the theme for the 1990 stein, which has gold rings accenting the overall tan color. Pictorials show the turn-of-the-century brewery on one side and similarly dated brewery workers on the other. The stein was again designed by a Heileman staff member and stands 10 inches tall, from its base to the tip of its pewter lid. Ilka Ceramics made 4,500 of these steins.

1991—King Gambrinus returns on this ceramic 9.5-inch-tall stein, which lists several Heileman brands. Text giving information about King Gambrinus is wrapped around the base. GERZ, a German company, made 4,560 of these steins.

1992—The home of Gottlieb and Johanna Heileman is featured on this ceramic stein, which has a tan background color accented with red bands and a red ribbon. The logos of the core brands are wrapped around the base, and text gives details about the Heileman house. The 10-inch-tall lidded stein was made by Custom Quality Ceramics of Beloit, Oho. The company made 2,494 of the steins.

1993—A Heileman office building, which burned in 1959, is the centerpiece on this 10-inch stein, which has three red bands breaking up its tan background color. Logos of the Heileman core brands arc over the building, with the House of Heileman logo featured at the top of the arc. Text at the stein's base gives some history about the building. Custom Quality Ceramics made 2,650 of these steins.

1994—The historic coin flip that determined ownership of the young La Crosse brewery is featured on this stein, which is dominated by a blue background color and stands 10 inches tall. A pictorial of City Brewery in the 1870s stands between portraits of its founders, Gottlieb Heileman and John Gund. Text details the brewery's history and the coin flip the co-owners used to divide their properties. Heileman won the coin toss and became the brewery's sole proprietor in 1872. This stein was the first designed by Kurt Friederichs, market services manager for Heileman and designer of the cover of this book. Custom Quality Ceramics made 2,600 of these steins.

1995—Johanna Heileman, Gottlieb's wife and the company's first president, is featured on this porcelain stein. A portrait of Johanna is on one side of the stein, which is the first porcelain stein in the series, and portraits of the Heileman children are on the other side. Text gives historical information about the Heileman family, and an eagle similar to the one that adorned the office building that burned in 1959 is centered on this 7.5-inch-tall stein. The eagle is significant because it was a predecessor of the eagle found in the Heileman logo. Friederichs designed this stein, and Concepts Unlimited Incorporated of Wilmington, North Carolina, made 2,800 of them.

1996—Emil Traugott Mueller, who helped run the brewery in it early years, is featured on this nearly eight-inch-tall stein, made of white porcelain trimmed with gold. His portrait is on one side and the original Old Style Lager is on the other. An eagle design and historical information about Mueller's accomplishments at the brewery fill the remaining space. This stein is the third designed by Friederichs. Illustrations for it were done by Burgandy Nilles, a freelance artist from La Crosse, and 2,800 of them were made by Concepts Unlimited.

Bibliography

Books

A History of The Brewing Industry in LaCrosse Steven Baier 1976

Ashes To Ashes—America's Hundred-Year War, the Public Health, and the Unabashed Triumph of Philip Morris Richard Kluger 1996

American Breweries Donald Bull, Manfred Friedrich, Robert Gottschalk 1984

Badger Breweries—Past and Present Wayne L. Kroll 1976

Beer Blast—The Inside Story of the Brewing Industry's Bizarre Battles For Your Money Philip VanMunching 1997

Brewed In America—The History of Beer and Ale In The United States Stanley Baron 1962

Breweries of Wisconsin Jerry Apps 1992

Citizen Coors An American Dynasty by Dan Baum 2000

History of La Crosse County, Wisconsin Western Historical Company Chicago 1881

LaCrosse In Light and Shadow Edwin Hill and Douglas Connell 1992

Price Guide to Beer Cans—Fifth Edition William E. Mugrage 1993

The Great Beer Trek—A Guide to the Highlights of American Beer Drinking Stephan Morris 1990

The New World Guide to Beer Michael Jackson 1988

The Pabst Brewing Company—The History of an American Business Thomas C. Cochran Phd. 1948

The Rise and Fall of Alan Bond Paul Barry 1990

Under The Influence—The Unauthorized Story of The Anheuser-Busch Dynasty Peter Hernon and Terry Ganey 1991

Wisconsin Biography Volume 5 - 1946

Newspapers

Bangor Independent

Capital Times

Chicago Tribune

Citibusiness News

Coulee Gazette

La Crosse Daily Republic & Leader

La Crosse Tribune

La Crosse Weekly

La Crosse County Countryman

Milwaukee Journal

Milwaukee Sentinel

Nordstern Newspaper

St. Paul Pioneer Press

Wall Street Journal

Wisconsin State Journal

Wisconsin Business Journal

Magazine articles

Bakery Production and Marketing September 24, 1987

Barron's July 3, 1967

Brewers Digest December 1969

Dun's Review June 1977

Dow Digest August 1968

Forbes September 15, 1969

Newsweek Magazine August 1, 1981

The Business Journal week of August 24, 1987

The Economist January 14, 1986

Time Magazine August 10, 1981

Web sites

beerismylife.com/breweries/us/or/432.htm

beernotes.com/northwest/articles/00049.html - Rainier Brewery - Rest In Peace

celebrator.com/9708/HENRYW.html

celebrator.com/9904/stroh.html - Last Call for Stroh Brewing Company

detnews.com/1999/biz/9908/07/08070118.htm

familySearch record for Gottlieb Heileman

home.earthlink.net/~mckennst/news1099.html

home.insight.rr.com/baileypage/Stroh/american.htm - History of Stroh Brewing and Brands

home1.gte.net/tjhoff/bchistp2.html

jadetech.com/~smallsha/interest.htm

mammer/prohosting.com/pentz/encycl/b4ency.htm

OCLC FirstSearch - Legal database of documents about G. Heileman Brewing Company

pfeifferbeer.com/history/history2.html

pixel.cs.ut.edu/library/towns/bowole.txt

seattletimes.nwsource.com/news/business/html98/rain_020999.html

thebeermuseum.org/gallery.html

www.americanbrewiana.org

www.antiquibles.com

www.bankruptcydata.com/NewsArchiveSample.htm - Bankruptcy 1996 History for Heileman

www.beerhistory.com

www.beertown.org

www.bizjournals.com

www.breweryage.com

www.cdcco.com

www.citybrewery.com

www.club-mgmt.com/dining/9712/beer.html

www.docpowells.com/tradition.shtml

www.findarticles.com/m3469/8_50/54237514/p1/article.jhtml

www.flagpole.com/Issues/03.04.98/beerhistory.html

www.fromsitetostory.org/sources/papers/mnarch98/98niv-bf-a.asp

www.grainbelt.com/history.htm

www.icsi.net/~mosnar/history.html

www.idem.org/library/palda2_en.html

www.jadtech.com/~smallsha/carling-.htm

www.jsonline.com/dd/dinmil/dec99/mobottle30122899.asp

www.ketupa.net/bond.htm

www.lacrossetribune.com

www.mi-brew.com/breweries/F/frankenmuth/index.html

www.newstimes.com/archive95/165/bzd.txt

www.oktoberfestusa.com/history.htm

www.pub.umich.edu/daily/1999/feb/02-09-99/news/news13.html

wwe.realbeer.com/news/articles/news-000813.html

www.roadsideamerica.com/set/drink.html

www.southerndraft.com/sodraft/9604/heileman.html

www.tinsel.org/beer/heileman.html

www.trib.com/scjournal.ARC/1997/NOV/Nov_16_99_

www.uic.edu/~pchalos/BENCHMARKING.html

www.utb/uscourts.gov/opinions/published/12br876.html

www.wisconsin-asa.org

Personal interviews and remembrances

Dozens of interviews were conducted by both authors.

Other sources

1946 "Two Way Street" - Heileman Employee Handbook

Email correspondence from Kirchheim unter Tech Germany archives

February 12, 1988 Heileman document to shareholders on vote to merge with Bond

G. *Heileman Brewing Company - A Brief History*

Heileman Annual Reports 1935 to 1987

Heileman Stockholder Report 1902

Heileman Baking Company Overview 1987

Heileman Employee's Pension Plan 1958

Heileman Local 81 Union Records

Heileman *What's Brewin'* Employee Magazines for August 1958 through April 1960

Heileman History paper by Tracy Meiner and Terri Waldron 12/01/1982

History of the Brewery - Early Years (from an article in a Heileman retirees newsletter)

House Of Heileman stein series

La Crosse City Directory

Milwaukee County Courthouse Real Estate Records Volume 50 Page 629

Old Style stein series

Plant Data Summary compiled by Walter Baltz dated January 31, 1989.

PPE Encyclopedia (web) - Alan Bond

Stroh - Giant Six Pack Facts

The House of Heileman History - A Brief History by David DeLano

Andrew Denton interview with Alan Bond

Thoughts from Author Paul D. Koeller

Paul D. Koeller, who was born and raised in La Crosse, is a software engineer who lives in Rochester, Minnesota. This is his first book.

Thank you to my wife, Karen, and daughter, Mara, for their love, support, and inspiration as I followed my dream. Thanks also to my co-author, David DeLano, for a great partnership that resulted in a much better book than either of us could have delivered alone.

Thank you to all of the people who took the time to meet with us and tell us their Heileman stories. Many people read early drafts and provided editing, corrections, and suggestions that greatly improved the book. It would be impossible to name them all, but special thanks to my mother, Beverly Koeller, and to Barbara Kroner, Clifford Sjolund Jr., and Beverly Pike.

Our editor, Fran Edstrom, with the assistance of her husband, John, did an outstanding job of editing our written words into a readable and well-organized book. Ken Brekke, Sue Knopf and the staff of RC Printing in La Crosse took the edited manuscript and turned it into a real book. Thank you to the staff of the La Crosse Public Library Archive Room, where I spent many afternoons researching. The staff at Murphy Library and the La Crosse County Historical Society helped us find all of the great historical photos.

Walter Baltz provided his personal historical archives, which were invaluable. Ron Buschman provided historical union documents that formed the basis for the union chapter. The Cleary–Kumm Foundation provided numerous photos and memorabilia. Gary Schultz graciously shared his awesome collection of Heileman memorabilia and advertising materials. Marian Pretasky and Adeline Kriese shared their photos and information about the Heileman sports teams. Larry Slezniko and Paul Currier from UW–La Crosse Educational Technologies photographed much of the memorabilia that appears in the book. Thank you also to Al Trapp and the staff of our publisher, the University of Wisconsin–La Crosse Foundation Incorporated.

Finally, thank you to all of the rest of my family and friends who supported and encouraged me during the project.

Thoughts from Author David H. DeLano

David grew up in Winona, Minnesota. He earned a degree in economics from Hamline University (Saint Paul, Minnesota) in 1973 and immediately went to work for the G. Heileman Brewing Company. David worked a total of 23 years for Heileman, all in some capacity within the credit department.

For the final decade of Heileman's existence, David served as corporate credit manager. During roughly that same period he also served as the company historian. David is married with two children and lives on the family farm near Winona.

What an enjoyable yet arduous project writing this book has been. I first had thoughts of writing a Heileman history book more than 20 years ago. At that point I realized how much interesting history the company had to offer. The more I discovered, the more I wanted to know, and so it started. Information was collected, notes were made and knowledge accrued over the years.

In 1996 the company was sold and my life, like that of so many of my Heileman co-workers, took another direction. However, I continued to think about writing a Heileman history book.

In the spring of 2002 I met Paul D. Koeller for the first time, and I was shocked to discover that he had independently researched the company's history from a completely different perspective and had book plans as well. We quickly joined forces and have since compiled a comprehensive perspective of the company's long and interesting journey through history.

Brewed with Style: The Story of the House of Heileman has been a labor of love. There are many, many people who contributed greatly to this project.

Thank yous have to start with my wife, Cynthia, whose support has been tremendous and whose attention to detail is without equal. Many thanks also to the scores of people who allowed us to interview them and capture unique perspectives about their Heileman experiences. Many of the accounts written in our book are a direct result of verbal recollections. Photographs and memorabilia bring history to life. We are grateful to the many individuals and organizations who allowed us to share their treasures in this book.

How about some kudos to all the wonderful Heileman employees? You truly were a great group of hard workers who were also fun to work with. I hope that your memories of working at Heileman are as fond as mine and that this book brings back the best of those memories.

Some personal thanks for their special help in bringing our project to fruition go to: Steve Carlson for his legal advice, Kurt Friederichs for the great book cover design, Randy Smith, Jon Reynolds, Lynden Gjerde, George Smith, all the folks Paul mentions in his kudos section, and to many more who aren't mentioned by name.

Thanks for the great memories.

INDEX

H

N

O

P

Q

R

S

T

U

Brewed
with
Style
The Story of the
House of Heileman